Stephen F. Berlinguette
Operation Làm Quen:
Motorcycling Rural Vietnam, One Landing Zone at a Time

Operation Làm Quen: Motorcycling Rural Vietnam, One Landing Zone at a Time
Copyright © 2025 Stephen F. Berlinguette
All rights reserved.
No part of this publication may be reproduced, stored, or transmitted by any means without the prior written permission of the author, except as permitted under U.S. copyright law.
ISBN (Paperback): 979-8-9988688-2-5
ISBN (Hardcover): 979-8-9988688-3-2
ISBN (eBook): 979-8-9988688-1-8
ISBN (Kindle Direct Publishing): 979-8-9988688-0-1
First edition
Published by Royal King Dynasty Press
Cover design by the author
Interior layout by the author using Microsoft Word

To Oscar, my life's greatest joy and love.
To Matt and Mark, whose memories and encouragement co-piloted me in every draft; I only wish I could have placed this final manuscript into your hands.

Acknowledgments
Author's Note
Note on Style
Introduction

IMPORTANT BACKROUND SECTION

Cub - Minsk
Cơm Bình Dân Quán Nhậu Tạp Hóa Nhà Nghỉ

SAIGON HINTERLANDS

Lai Khê
Sông Bé
Tà Thiết
Lộc Ninh
An Lộc
Fire Support Base Burt
Ka Tum
Núi Bà Đen
Dầu Tiếng

CENTRAL HIGHLANDS

Ia Drăng
Plei Djereng
Kon Tum
Hill 601
Đăk Tô
Bến Hét
Khâm Đức
Hải Vân Pass

DMZ

Quảng Trị
The Tape
Leatherneck Square

Western DMZ
Quảng Bình
Đường 20 Quyết Thắng
Afterword
Glossary
About the Author

Acknowledgments

I finally met Jonas Thorsell in February 2020, when he returned to Vietnam and we took a three-day motorcycle trip to explore Vietnam War-era sites in the Mekong Delta. Before then, we only knew each other online. I was living in Saigon at the time and first encountered Jonas through "Climbing Hamburger Hill 50 Years After the Vietnam War's Brutal, Haunting Battle," a May 2019 *Washington Post* article by journalist Paul Schemm. Schemm had accompanied Jonas and guide Văn Ngọc Vũ on a hike to the summit of Hamburger Hill for the story.

The article linked to Thorsell's Nam War Travel website[1], where I found a loose-knit community of amateur archaeologists and historians—Vietnamese and foreign—drawn to the remnants of battles, bases, and other wartime coordinates on the map. They traveled to these places, photographed them, and wrote about them.

Though Jonas is Swedish—his country never participated in the Vietnam War—and not a trained historian, he has become one of the world's experts on the 1969 battle of Hamburger Hill. He's read nearly every memoir, history, article, and after-action report written about it. He's befriended veterans of the U.S. Army's 187th Infantry Regiment, the "Rakkasans," and walked the hill with them, documenting each contour through film and interviews. He's even been a guest at their reunions—drawn into the circle because of his care for and persistence with their history.

Thorsell has spent years walking former battlefields across Vietnam. We're roughly the same age. I recognized in him a familiar generational thrill: the urge to circle back and try to touch something we grew up with but were too young to live through.

Văn Ngọc Vũ operates Annam Tours in Đông Hà, the capital of Quảng Trị province. His knowledge runs deep, having grown

---

[1]. https://namwartravel.com

up along the former Demilitarized Zone in the years just after the war. Like Jonas, Vũ has long felt the war's pull, and now makes his living guiding veterans and curiosity-seekers to storied battlegrounds and forgotten base camps. He seems to know every inch of central Vietnam, and can produce details as minute as where a particular fuel drum was stored at a particular Landing Zone.

I'd been casually visiting Vietnam War sites for fifteen years when I read that *Washington Post* article. I'd toured the DMZ with Vũ a couple of times. But I hadn't heard of Nam War Travel. It was next-level. The community had a shared, if informal, methodology: they freely exchanged GPS coordinates, research, and on-the-ground advice. The site had a dedicated following of American veterans, many of whom filled the comment sections with stories, questions, and corrections from their time in-country.

It wasn't just a website. It was a kind of platform—a space where intergenerational memory work played out in real time, shaped by photographs of what these places look like today.

I reached out to Jonas immediately. Not long after, I started taking more motorcycle trips and contributing to Nam War Travel. I learned by doing—picking up exploration skills and writing more.

Though he'd since moved back to Sweden, Jonas was involved in this project. He helped me problem-solve and locate many of the sites in this book—often on the fly, as I pulled over and called him from remote places like Ka Tum or Đắk Pék. Vũ, who appears in later chapters, played a similar role: he had my back through much of the book's third section. Booking a tour with Vũ is always a good investment. He knows where to find things, and he knows what happened there.

Both of these gents are good friends of mine, and this project probably wouldn't have happened without their counsel.

Nam War Travel website:
https://namwartravel.com/

Vietnam War History Travel Facebook:
https://web.facebook.com/groups/229153984813510
Annam Tour Facebook:
https://web.facebook.com/dmztours

Thank you to Sam Oglesby for early feedback on and care about this project.

Thank you to Daniel Lane for narrative shaping and encouragement, over lagers in Saigon.

Thank you to Bố Trạch District's unofficial ambassador, Ben Mitchell.

Thank you to Tuyen D. Nguyen for elevating my already overwrought theory on "Hello," by Lionel Richie.

Thank you to Dan Dockery for the origin story of the Hanoi Minsk Club.

Thank you to Scott Robertson—my favorite riding buddy—for thousands of motorcycle miles logged together in Vietnam and Laos, where some of the stories and ideas in this book first germinated. Though Scott wasn't on this trip, I wish he had been.

Finally, thank you to Laura Vogel, Barbara Noe Kennedy, and Tatiana Wilde for their exceptional editing and insight on early drafts of this book.

Disclaimer

The views and opinions expressed in this book are those of the author and do not necessarily reflect the official policy or position of the United States Government or the United States Agency for International Development (USAID).

Author's Note

Vietnamese have no aversion to small talk. The title of this book includes the Vietnamese phrase *làm quen*, which roughly translates as "to get acquainted" or "to get to know." In Vietnam, this describes the casual process of becoming familiar with someone through small talk—usually through a battery of direct questions: How old are you? Are you married? How many children do you have? Where are you from? And for foreigners: How long have you been in Vietnam?

Since having an English language repertoire is now prevalent among younger Vietnamese, foreign visitors are no longer sheltered from this interrogation. Western travelers in particular sometimes find these questions abrupt or invasive—many don't want to discuss their family status with a person they just met and likely won't ever meet again. But in Vietnam, *làm quen* is just how conversations begin. It's a friction-reducing ritual, especially in rural areas.

In these pages, *làm quen* means more than just small talk. It's a gesture. A way of noticing. A way of stepping into someone else's frame without pretending to belong there. It became shorthand for how I moved through rural Vietnam—through its past and present—and how, in quiet moments, that movement was sometimes reciprocated.

Note on Style

Vietnamese words appear with full diacritics wherever possible, out of respect for the language and how it's used in daily life. Widely anglicized names—like Vietnam, Saigon, Hanoi, and Ho Chi Minh—are left in their common English forms for readability. When spelled out, acronyms like ARVN and PAVN retain Việt Nam to reflect their source language and structure.

I did my best with the Vietnamese throughout. Any misspellings, awkward phrasings, or tonal misfires are mine alone—and I'm grateful for the generosity of those who've helped me get as close as I could.

Introduction

"Yes, you may take the elevator to the rooftop," the man at the front desk said warily, in Vietnamese. "But please be considerate. People live up there." He'd had to share those instructions with unannounced visitors before.

I entered the tiny elevator and rode it to the eighth floor. Empty offices greeted me when the door slid open: doors locked, shades drawn, and unoccupied desks resting in the dark. Turning right, I hiked up a staircase and found myself on the roof of the Pittman Apartments building in Saigon's District 1. Even in middle age, I still feel chills when I find myself in a historically momentous place I know well from photographs, when the imagined and actual images merge for the first time.

This was one of those times. Soon, I was standing in the shadow of a lonely rooftop shed. It was squat and sun-faded, a forgotten box with a single air vent, against which rested a tired bamboo ladder. The air held a mineral tang: rusted iron, sun-baked concrete, and something vaguely organic, like old water and dust.

Dutch photographer and journalist Hugh van Es photographed a UH-1 Huey helicopter hovering over this simple shed on April 30, 1975. There was a queue of Americans and South Vietnamese friends of the United States urgently waiting for their turn to board and evacuate the city, extending down a ladder and onto the rooftop. One American man in a white shirt on top of the shed is directing the action. This photo announced to the world that Saigon was falling and the Vietnam War was finally ending. It appeared on the front page of newspapers in the U.S. and elsewhere, cutting through all of the information, misinformation, and spin that the world had tried to make sense of for twenty years: it was all over.

On that day in 1975, the roof of this shed was one of several makeshift helicopter landing pads in Saigon for Hueys whisking evacuees to U.S. Navy vessels in the South China Sea. Vietnam's largest city was surrounded by several North Vietnamese Army divisions that were expected to launch an all-out military assault soon. These were the waning hours of South Vietnam's existence as a state.

The Pittman Apartments building is situated a few blocks from where a cluster of go-go bars clustered on Rue Catinat (renamed Đồng Khởi—meaning "uprising"—Street after 1975) catered to the U.S. G.I.s during the war. Today, Pittman's faded balconies stare directly into the polished face of modern Vietnam.

Vincom Center, with its twenty-nine stories, is a mixed-use skyscraper that houses the biggest shopping mall in Ho Chi Minh City. At the right hour of the morning, the Pittman sits in Vincom's solar shadow. Scanning the Saigon skyline today, the Pittman Apartments and its shed aren't immediately obvious. But once you spot them, you know exactly what you're looking at. Anyone familiar with Hugh van Es's iconic 1975 photo would recognize it instantly.

The exterior looks much as it did then; many parts of central Saigon still do. Yet, inside, it's contemporary, spartan Ho Chi Minh City, not glamorous pre-1975 Saigon. The ground-floor lobby is spacious and largely empty. Cheap sofas sit in the lobby, still wrapped in peeling showroom cellophane. Previously, every time I passed by the Pittman Apartments building, I seemed to notice men loitering on those couches, phones in hand, smoking cigarettes, cutting deals of some kind. It's such an ordinary Vietnamese scene for such an extraordinary place.

My visit took place close to the fiftieth anniversary of the Fall of Saigon. At 2:00 p.m., it was lethally hot on that roof. Unlike many of Saigon's more recent constructions of questionable build quality, the Pittman Apartments building was made to last. It's still in good shape.

Ironically, the Ho Chi Minh City government has been discussing razing the structure for years (after the war, Saigon was renamed "Ho Chi Minh City"; the term is generally used in official circles, but "Saigon" still applies in most other contexts, probably similar to how Russians once managed the Leningrad versus St. Petersburg nomenclature). Real estate is too valuable in Saigon's central business district; this plot could easily generate more revenue as a modern office building.

However, it could also be because the Pittman represents a strain of the country's past that doesn't assimilate well with the city's push to transform Ho Chi Minh City into a place without history. Saigon's elegant French-era post office and the Notre Dame Cathedral tell relatively straightforward stories of colonialism: most Vietnamese were subjected to its severity, and these French constructions now stand as reminders that Vietnam prevailed—that these are Vietnamese places. Colonialism, for all its violence, was endured collectively.

But mid-century structures like the Pittman tell a more complicated story—one shaped by competing notions of patriotism and mobilization. A different narrative. It seems apt, then, that the Pittman Apartments and its rooftop shed aren't marked, aren't marketed, and aren't accessible to the public, at least to tourists who don't know the unstated rules of this place, which include negotiating with a door attendant and keeping a low profile. Furthermore, it faces a brand-new skyscraper representing consumerism, wealth accumulation, foreign direct investment, property development, and modernity. Yet, for all the talk of razing Pittman, the authorities haven't done so yet.

Until 1975, the Pittman was a high-rise apartment building leased by the United States for government officials and those attached to the embassy in Saigon. What's in the Pittman Apartments building today? Weirdly, all tenants—half a dozen different state-owned enterprises or state-connected enterprises—do business in the chemicals sector. Where embassy families once lived, now: particle board desks, Venetian blinds, and chemical supply pamphlets. Neither the cracked floor tiles nor the outdated calendars hinted at the building's previous life.

The rooftop doesn't seem to have changed much. The famous shed is, at least in appearance, as it was in 1975. There's a rusty door to get into the shed itself, but it's locked. Someone used a key to scrawl "The Fall of Saigon" in English into the rust, in the half-cursive, half-block letter handwriting familiar to almost everyone who learned to write in a Vietnamese public school. Perhaps odd to a visitor but extremely routine for Vietnam is what's *on* the roof: it's home to two gardens, ubiquitous concrete tables and benches, tea sets, and a *thuốc lào* bamboo water pipe for smoking tobacco, all of which are part of the landscape wherever people gather, loiter, and make small talk in this country.

We'll need this for later: a *thuốc lào* is a water pipe/bong made from a section of bamboo. Vietnamese men pass the time by smoking a highly potent tobacco through this communal pipe. The sound of air inhaling through the bamboo is like a whistle ascending in pitch: one can deduce that they're strolling through a working-class neighborhood when they hear this sound in the background.

In one corner was an awning hanging over a hammock, a few tubs and dishes, and a small locked cupboard. Someone, indeed, lives up here. It's a serene spot, a stark contrast to the frenetic streets below.

I opted to walk down from the rooftop rather than take the elevator. I peeked into the chemicals company reception areas that were previously penthouse-floor USAID apartments and saw the omnipresent red banner with gold font reading *Đảng Cộng Sản Việt Nam Quảng Vinh Muôn Năm!* or "Long Live the Glorious Communist Party of Vietnam!"

Otherwise, there were empty rooms, copiers, cardboard file boxes, particle board desks, ashtrays, discarded boxes of White Horse cigarettes, calendars, and wood paneling. It could have been any small office building in Vietnam. Yet, no people. The offices were empty. As it was around 2:00 p.m., this was probably evidence that state enterprise employees like to leisurely sip iced coffee on the sidewalk after taking long lunches and before returning to work.

As I made my way down the stairwell, the scene from 1975 was easy enough to imagine. This passage would have been packed with Army of the Republic of Việt Nam (ARVN) military, nervous South Vietnamese civilians, and the odd American trying to make their way to the roof. There would have been more people in the lobby among suitcases, bags, or whatever one grabs when fleeing a war zone. Probably a few escapees dressed in evening wear, unprepared for a sudden and life-changing helicopter flight to an offshore United States Navy aircraft carrier.

There would have been muscle: South Vietnamese military police and plainclothes Americans guarding the front door and trying to ensure the Pittman wasn't overwhelmed by crowds. There would have been noise. Loud chatter, shouted commands, choppers making ingress and egress flights. Arguments, aggression, frantic street traffic. The sound of ordnance and gunfire—both near and distant. After the final chopper departed, those still present would have eventually had to start figuring out a Plan B or C and find the motivation to get moving again. They were probably stunned.

I stumbled upon a first-floor canteen that presumably serves all of the chemical company staff in the Pittman building. I interrupted two cafeteria ladies who were cleaning the kitchen and washing dishes. Like most Vietnamese people who serendipitously meet Westerners, they were charming. They hammed it up for photographs. Then I told them I was interested in the building's history, and they blankly replied, "Well, the cafeteria is closed. Sorry."

No tour, no insider conversation about the Fall of Saigon. Just two women scrubbing pans, laughing, and sending me on my way. A perfectly Vietnamese anticlimax.

*　*　*

Few people who live in Vietnam have much interest in visiting the war's bunkers and deteriorating runways that have been sitting silently in the villages and jungles for fifty years. Still fewer have any penchant for the amateur archaeology I adore, combing through the soil for the leftovers: cartridges, sandbags, poncho scraps, or the occasional 50-year-old Budweiser beer can.

Apart from a handful of foreign and Vietnamese amateur historians I've befriended, this isn't really a done thing. The real thrill isn't just knowing what happened in these places—it's feeling it press up against the now. When the jungle parts and a leftover bunker or fragment appears, it's not just discovery. It's a strange, physical buzz I only get when history feels that close. The hairs on my arms stand up, and it's as if time has circled back to let me in for a little while.

I like to think it's about remembrance. And maybe it is. But there's something else in it too—something I don't always want to name, though I know it's there.

Why would anyone go all the way to dusty Khâm Đức, out by the Lao border, to see the shell of a 1968 U.S. airbase, when they could much more easily tour the celestial Hạ Long Bay or bask in Phú Quốc's white-sand beaches and cerulean waters?

It's a fair question and one that comes up sometimes. Indeed, the Vietnamese government would prefer tourists to be corralled in these more conventional and welcoming places rather than snoop around in frontier areas or the countryside. The services are light-years better in Hạ Long Bay and Phú Quốc than what one finds in Khâm Đức. The photographs are probably glossier and more social media-friendly in these heralded places.

But that sheen comes at a cost. After moving back to Saigon several years ago, it finally occurred to me to start visiting the sites of bases and battles from the Vietnam War before these places were swallowed by the country's rapidly moving modernization drive.

* * *

I was born in 1970. I vaguely remember seeing evening news footage in 1975 of American sailors pushing UH-1 Huey helicopters off of the side of aircraft carriers into the South China Sea. It's one of my earlier memories of television—blades spinning, helicopters tipping, a gray sky over gray water. I didn't understand what was happening, but I remember the noise.

The ships weren't designed to handle the kind of mass, chaotic helicopter evacuation during the Fall of Saigon. Flight decks quickly became jammed with Hueys, which were too large to store or move below. With more approaching—some low on fuel and unable to turn back—the U.S. Navy made a grim but necessary decision: push the choppers into the ocean to make room for incoming aircraft and save more lives.

By the time I was ten, *The Deer Hunter* had already made its run in theaters and arrived on television. Like much of New England, my family watched it in three nightly parts around 1981, on *The Movie Loft*—the hosted film series on Boston's Channel 38. One moment stuck. It was a scene where Michael, played by Robert De Niro, returns to Saigon after his combat tour to find his friend Nick, a young Christopher Walken. After serving a tour together, Nick never came home, opting instead to stay behind and become a professional Russian roulette player.

Michael eventually locates Nick in a warehouse, seated across from another man. A revolver gleams on the table. Around them, a sweaty crowd of Vietnamese gamblers jostles and shouts, placing bets with a bookie. Michael somehow squeezes through the crowd and pleads with Nick, who is drugged up and doesn't recognize his friend. Nick goes first. He lifts the pistol to his temple and pulls the trigger. Empty chamber. He passes the gun to his opponent, who pulls the trigger and dies instantly. Nick bolts from the room and jumps on the back of a Vespa. Michael follows, mounting another scooter.

The chase barrels through crowded Saigon streets and alleys, flooded in darkness, neon signs, gangsters, prostitutes, American G.I.s, street hawkers, and jostling motorbikes pushing through the horde. Shadowy, simultaneously menacing and ravishing, that street scene rewired the neurons in my young brain.

* * *

I finally visited Vietnam in 1998. On my first night in Saigon, I landed at a *quán nhậu,* or working-class sidewalk bar and grill. Quán Loan (Ms. Loan's Restaurant) sits on the corner of Hai Bà Trưng and Lý Tự Trọng Streets in central Saigon, in what was once a district of bars, restaurants, and brothels that catered to American soldiers. Quán Loan is still there today; the restaurant sits at the street level of a gorgeous mid-century modern building that originally housed the United States Information Agency (USIA) headquarters in Saigon, a block or so away from the Pittman Apartments building. Since repurposed into apartments and shops, the old USIA building and its tenant, Quán Loan seems bolted to this Saigon street corner.

I sat on a red plastic stool, drinking southern flagship brand Bia Saigon on ice, gazing at the busy intersection. Saigon was a mesmerizing circus. Parades of vintage 1960s Honda Cubs and '67 50-cc motorbikes buzzed by in the darkness, some with five passengers. There was no working traffic light at this junction, and few overhead streetlights lit the sidewalk below. Rickshaws ambled through, with motorbikes swerving and pedestrians pausing. A singer who'd lost limbs, likely a legacy of the war, shuffled through the chaos and crooned into a microphone wired to a battery-powered amplifier. A friend of the singer held a pith helmet out for donations.

Homes and shops were open to the sidewalk, barely illuminated by low-wattage lights, casting a cream-green shadow on shirtless men guarding stacks of cigarette cartons—their family business investment—for sale. Women wearing *nón lá* conical hats peddled their bicycles the wrong way in the center of the one-way street, balancing towers of Styrofoam takeout containers tied down to bicycle luggage racks. Touts stopped here and there, pitching sunglasses, UH-1 Huey helicopter replicas made from empty beer cans, chewing gum, and vintage dog tags to men drinking beer together on the sidewalk. Couples and families, middle-aged and young, were out for a stroll in central Saigon in December, the month with the city's freshest climate. Saigon hadn't changed all that much since the early 1970s, it seemed. It felt curated, which made it all the more hypnotic. I had dropped myself into that motorbike chase scene from *The Deer Hunter*.

* * *

Growing up in the 1980s meant I was privy to a reexamination of the war that was happening in the United States at that time. There was an appetite for Vietnam War stories in books and on screen. Sylvester Stallone, Neil Sheehan, Francis Ford Coppola, Stanley Kubrick, Chuck Norris, Stanley Karnow, Oliver Stone, and Michael Herr told us those stories. The decade's pop stars—Bruce Springsteen, Paul Hardcastle, Billy Joel—also weighed in. But the stories they told were mostly about us. America's grief. America's shame. America's haunted mirror.

Vietnam was there in the frame of these stories, as a supporting actor or a silhouette, but almost never as the subject. That part, we didn't yet know how to look at. Fifty years later, most of us still don't. I'm not exempt. Even now, some part of me leans in. I still find myself lit up by the American frame—the silhouette, the script—even when I know better. And if I'm being honest, that frame is what brought me here in the first place.

The United States was taking its first steps toward atoning for the wounds it caused its people and gradually piecing together a more modern and fair domestic narrative of the Vietnam War, one that undercut the previous reductive tales of hawks and doves and explored the boundless personal and collective emotions that our foreign policy unleashed. None of this was clean. It was a decade full of venting and noise, stubbornness and magnanimity, as a generation associated with self-absorption tried to process what had happened and what to do next about Vietnam, Agent Orange, Vietnamese refugees, post-traumatic stress disorder, late-Cold War communism, Americans missing in action, and the destruction we'd wrought in Southeast Asia.

Many combat veterans went through a brutal adjustment. One of my cousins did three tours in Vietnam. He came back, regularly drank to excess at a Manchester, New Hampshire, biker bar called The Zoo, got into violent fights, and finally died from cancer before he was forty, most certainly from extended exposure to Agent Orange. He never had much of a shot at a normal life. He and others like him seemed alone—somehow, the United States had concluded that the best way to address all the pain we'd caused our veterans and the people of Vietnam was vengeance: twenty years of punishment and isolation for the reunified country now known as the Socialist Republic of Vietnam.

* * *

As a teenager, I gained some sense of where the war took place, be it Cồn Thiên Combat Base or in Saigon. I read *Bloods, Dispatches,* and *The 13th Valley,* among others. I've watched the entirety of *Vietnam: A Television History,* the thirteen-part PBS documentary that came out in 1983, probably sixty times.

As I've gone deeper into this world of the lightly mapped geography of the war, I've learned much by superimposing GPS coordinates onto maps. Americans, the National Liberation Front (NLF), the Army of the Republic of Việt Nam (ARVN), the People's Army of Việt Nam (PAVN), friendlies, and hostiles draped this country's cities, towns, villages, and countryside.

Put your finger on a random spot on a map of Vietnam. Chances are good that something was located there, or something war-related happened there. A firefight, a Strategic Hamlet, a secret NLF base in the jungle, a French army camp, a village whose leadership unofficially changed hands every night and morning, an American base, a cache of Soviet rifles or rice buried under a tree, a Special Forces camp, a tunnel complex, or a shantytown of bars, massage parlors, and corner stores selling black market goods outside the gate of a military facility. Every village, at some point, was probably contested or somehow touched.

Vietnam is saturated with these once-violent and politically charged places; many of these remote sites that I'd read about as a teenager are still there. On the one hand, that's obvious. But on the other, it's a revelation: few of these base and battlefield sites are on the map. Even fewer are officially recognized. Few people here care, there aren't many museums or memorials, and fewer and fewer aging American veterans travel to these places anymore.

A population that's doubled since 1975, a twenty-year real estate boom, and nonstop development now threaten these places. It's a race—progress at one end, erasure at the other.

***

This book chronicles solo motorcycle trips across Vietnam, in which I chase down forgotten war sites before they vanish. Put simply, I wanted to see what these sites look like today and try and record new chapters of their stories before they are one day swallowed by the country's development drive. I grew up when Vietnam was still the center of a loud national dialogue. It's a personal archaeology now—a way of touching the war that shaped my country and never quite let go. Not closure, but an opening. A way in.

Moreover, I wanted to perceive what these places feel like today, in some sense to test the idea that the past can resonate in the soil, on the concrete, on longitude and latitude coordinates where something monumental happened over fifty years ago. Finally, I wanted to find out if this history would manifest itself in rural Vietnam itself, its people, institutions, and personality. To see if time might circle back and open the door, even briefly.

***

Urban Vietnam has undergone enormous change since 1975. The country's major cities are globalized, have flamboyant skylines, and increasingly look and feel like other Southeast Asian cities, such as Bangkok, which experienced its own growth spurt beginning in the 1980s. Urban Vietnam is catching up.

Rural Vietnam, not so much. Visually, the country's villages aren't terribly far removed from what we see in photos taken in 1969 or '70, during the war. And the core identity and fundamental human traits, or the village DNA, are essentially the same. The people one meets in the countryside either grew up during the war, or their families were participants, and they carry that history with them. Few Vietnamese move from city to country; migration usually goes in the opposite direction. So that's where I went, endeavoring to travel through time on a motorcycle.

The sites of battles and military bases that I cover here were consequential, but they're neglected now. They are not a substantial part of what Vietnam presents to tourists as the country's history. Once, they were in the headlines and inundated with noise, emotion, laughter, and pain; now, they get little attention. They're empty lots, dumping grounds for discarded furniture and tires, cassava plantations, construction sites, residential areas, and farms. With luck, one can stumble across evidence and memory at these sites: remnants of concrete structures, bunkers, American G.I. garbage, unexploded ordnance, spent cartridges, and bomb craters.

One can go to these places and breathe the air of one of the twentieth century's most momentous conflicts. Visitors will have these places to themselves; they're not very interesting to most people. Most are not memorialized places in Vietnam, and that's part of the appeal.

Why would I vacation in Bến Hét or Cồn Thiên instead of Phú Quốc or Hạ Long Bay? I suppose it's because Bến Hét and Cồn Thiên won't be there forever. They are exalted in American history, books, documentaries, and veterans' stories. They're fallow, but not quite gone. Memorializing them would mean cleaning up these places, politicizing them, polishing them, and building a visitor center.

Enough of these places are today approximations of what they were like when they were abandoned fifty or so years ago. They carry emotions and a spirit that is sometimes tangible. And if one spends time in and around these places, one can learn something about modern Vietnam and Vietnamese people, those whom America, as a country, never really got to know during the war. Despite all of the growth and change, the twentieth century pervades Vietnam. It's all still here, but like any amateur archaeologist, one has to dig a little.

IMPORTANT
BACKROUND SECTION

Cub - Minsk

Back in 2003, I was living in Hanoi. A friend from the United States was visiting, and one Saturday morning, I invited him for a coffee. We rode my Belorussian Minsk 125-cc two-stroke motorcycle to a café. It was 7:30 a.m. The street was empty. We arrived at a red traffic light, and a forty-something man pulled up next to us on a beat-up, thirty-year-old 49-cubic centimeter Honda Cub that had long since been converted from a commuter motorbike to farm duty.

He was straight out of the countryside. The morning was already warm, and his bike radiated a scent that was part hot lubricant, part livestock. He wore an oversized striped Oxford shirt with oil stains on it, yellow *dép tổ ong* sandals, a dirty ball cap, aviator sunglasses, a mustache, and teeth blackened by years of chewing betel nut. Welded onto the back of his old Cub was a homemade apparatus of probably twenty small cages, each containing two or three chickens.

Those *dép tổ ong*—cheap, durable polyvinyl chloride (PVC) rubber shower sandals with a honeycomb pattern—have been a staple of working-class and rural menswear in Vietnam for forty years. They are a symbol of the country's self-reliance during the economically tough '80s and '90s. Still widespread and ever practical despite their reputation as ugly and outdated, these sandals retail for about a dollar at any traditional market, and they're typically suitable for daily wear for two to three years. Vietnamese women prefer to see *dép tổ ong* in a museum; they despise this hideous, but enduring, footwear.

We smiled at him, nodded, and he smiled back. The light turned green, and we proceeded. A moment later, we found ourselves waiting at another red light beside the same fellow. I asked him how many chickens he had.

"About forty," he said. "I'm taking these chickens to the market."

Very well. The light turned green again, and we accelerated. This time he gunned his engine, trying to keep pace. We neared another light, just turning from green to red as we slowed down.

He was next to us again, so I smiled once more. Then he asked me a question. I thanked him but shook my head. I told him my friend and I were headed to get a coffee and that we weren't interested. The light turned back to green, and I accelerated.

My friend leaned in. "I heard the words 'boom-boom,' but the rest was in Vietnamese. What just happened?"

"Well, that gent just asked us if we'd like to have sex in a hotel room after he drops off the chickens," I replied.

"Jesus. The guy wanted to have sex with us?" My friend shuddered. "Christ. I haven't even had my coffee yet."

* * *

Riding a *xe máy* (motorbike) on Vietnam's streets can be an intimate affair. There's no faster way to know Vietnam than on two wheels. You join the chaos. When one finds oneself on a motorbike in Vietnam, one instantly joins an informal hundred-million–member outlaw motorcycle club, probably the biggest in the world.

It's hard to appreciate Vietnam, rural or urban or anything in between, without appreciating motorbikes. They're not just transit. They're texture, woven into everything. Ask a Vietnamese uncle about his first motorbike, and he'll probably name one of two machines: the Honda Cub or the Minsk. The Cub ran the South. It was compact, dependable, Japanese. The Minsk handled the northern highlands. It was bigger, legendarily uglier, Soviet. On one level, they were just transportation. But they were also statements of style, place, time, and Cold War political orbit.

This isn't strictly a motorcycle memoir, but motorbikes are in nearly every scene.

This motorbike club's numbers started small in the mid-twentieth century, riding Mobylettes, Vespas, and Lambrettas, but grew exponentially after the introduction of the Honda Cub. The Honda Motor Company exported twenty thousand Super Cubs to South Vietnam in 1967, and the bike gained a 90 percent market share by the early 1970s. Southerners fell in love with the Honda Super Cub during the war. They were small but hellaciously reliable and strong for their size. People learned that a Cub would, without complaint, do just about anything they told it to do; the bike served as South Vietnam's station wagon, pickup truck, hot rod, taxicab, and delivery mule.

In those days, Honda Cubs essentially came in one color: olive green. Like old Fords in Detroit or Chevrolets in Havana, these bikes still roam the streets of southern Vietnam. Locally nicknamed the "Honda Dame," these rare pre-1970s models inspire the most nostalgia in southern Vietnam. The bike has a certain sex appeal for one demographic in particular: southern Vietnamese men over sixty, who associate them with life in pre-1975 Saigon. Back then, they were young university students, workers, or soldiers, spending their free time courting women, idling at cafés, and perhaps even catching a CBC Band concert at Saigon's Sherwood Forest nightclub—all on a green Honda Cub.

Saigon before 1975, or *Trước '75*, was a vibrant (or decadent, depending on one's point of view) place. The city experienced the same 1960s youth culture explosion as the West, though perhaps not to the extremes of San Francisco. Saigonese grappled with a version of the same tension between youth-driven utopianism and the Vietnam War that Americans did, reflected in the city's activism, art, politics, fashion, literature, and music. South Vietnam even had its own Woodstock—an all-day rock festival in 1971 at the Saigon Zoo.

One of wartime Saigon's most famous venues was Sherwood Forest, a downtown club with nightly rock music performances attended by mixed Vietnamese and American audiences. The acid-rock CBC Band was one of the city's biggest acts, regularly appearing at Sherwood Forest. As to their sonic cues, think heavies such as Big Brother and the Holding Company, Iron Butterfly, and Blue Cheer. On tour when Saigon fell in 1975, the CBC Band couldn't return—stranded in exile, they eventually resettled in Texas, taking the sound of wartime Saigon with them.

To say that millions of southerners who fled or remained in Vietnam after the war are nostalgic for this era would be an understatement: for many, it was a paradise lost in 1975. That version of Saigon lived on—in song, in memoir, and in private corners of postwar Vietnam where the past wasn't erased, just quietly held. It also migrated with the diaspora to places like Westminster, California—the largest and best-known of the constellation of exiled overseas Little Saigon communities—where the pre-1975 South Vietnamese flag still flies above shopping centers and karaoke bars.

Trước '75 Saigon popular culture really ought to get its own book.

* * *

Much like Americans have a love affair with their automobiles, the Vietnamese are passionate about motorbikes. There are well over fifty million on the road here, enough machines for half the entire population to ride simultaneously. And it often feels like they are: unless one is scuba diving, at any time or place in Vietnam, an observer will probably see one, or dozens of them, wherever they cast their glance. This country's soundscape is distinguished by the intermittent Doppler shift and buzz of a 125-cc motorbike engine coming or going close by, or somewhere off in the distance.

That buzz, that density, it's not just transportation. It's national identity. And the Vietnamese know it. I saw this self-awareness when I had the opportunity to sit in the cheap seats for Vietnam's negotiations with the U.S. government to join the World Trade Organization in 2007. During one meeting, a U.S. Trade Representative team questioned Vietnamese officials about trade barriers, specifically regarding the import of Harley-Davidsons.

"So, tell us about motorcycles in Vietnam. Are they popular?" one American negotiator asked.

A Vietnamese Ministry of Trade representative chuckled before responding, "Well, yes. Motorbikes are something like a religion in Vietnam." The Vietnamese side of the room erupted in laughter, while the Americans sat confused as to what had just been said.

* * *

This isn't a story of motorbike breakdowns leading to digressions, serendipitous sub-plots, and friendships. The bike held up and the detours were intentional. This long digression into Cub and Minsk history isn't just indulgence. Perhaps the latter more than the former, these two bikes attracted the kinds of people who would go on to build a riding community that still exists in Vietnam.

Before I began taking motorcycle trips here, as well as the trip covered in these pages, there was already a group of Westerners who explored Vietnam by motorcycle that started after the Cold War ended in 1991 and the country gradually reopened. It became easier to enter, tour, work, and invest in Vietnam in the mid-1990s, and Australian, English, French, and American expatriates trickled in. Some came to experience a reclusive republic just waking up to the world after twenty years of slumber; others came here to find business opportunities in a country dismantling socialism, a nascent market with high upside.

Bewitched by Vietnam, many of these émigré long-termers discovered that the Belorussian Minsk motorcycles that were at that time the daily riders for many northern Vietnamese were perfect for exploring Vietnam's hinterlands, particularly the Hoàng Liên Son mountain range in the northwest, on the Lao and Chinese borders, with its scattered Hmong and Thai ethnic minority villages, the site of the 1954 battle of Điện Biên Phủ, waterfalls, local moonshine, karst formations, and more natural riffs on the color green than I have ever seen.

The northwest was simultaneously wild and prosaic; neither state nor Communist Party control was as pervasive in the highlands as it was in the Red River Delta area around Hanoi. Taking wobbly Soviet two-stroke motorbikes deep into the outback on lousy dirt roads was an adventure, full of problems and rewards, but rarely unsatisfying.

The legacy of foreign explorers on Minsks reached a height with the founding of the Hanoi Minsk Club. Formed in 1998[1] by a group of eighty-five expats and Vietnamese, the club would ride the countryside, meet at *bia hơi* taverns in the capital, and organize the annual "Minsk Olympics" at a resort outside of Hanoi—a series of motorcycle competitions capped off by a blowout party.

One of the club's more storied accomplishments was orchestrated by Dan Dockery, a longtime English expat and a founding member of the club. In 1999, while teaching a business English course, Dan learned that one of his students imported Minsk motorcycles. The student, aware of Dan's involvement in the Minsk Club, offered to introduce him to the CEO of the Minsk Motorcycle and Bicycle Plant in Belarus, who would be on a business trip to Vietnam in a month's time.

Dockery did more than show up at a meeting; he organized a VIP welcome for the CEO at Nội Bài International Airport. As the CEO stepped off his flight, he was greeted by Vietnamese women in miniskirts offering him shots of vodka and bouquets of flowers. Waiting for him outside was the Hanoi Minsk Club astride their bikes, along with a cooler full of vodka. Receiving a standing ovation from the crowd, the CEO looked stunned but kept a sedate official composure. On their motorcycles, the Hanoi Minsk Club escorted the CEO's sedan 20 miles to his hotel in the city.

Vietnam stopped importing Minsk motorbikes from Belarus sometime in the mid-2000s, and their numbers have dwindled. Yet some are still on the road, and lifelong fans still entertain each other with postings of photographs of outlaw-looking locals riding Minsks in Afghanistan, Tehran, the Caucasus, Angola, Ukraine, or Maputo, often shouldering a Kalashnikov.

* * *

In the summer of 2002, I took my first Minsk ride on the fabled northwest Hanoi–Điện Biên Phủ–Sa Pa–Hanoi Loop; it was the most exuberant thing I'd done in my life to that point. Since then, I've passed through every one of Vietnam's sixty-one provinces and cities on a motorcycle. For the trips covered here, I rode a 2009 Kawasaki W650.

W650s didn't take off in the United States when Kawasaki began exporting them in 2000, and I'll never quite understand why. Officially, the W650's design was a nod to the early 1960s Kawasaki W1, but the reality is that its appearance is closer to a 1968 or '69 Triumph Bonneville than it was to the Japanese twin. The W650 was exported to the U.S. for only two years, 2000-2001, and it didn't sell terribly well. The country was still in the late-stage Cruiser Era, and Americans didn't like the motorcycle, apparently.

During the late-stage Cruiser Era, Americans still preferred wide, comfortable, large displacement, low-riding cruiser motorcycles to the more compact styling of 1950s and 1960s British Twins. My hunch is that had Peter Fonda rode a 1968 Norton Atlas, with

Dennis Hopper on a 1968 BSA A65, in the 1969 film *Easy Rider*, the United States might have entirely avoided the thirty-plus-year Cruiser Era of fat, and over time fatter, Harley-Davidsons, as well as the millions of Japanese bikes styled after Harleys. That said, in this alternate reality, by 1990 or so, the sight of overweight American Baby Boomers wearing baggy Levi's jeans, white T-shirts, white Reebok sneakers, and black leather jackets riding Norton Atlases would probably have been unavoidable.

In any case, we can thank England for perfecting motorcycle design and thank Christ that the Kawasaki W650 has found a popular following in Asia and the Pacific Rim. The W650 is an elegant, fun, and reliable bike that doesn't fuss or grumble. Unlike a Minsk, it doesn't break down repeatedly and require endless problem-solving on a long-distance trip. Instead, the W650 is like a quiet but loyal companion—something I've come to appreciate at my age. The Minsk originally brought me to Vietnam's back roads, yet the W650 lets me loiter there longer. It's not a Vietnam heritage bike. But it took me to some heritage places.

Cơm Bình Dân Quán Nhậu Tạp Hóa Nhà Nghỉ

Let's return to that Saturday morning in Hanoi, when the farmer balancing cages of chickens on his old Cub, wearing the stained Oxford shirt and yellow sandals, pulled up at a red light and propositioned us.

A Vietnamese would describe this farmer as *người bình dân*, which roughly translates to "common person"—or, in a less courteous but more earthy sense, *nhà quê ra tỉnh* (redneck straight out of the province). To many, *bình dân* evokes "easygoing but penniless people who live simply." Particularly to an older generation that grew up with *bình dân* stories and jokes, *bình dân* people are charming simpletons in television dramas who do funny things.

But such reductionism is probably unfair. Since the past 100 years of Vietnamese history and identity is about nothing if not the tensions between capitalism and socialism, and the class consciousness these tensions embody, one can read some Marxism-Leninism into the term *bình dân*.

Simply put, *bình dân* people are the proletariat. They till the soil, labor in factories, catch fish, mine caves, fight wars, drive taxis, construct buildings, and collect garbage. Colonial rulers exploited their ancestors, and their sons and daughters joined the army and the revolution. Although many of Vietnam's revolutionary leaders came from educated Mandarin families, the revolution was waged on behalf of the *bình dân* population.

After the war, when Hanoi implemented socialism across the country, *bình dân* people worked collective farms in the countryside and rebuilt the country's cities. The new economic order was meant to benefit the proletariat: in Vietnam's postwar two-decade "subsidized time," private enterprise was abolished and state-owned enterprises distributed rice through coupon systems. Government canteens sprouted up to serve workers cheap meals, and housing, utilities, fuel, and consumer goods were subsidized. *Bình dân* people inherited the country of Vietnam after the war, at least in theory.

Bình dân Vietnam is something of a window into this country's past, a window that increasing globalization and rising incomes are probably closing. Younger Vietnamese, rural and urban alike, are forward-looking: keen to join the world, speak English, and adopt interconnected global ways of living. Fortunately, the *bình dân* world is still the counterpoint to the language of globalization, and Vietnamese are bilingual. It's part of why I prefer the countryside; not wholly out of nostalgia, exactly, but for affection, too.

Riding a motorcycle through rural Vietnam with our shared history in mind can feel like time travel. The people carry the same literal, or at least cultural, DNA. The villages still resemble what we see in photographs from fifty or sixty years ago. The food and drink haven't changed. And at many of these sites, there's just enough evidence to let us transcend the decades.

Furthermore, we don't get to know Vietnam's proletariat very well through English-language narratives of the war and the country. So we miss it, the charisma that lives in *bình dân* people and places. That charisma, it turns out, is bountiful.

Let's start with the midday meal. *Cơm bình dân* means "ordinary person rice" and is a marketing classification for a certain type of universal canteen-style restaurant that delivers cheap, quick, and filling proletariat lunches. The descendants of subsidized-era canteens, *cơm bình dân* are usually curbside buffet-style places with communal aluminum tables and stools and an extensive open frontage that pulls in the noise and pollution from the street. Familiar *cơm bình dân* recipes are deep-fried freshwater fish, omelets, pork-stuffed tofu in tomato sauce, boiled bamboo shoots, fried cabbage, squid with pineapple, sautéed morning glory, and boiled bitter melon.

Cơm bình dân tends to be delectable, if not a bit of a guilty pleasure: I've left *cơm bình dân* restaurants reeling from face numbness after consuming too much MSG. Though celebrity chefs like Luke Nguyen and Anthony Bourdain have extolled Vietnamese cuisine as the healthiest in the world, the country does have its share of junk food.

Save for the sounds of chewing, grunting, belching, slurping, gnawing, and the unraveling of toothpicks from paper sleeves, *cơm bình dân* restaurants aren't noisy places. They are pit stops for men in a hurry; there's no ceremony to a *cơm bình dân* lunch. Not a typographical error: ninety percent of the clientele at a *cơm bình dân* canteen are male. In my experience, women tend to dine at slightly cleaner and classier places, such as cafés that serve bespoke rice dishes from a menu.

The core *cơm bình dân* demographic is people who wake at four or five in the morning to work. So lunch can start at 10:30 a.m. and the rush usually finishes at around 12:30. Only a fool shows up hungry at a *cơm bình dân* at noon with high expectations; by that point, the buffet has largely been consumed, and the floor buildup of used napkins, chicken and fish bones, toothpicks, spilled soup, and cigarette butts is sometimes ankle-high.

* * *

If *cơm bình dân* is lunch, then its evening counterpart is the *quán nhậu* in the south or the *bia hơi* beer garden in the north. In other words, a working-class tavern. In southern parlance, *đi nhậu* means "to eat and drink [to excess]," and the term *quán* means "restaurant, store, kiosk." Like *cơm bình dân*, *quán nhậu* are raucous but unadorned places with primitive restrooms, decent food, and uncomfortable furniture. Essentially the same institution, but with flowing beer.

They spill onto the sidewalks, absorbing the chatter, motorbike rumble, and drifting scents of grilled meat and puddles of beer on the pavement. Like *cơm bình dân,* the floors at these places build over time with chicken bones, empty crushed beer cans, napkins, and cigarette butts. Given the geography of this book, we'll focus on the southern variety of these working-class taverns.

But a slight detour is in order: *bia hơi* is too central to working- and middle-class Vietnam to leave out. In Hanoi and the north, *bia hơi* is a magnificent, locally made pilsner that has been around for more than a century, historically priced for the proletariat. It's served in small sidewalk bars or, in some cases, grand beer gardens where a sea of red plastic stools ready to accommodate 1,000 patrons stretches out under the night sky. Though the settings vary, the crowd is usually the same.

Not exactly a history lesson, but maybe a better introduction to Vietnam than any policy brief: like motorbikes, *bia hơi* also made its way into Vietnam's aforementioned World Trade Organization negotiations in 2007. During one meeting on opening Vietnam's beer market to global competition, U.S. negotiators probed the Vietnamese team about this *bia hơi* product, curious if Budweiser could compete fairly in the local market.

"Who drinks bia hơi? What is this demographic?" the Americans asked.

"Mainly government officials," the Vietnamese lead answered, deadpan and delighted with his timing. He and his team were puzzled as to why the American negotiators weren't laughing along with them.

* * *

Tạp hóa are Vietnam's general stores, family-run groceries, corner stores, bodegas, and convenience stores. Though they are slowly being replaced by 7-Elevens, Family Marts, Circle Ks, and other chains, *tạp hóa* are still everywhere.

Tạp hóa usually occupy the ground floors of shophouses, the commercial extensions of family dining rooms and living spaces onto the sidewalk. Should one walk up to one and buy a bag of potato chips, the man of the house might rise from a chair and the television in the living room broadcasting state-run VTV, unhurried in his underwear and grumbling about the heat, to come and take your money.

Country *tạp hóa* are a bit less formal and more closely resemble general stores. Some are hastily tacked onto houses, made of plywood and corrugated roofing. They look half-built, with gaps between the boards, holes in the walls, and a layer of road dust blanketing everything for sale.

Inevitably, a *tạp hóa* will have a few red plastic chairs or stools around a red plastic table out front. Customers might sip iced tea from cloudy, aged plastic cups, trade gossip, and let the hours slide by. A *thuốc lào*, or a bamboo water pipe kit, will likely be handy, so patrons can take a pull when they feel like it.

* * *

Nhà nghỉ translates to "rest house," and these inexpensive, simple, family-run hotels are where I take my lodging on motorcycle trips.

Let's get this out of the way: though not all *nhà nghỉ* fit the description, some of these rest houses serve as "love hotels," and extramarital affairs or certain dating rituals might be conducted here. Giveaways are a flashy neon sign outside that advertises hourly rates, or the rooms themselves might have odd, ergonomically shaped vinyl Valentine's Day-red couches inside. Every so often, news will break about some VIP caught at a *nhà nghỉ* "taking care of" a close friend's wife, or having a woman deliver "special medicine" for them, or simply "resting" with women who are not their wives.

But most *nhà nghỉ* are more mundane—especially outside urban red light districts.

In rural Vietnam, *nhà nghỉ* hotels don't often market themselves as love hotels, instead pitching to truck drivers or families. They don't see a lot of foreign customers, but they're not chasing this demographic anyway.

So, a Westerner on a motorcycle seeking a room at a *nhà nghỉ* is something of an oddity; sometimes, when I arrive at a village *nhà nghỉ*, the owner will try to wave me off, assuming there will be communication difficulties and hassle. Fair enough, so there's usually a conversation where I must demonstrate my bona fides. They invariably relent after some more badgering, and I'll move in for the evening.

*　*　**

With that primer digested, it's time to hit the road.

This book is organized into three sections, titled Saigon Hinterlands, the Central Highlands, and DMZ, reflecting my route. While the trip connects with some of the war's watershed moments and places, it wasn't mapped to the war's chronology in any way. This would have been impractical: geography and time didn't synchronize linearly all that often during the Vietnam War in the way that perhaps the Allied liberation of Europe during World War II did. There's no defined historical path to traverse.

There might be a metaphorical connection, however—much like the war itself, my route moved through different regions and layers of history, highlighting the magnitude of the conflict's footprint and devastation. My aim is not to provide a comprehensive story of the war but to capture themes, moments, and places that reveal how the narratives I grew up with can somehow manifest themselves when standing on a particular patch of real estate.

Simultaneously, we will encounter the revolutionary narrative that both framed and resulted from Vietnam's experience—an account whose omnipresence is gradually receding before the pressures of modernity, even as alternative perspectives, such as the unresolved and painful legacy of the Republic of Vietnam, endure in diaspora communities and private memory.

Quán nhậu taverns, *cơm bình dân* canteens, and *nhà nghỉ* hotels will be the stage set for this story. They helped me better engage the everyday life around these war sites, where the war still overlaps with rural normalcy, where a bomb crater might sit behind a vegetable garden, or a bunker might share a hillside with a hammock.

SAIGON HINTERLANDS

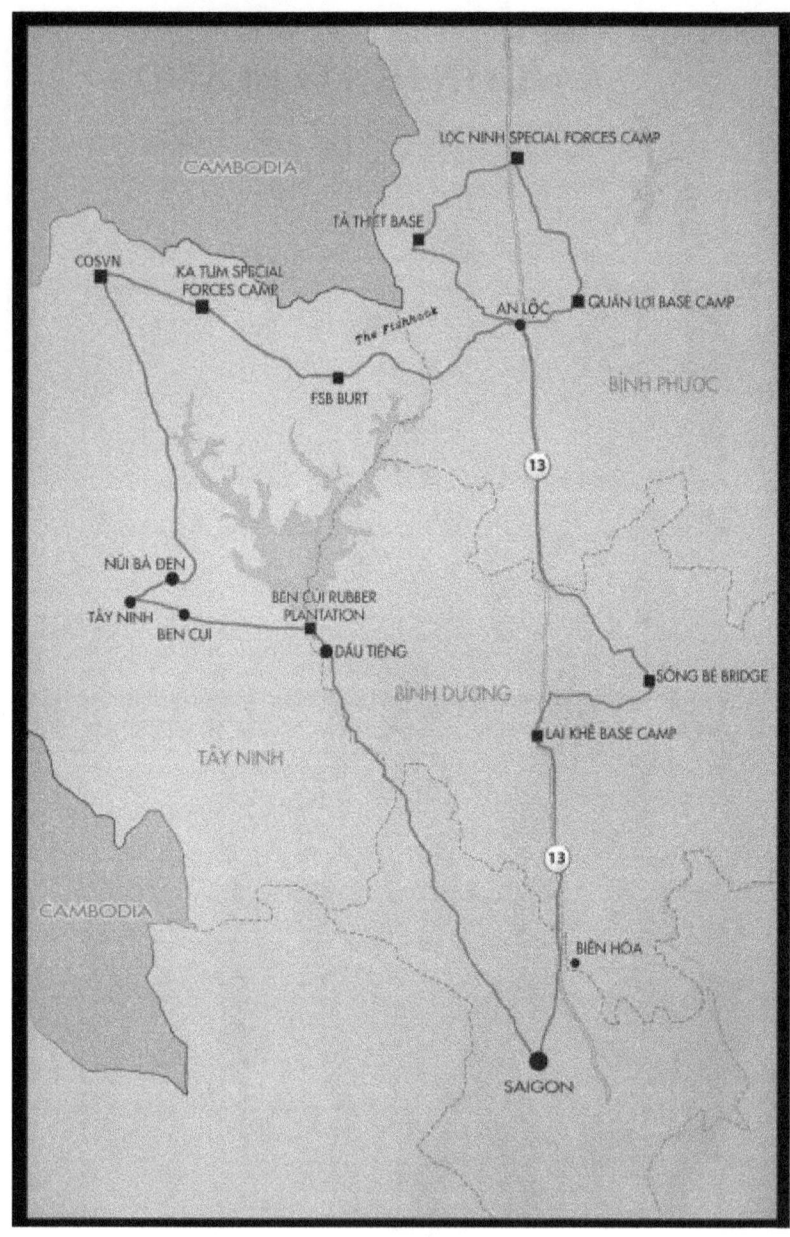

MAP: SAIGON HINTERLANDS

Lai Khê

Saigon's footprint spans over 800 square miles. It's a city without end. Foolishly, I chose to depart on this project's maiden ride from the commercial capital to the countryside to visit war sites on a Friday afternoon. This timing fell on one of Vietnam's few holiday weekends. The country was commemorating Reunification Day on April 30th, the day South Vietnam surrendered in 1975, and International Workers' Day on May 1, the global celebration of labor solidarity.

Vietnam has about the same number of national holidays as the United States, around ten or eleven annually. Tet Lunar New Year claims most of them. It's when the country closes shop and families head back to their home villages. The rest of the year is a bit thin, and these two anniversaries typically form a long weekend in a country with few. Even on a good day, leaving or entering Saigon takes hours; the city's mid-twentieth-century urban infrastructure is well-strained.

Renamed Ho Chi Minh City in 1976, Saigon was the capital of the former South Vietnam. As such, the capital's hinterland faced constant pressure from both indigenous and northern Communists who operated in the jungles of the countryside. The American and South Vietnamese presence in the region was enormous. Consequently, it's a domain of former base and battle sites. And they're gradually disappearing.

That Friday afternoon, I was crammed onto one- or two-lane roads packed with 18-wheelers, pedestrians, motorbikes, bicycles, wheelchairs, and tractors. The same roads that once ferried American and South Vietnamese soldiers and supplies to the bases of the capital's backyard. Everyone was seemingly escaping the city for the holiday weekend.

* * *

Saigon very slowly unfurled into suburbs over a few hours of slow traffic. Visually, the lines between the city's urban, suburban, and exurban edges dissolve. Greater Saigon's roads are lined with family-owned shop after family-owned shop, merchandise on the sidewalks, sleeping men slumped in storefront plastic chairs, restaurants, factories, and hawkers selling lottery tickets.

I planned to ride a loop over several days, heading north from Saigon through Bình Dương province to the Cambodia border along Highway 13, first to a town called Lộc Ninh. From there, I would turn west and ride along the frontier, in a region once referred to as "The Fishhook," which separates Battambang province in eastern Cambodia from Bình Phước and Tây Ninh provinces. Sleepy Bình Phước welcomes about nine hundred tourists a year, making it one of the country's least-visited provinces.

This area was named due to the shape of the frontier line between the two countries. Simply put, the salient resembles a fishing hook. During the war, the Ho Chi Minh Trail terminated at several points in Cambodia's Battambang province, where the People's Army of Việt Nam (PAVN) stockpiled supplies and troops to be sent into the war in the south. The Communists were massed on the Cambodian side, a mere 50 miles from the capital in Saigon.

However, due to Cambodia's official neutrality in the war, the United States and South Vietnam couldn't legally invade and take the war to the PAVN. Legal limitations didn't stop either army, however: the U.S. and ARVN made clandestine incursions into Cambodia all the time. So, the U.S. Army blanketed the buffer area between Cambodia and Saigon with military bases and regularly clashed with the communist guerrillas and North Vietnamese troops that infiltrated and quietly roamed Saigon's outskirts.

After passing through the Fishhook, I would visit Tây Ninh city and turn back south toward Saigon. Along this route, I planned to stop at about a dozen places, locating them via GPS coordinates shared through an online community of Vietnam War base and battle site enthusiasts (For that online community, start here: https://namwartravel.com/[1]).

* * *

American vehicles stayed off Highway 13 at night. Once nicknamed "Thunder Alley" by G.I.s that rode supply convoys from Saigon to the many bases on the road, Highway 13 was deadly. Vehicles and troops came under frequent ambush along the road, and the Americans and South Vietnamese had to post 24/7 sentries on the road's bridges and other infrastructure, sending out foot patrols every night across the environs.

The region between Saigon and the Fishhook in Bình Dương province also had a nickname: "The Iron Triangle." The Iron Triangle denoted a roughly 120-square-mile patch of land that concealed a staggeringly broad Việt Cộng underground tunnel network that moved supplies and men from Cambodia into Saigon's suburbs. American efforts to bomb, bulldoze, defoliate, and expose these Communist tunnel positions were indiscriminate, and swaths of forest were vaporized. Highway 13 likely traverses sections of the former underground tunnel complex, and it once resembled a moonscape: stumps, scorched earth, and scarred foliage.

As much as the U.S. tried to impose order and predictability on Saigon's hinterland by destroying the landscape, the violence never really abated. Communist troops and materiel flowed through the tunnels, which stretched for hundreds of miles. The Americans had ideas on Communist force levels in the region but these were likely

---

1. https://namwartravel.com

severe underestimations. Bình Dương, Bình Phước, and Tây Ninh were heavily militarized.

* * *

On the road, Bình Dương's air was weighed down with dust, exhaust, and other contaminants. The soupy atmosphere was accompanied by rows of industrial parks, flat delta heat, truck horns, truck engines, and street food stalls playing endless tape loops of a middle-aged male voice calling out, "Bánh mì ... bánh giò!" on a portable audio system.

Bánh mì is, of course, the world-famous Vietnamese sandwich of barbecued pork, pickles, herbs, and pâté enveloped in a personal-sized loaf of French baguette, and *bánh giò* is a glutinous rice ball filled with pork and sweet soybean paste. Both are found everywhere on the streets in Vietnam. The charming detail about the tape recording of a hawker announcing *bánh mì ... bánh giò* is that *all* vendors of these products seem to use the same original recording, done by the same man, some afternoon long ago. Not much is known about this spokesman and his famous voice, but this recording was his gift to the soundscape of Vietnam.

Eventually, things quieted down and tidied up, and Bình Dương became pleasant. The thoroughfares emptied a bit, and the chaos turned into a paved two-way road that revealed municipalities less concerned with industrialization at all costs. Despite being covered with a thin film of grease and dirt, and after picking a few flies out of my teeth, I began to relax and cool off as I finally had room on the road to accelerate.

Towns planted flowers in road dividers, and red-and-gold Communist Party propaganda banners began appearing. Some banners stretched across the road, nine to twelve feet off the ground, while others were vertical signs planted on town center sidewalks aimed at passing motorists.

Having grown up in a country without a lot of conventional propaganda, I have a certain attraction to these Communist Party communiqués. For Vietnamese people, propaganda is simply part of the party background noise that pervades daily life. The Party celebrates anniversaries, no matter how obscure, and many Vietnamese tune out the calls to mark the country's dozens of remembrances throughout the year.

Though no one expects Vietnamese citizens to mark, say, the 1930 Unification Conference in Hong Kong—when Ho Chi Minh and other exiles merged three factions into the Communist Party—the Propaganda Department still makes sure everyone's reminded, through billboards and public messaging campaigns.

The underlying message is: *Don't forget about the Communist Party*, with red-and-gold hints recalling the country's historical moments when the party was critical and celebrations of modern Vietnam's achievements and origin story. Sometimes, the banners are even endearing in their attention to detail. That day, I rode under street-width banners that read *Chúc Mừng Kỷ Niệm 23 Năm Ngày Tại Lập Tỉnh Bình Dương*, or "Celebrating 23 Years Since Bình Dương Province Was Created," as well as *Nhiệt Liệt Chúc Mừng Đại Hội Đảng Bộ Các Cấp Nhiệm Kỳ 2020–2025*, or "We Warmly Congratulate the Party Committee Congress at All Levels for the Term 2020–2025."

In bustling Bình Dương, propaganda reminds us that the Party is, in some sense, achieving its dream. While While past propaganda campaigns focused on mobilization and war, today's messages lean towards science, technology, and agriculture. Revolutionary anniversaries are still ever looming, but the core message is that a better future is arriving. The drive to build socialism permeates: increase production, integrate agriculture and industry, conserve resources, process commodities, build hydropower, industrialize, modernize, plant forests, boost electricity, build tractors, and transform battlefields into farms and factories. In short, produce more, consume less, and export the surplus. And in these banners, we see the state trying to narrate its version of legitimacy and continuity: from battlefield to factory, from rifle to rice harvester.

* * *

The goals for the next few days were Lai Khê Base Camp, Lộc Ninh, and An Lộc town. Lai Khê was once a massive U.S./ARVN base protecting the road to Saigon, and An Lộc was famously besieged by a PAVN invasion from Cambodia in 1972. Saigon finally gave way to proper countryside after a few hours of riding, and soon, I found myself nearing Lai Khê hamlet. Highway 13 shrank to a two-lane road crowded with shophouses on both sides, clustered with people, motorbikes, and stray dogs.

I had a rough idea of where Lai Khê Base Camp was, so I began surveying Highway 13. I looked for any features that would signal I was near the old U.S. and South Vietnamese Army installation that once protected Saigon. The road cleared. Rubber plantations and fields of weeds stretched out on both sides. There were also motorbike tracks and bits of trash from passing cars. The dearth of infrastructure had me thinking that Lai Khê might still be here in some form, not yet bulldozed for new buildings. Then I saw a large square concrete mass, three feet high, on the left side of the road.

Honing in on it for clues, I approached the structure and noticed slits in its walls. It was a Vietnam War–era bunker with portholes for rifles and machine guns. Most of the slits faced south, back toward Saigon. Dismounting my bike, I trudged a few feet from the road through thick weeds, eventually joining a small path that led around the rear of the bunker to its entrance. Motorbikes and cars zoomed by on Highway 13. Drivers and passengers looked at me, curious about what I might be doing on the side of the road.

This structure was solid, with reinforced cement walls that looked 10 to 12 inches thick. Built to resist armed attacks, neither climate nor vandalism seemed able to age or harm it. I ducked into the entrance and found myself inside. The floor was dirt. A few empty Red Bull cans lay around. There were white Styrofoam clamshell takeout containers and translucent plastic bags resting on the ground. A faint aroma of urine lingered in the air. Afternoon light made its way through the three slits and did its best to cut the darkness inside.

I activated my phone's flashlight and surveyed the floors and walls. Shadows, more garbage, and cobwebs lined the room. A traveler or two had used this bunker as a way-station, a spot to escape the region's oppressive midday heat, a place to pull over and meditate in the dark while sipping an energy drink and eating takeout. Bunkers are also often used as country restrooms.

Somehow, these signatures deepened the eerie atmosphere inside, as though the garbage competed with the emotional resonance that I started to feel in the place. I wondered what pulling overnight duty with another soldier or two in this small, dark space might have been like. Their eyes would have to adjust to the dark. Each evening, they would have watched out of the slits, scanning southward. They would have focused on any movement or anything out of the ordinary in the landscape. Any shadow that could shift them from vigilance to a firefight in an instant.

"The Việt Cộng owned the night," it's been said many times about places like this; all of the American bases on Highway 13 became increasingly vulnerable as the sun went down. Soldiers would have geared up at dusk and made their way to bunkers like this one, sleeping in shifts and silently contemplating the darkness for hours. I was squatting in a structure that had existed on this spot for seventy or eighty years, and its walls knew the night terror of both French and American conscripts. Somehow, their presence lingered.

* * *

Back outside and into the light, I studied the rubber forests on both sides of Highway 13 and relaxed. I was very likely in Lai Khê, and if this bunker was still here, there might be more. Across the road, a rusting white-and-chalk-green fence caught my attention—an unusual sight in rural Vietnam, where walls and gates are typically more utilitarian. Landscapes give hints. The fence's curves and faded colors suggested a 1960s origin. Unlike modern chain-link or cinder block structures, it had a distinct period aesthetic.

I was a debutant in this kind of amateur archaeology, just beginning to navigate the process of uncovering Vietnam War remnants, relying on little more than instinct and scattered clues. My hunch was that it predated 1975, though dating twentieth-century Vietnamese architecture isn't always straightforward.

Mid-century modernism was widely reinterpreted in southern Vietnam, its geometric forms and futuristic flourishes taking on local character—at times bearing echoes of Soviet modernism, which held in the north. Both styles conveyed innovation and progress—the optimistic mid-century modernism integrated more with nature, while the more austere Soviet Modernism celebrated engineering and labor. After reunification, Soviet Modernism spread south and remains the standard for government buildings, party offices, war memorials, and state-owned hotels. Even constructions from the 2010s may carry design signatures from the early 1960s.

This can confuse. So paint schemes, structural weathering, and unconventional geometric flourishes must serve as clues. Surveying the fence across from the bunker—its white concrete base, iron oval structure, and turquoise-green vertical rungs—I felt certain: this was an original part of the site of the massive Lai Khê Base Camp, once one of the most rocket attack–prone U.S./ARVN military installations in South Vietnam. Turquoise green was not a revolutionary or post-reunification color in Vietnam. The fence was *Trước '75*.

* * *

I mounted my motorcycle and rode through the gate into a rubber forest that extended as far as I could see. The light dropped off quickly. This forest had a grid of 60- to 70-foot-high rubber trees meticulously spaced apart. These trees seemed to lose their balance at their heights, curving inward and blocking sunlight from reaching the network of dirt roads that meshed the shady forest floor.

Chugging along, I searched for a base camp. Motorbikes were parked by the road. I noticed groups of two to three workers together in green uniforms. They were pouring liquid latex from cups mounted on tree trunks into larger buckets. More often than not, one worker would be perched nearby, seated on the ground next to their teammates, gazing back at me, drawn by the sound of my engine.

I took a right and turned left at some point, but the forest and the road network were a maze. It all looked the same. Unexpectedly, a worker on a motorbike overtook me from behind. I passed a couple in their sixties, the husband in grubby work gear and Wellington boots on the ground, smoking a cigarette. His wife was next to him, in colorful polyester trousers, a sweater, and a fishing hat, holding a thermos. They waved.

As I turned back from the exchange, I noticed a mound of concrete in the distance. Shadows began to envelop the forest, but this looked promising. Turning on my headlight, I realized I was right; it was another bunker and gun post, stranded in the middle of the trees. This one had deteriorated much more than the first. It was about the same size as the one on the highway, and boxy. Either it had been hit by a rocket at some point, or fifty years of nature had decayed this once-impregnable structure.

Concrete slabs had broken off the bunker and lay scattered across the ground. A 50-foot-tall rubber tree grew from its center. I stepped closer and turned on my flashlight. Two more slits for rifles came into view. Unlike the roadside bunker, there were no signs of R&R here—no Red Bull cans, no cigarette butts, no takeout containers. While I stood on a three-foot-high heap of broken concrete, a phantom rubber worker approached on a motorbike and rode around the bunker, eyes fixed forward, as if I wasn't there. In the dark forest, it was an eerie moment.

The entrance to Lai Khê Base Camp once read "Welcome to Rocket City," a nod to the relentless Communist rocket attacks it endured during the war. The ARVN Fifth Division, known for its true believer *esprit de corps*, was based here. In the postwar American narrative, the ARVN became a stand-in for the war's failure; easier to blame than to understand. It's often forgotten—or dismissed—that so many South Vietnamese fought with tenacity, loyalty, and staggering loss.

If forests could absorb sentiment and memory, this one would be saturated.

Lai Khê was a South Vietnamese stronghold, coordinating air assaults, search-and-destroy missions, night patrols, and recon across the capital's hinterland. Within the base walls was a vast facility: barracks, officer quarters, mess halls, field hospitals, fuel and supply infrastructure, warehouses, an airstrip, helicopters, other vehicles, and thousands of combat and support troops. Rocket City earned its name: Lai Khê was likely the second-most bombarded site of the war, behind only Khe Sanh in Quảng Trị province, where U.S. Marines endured a prolonged PAVN siege in 1968.

When I returned to my earlier spot in the rubber forest, the couple was still there, collecting latex. I approached and asked if they'd seen any war relics.

The gent pulled his cigarette from his mouth and said, "Yes, there's something right on this road, further," pointing behind me.

Realizing he was sending me back the way I came, I asked if there might be another. There was—he pointed me the other way.

It was past dusk, and the rubber trees seemed to hang lower. I kept moving, hoping my headlight would catch another piece of rubble. I felt a flicker of exhilaration—this was my first solo Vietnam War archaeology mission—and at the same time, a steady alertness from being swallowed by this eldritch forest. Just a few hundred yards away, Highway 13 still pulsed with life. Through the trees, I glimpsed the occasional motorbike drifting past. My beam caught an owl flapping low across the road.

My light swept across the darkness and caught the spectral jagged outline of another collapsed bunker. It had crumbled into concrete slabs, tangled rebar, and a single wall that, somehow, was still standing. I perused the wreckage on the forest floor.

Here I was, among the bones of a decomposing base camp once central to the war. Whether the bunker collapsed from battle, vandalism, or time, I couldn't say. The air felt unusually full—too still, as if holding breath. Rebar curled from the rubble like branches from a dead tree, frozen in the moment of collapse.

It felt like history at the time. Maybe it was. It passed for history, or maybe I just needed it to.

I glanced back at the highway in the distance, noticing another lonely motorbike prowling by with two passengers. They were probably headed home. Though it was only 6:30 p.m., it suddenly felt like it could have been 3:00 a.m. in that forest. I exhaled and decided to return to the road to find a *nhà nghỉ* nearby. No longer "owned by the Việt Cộng," this particular night and place on Highway 13 suddenly felt like a new shift was beginning.

* * *

I rode out of the forest, with its own set of mystical anxieties, and turned left on Highway 13 to a more worldly set of hazards. Always avoid riding a motorcycle in the Vietnamese countryside after dark. There are no real streetlights. Half-cut drivers. Buffalo. Motorbikes cruising with no headlights or taillights. Chickens. Dogs. Bicyclists appear suddenly. Aggressive trucks.

Recalling a showy-looking *nhà nghỉ* a half-mile back toward Saigon, I retraced my steps. It was situated down a decline in the forest on the right side of Highway 13, just before a small bridge over a creek. On the roadside, an LED sign shaped like an arrow pointed into the forest, flashing "NHÀ NGHỈ" in red.

I slowed the bike for the dirt path that declined off the highway. It was lush. As I moved down the path, short trees with big, shamrock-green elephant-ear leaves brushed my helmet. Low-wattage lights glowed faintly ahead, casting the scene in the twilight of a lakeside camp house. A concrete gate and fence, shaped and painted like logs, corralled the installation. I rode in.

This *nhà nghỉ* occupied the edge of a creek, its sluggish, visibly polluted waters rolling past about a meter below the bank. Plastic cups and other debris had gathered along both sides, trapped in stagnant eddies. More of a rustic retreat than the more conventional above-ground bomb shelter *nhà nghỉ*—boxy cinder block structures divided into windowless motel-style rooms—this place had a different charm. A gazebo, fashioned from concrete and rebar to resemble rough-hewn logs, stood in the courtyard. Four or five cylindrical bungalows mirrored its design, their thatched roofs softening the design. Among them, tropical trees and dense foliage wove the setting together. It was, I had to agree with whoever conceived this *nhà nghỉ*, a romantic place.

* * *

The front desk was in the owner's residence, a stock one-level, two-room concrete Vietnamese country house. I approached a middle-aged woman. She was outside on the terrace, watching a television propped on a windowpane.

I handed over my passport. As she checked me in, I peered at the television—a music video of six girls, maybe eight or nine years old, skipping across a beach, harmonizing to a sing-along patriotic song. She was watching *Thế Hệ Trẻ*—The Young Generation—reruns. The video looked at least a decade old, and it brought me back.

There was a time when I found this programming a little strange. In the early/mid 2000s, it seemed every third channel on Vietnamese television was showcasing children on stage, singing. It was simple, wholesome entertainment, and shows like *Thế Hệ Trẻ* had multigenerational appeal. Vietnamese love children, and they love youthfulness.

"Looks like you're watching Thế Hệ Trẻ," I said.

She smiled and handed me my key. "That's right."

She motioned to my bungalow. It was the closest to the owner's house. Maybe they wanted to keep an eye on me. A Honda Wave motorbike was parked next door, the lights low inside.

After a shower, I ambled to the dining room. The Honda Wave next door was gone. Just as I dropped my room key at the head of an empty, thirty-seat rectangular dining table in the gazebo, the owner's daughter appeared and handed me a twelve-page menu of Vietnamese comfort foods. *Đậu phụ sốt cà chua* (fried tofu and tomato sauce) and *rau muống xào tỏi* (sautéed morning glory with garlic) were on the first page and all I needed to see.

Dinner arrived in three minutes and was consumed in seven. I wiped my lips with a few squares from the toilet tissue roll on the table, then made my way to a communal table at the bank of the creek. Almost every public-facing business in Vietnam has a communal table, with an oft-used tea set and a *thuốc lào* tobacco water pipe nearby. I saw the silhouette of someone sitting there. I descended and joined him. No invitation was necessary.

I sat, crossed my legs, and gazed at the passing creek, saying nothing.

He inhaled and stilled. "How tall are you?"

I turned and smiled. Next to me was a Vietnamese man of about seventy, wearing a striped polo shirt, slacks, and yellow *dép tổ ong* sandals. He was slight and balding, a handsome man with a gentle face. I paused and considered, giving him my height and adding my weight.

The dialogue was unfolding country-slow, and he silently processed my answer. This gent was the security guard for this *nhà nghỉ*, and he had just begun his shift. Now in possession of the intelligence he wanted, he lit up the *thuốc lào*, took a big hit as the whistle ascended skyward, stood, exhaled a dense cloud, and silently returned to do his foot patrol. My friend passed by several more times over the next twenty minutes, stopping briefly for another wordless visit with the *thuốc lào* before continuing his nighttime tactical operation.

Sông Bé

Waking at six, I heard the distant signature of a karaoke singer wind its way through the creeks and rubber plantations. Closer in, the roar of long-haul trucks passing on Highway 13. The sounds of life stirring in the countryside. I rose and returned to the gazebo dining room, taking my compulsory two fried eggs, a small baguette, two sliced cucumbers, two sliced tomatoes, soy sauce, chili sauce, and fresh orange juice on ice. After vacuuming up this perfect meal, I carried a coffee back down to the communal table.

My friend from the previous evening was there, studying the creek. I doubted he'd been up all night guarding the hotel. He looked relatively fresh, despite wearing the same apparel. His shirt was still tucked into his slacks, cinched with a pleather belt imported from China.

Next to him at his seat was a small monkey, tied by the neck to a table leg with a length of string.

"Who's this guy?" I asked him as I sat down.

"He's a monkey. He stays here with us." He fed him some peanuts.

Maybe the man had brought the monkey out on patrol that morning to introduce the two of us. He treated him more like a companion. Somehow, it seemed intuitive that he might.

"Well, he seems like good company," I said.

After a moment, he cut through the hush.

"Did you find a woman last night?"

"Um, no. I wasn't looking for a woman. I'm on a motorcycle trip, and I had a look at Lai Khê yesterday. The base over there," I replied, motioning behind my back.

"Ah," he said, and let that information settle.

"Are you from this area?" I asked.

He was. For years, he'd lived across from the old Lai Khê Base Camp. His polo shirt sleeve ended halfway down his bicep. On his forearm was a faded black tattoo in the Khmer script. I've seen these tattoos before, usually found on men of conscript age in the late 1970s into the 1980s.

Tattooed in Cambodia. That mark placed him in a generation drafted into the long war that came shortly after reunification—Vietnam's twelve-year campaign against the Khmer Rouge. The conflict began in 1978, after years of Khmer Rouge cross-border attacks into Tây Ninh and several Mekong Delta provinces. Their aim was to reclaim territory the Khmer Empire had lost to Vietnamese kingdoms centuries earlier.

It was one of history's dumber miscalculations. Vietnam had been fully mobilized for three decades, and in that time dispatched the French, the Americans, and the ARVN. In December 1978, Hanoi sent 150,000 seasoned troops across the border, captured Phnom Penh, and toppled the Khmer Rouge in less than two weeks. The PAVN stayed for another twelve years.

Given his age, there was a good chance he'd also fought in the earlier war's closing chapters, perhaps against the Americans. This laconic man had seen more than he let on. There was something measured in his pace, as if he was conserving energy. Or trust. He rose without a word, freed the monkey, and the pair vanished together.

* * *

As I motored away from Lai Khê on Highway 13, I basked in the vastness of the rice paddies alongside the road on an exceptionally bright morning. I could sense the stoic misery of the farmers I passed, who tended their fields in long pants, long-sleeved shirts, and conical hats. It was 7:30 in the morning, nearing 100 degrees already.

April and May are southern Vietnam's hottest months, as the region's bloated skies climax with heat and humidity just before the rainy season begins in June. I then realized it was Reunification Day, the anniversary of the decisive northern push to take Saigon.

It would have been barbarically hot when they fought across South Vietnam's flat plains and into the capital. I imagined the soldiers maneuvering under that same brutal sun, boots and sandals kicking up the dust now tilled by these unflinching farmers. A different time, but the same soil. The heat, the monotony, the weight of it all remained unchanged.

Indeed, Vietnam is a beautiful country. But large stretches are mundane. Saigon's inland surroundings, especially the section I was riding, are flat, hot, dry, dusty, and dull. It's the outer edge of the Mekong River Delta. Photos from the 1960s and '70s back this sentiment. Through the snapshots of American G.I.s, the provinces of Tây Ninh, Bình Dương, and Bình Phước look oppressively blazing. These photos always seem washed out, with soldiers raising their palms to block the bright sunlight.

* * *

My first stop was the Sông Bé Bridge, built in 1925 by the French colonial administration. It later became a key choke point on supply routes during the Việt Minh's war with the French Colonial Army—the Việt Minh being the revolutionary predecessor to the 1960s National Liberation Front, or Việt Cộng.

An interruption shook me as I rode through a town called Phước Hoà. At first, I thought I'd driven through dust kicked up by some roadside machinery. Sadly, it was a swarm of thirty or so bees, hovering in front of a sugarcane crusher beside a tạp hoá country store. I passed straight through them.

Pulling over, I opened my jacket. One dying bee wiggled out of my shirt and fell to the pavement. His barb stuck in my chest, it was traumatic. I'm the kind of man who is terrified of bees.

I recovered and continued toward the bridge. Crossing a modern, paved, four-lane span over the Bé (small) River, I stopped midway and looked upstream. There it was: what remained of the 1925 Sông Bé Bridge, about 100 yards upstream. What once connected two sides now stood frozen from 1947. The midsection was gone.

The ruined bridge stretches about 100 feet out from each bank of the Bé River, ending in a sudden 50-foot gap where the two halves once met. Beneath that gap flowed the muddy, slow-moving Bé. Bougainvillea, cashew, mango, and Rangoon Creeper trees lined the riverbanks, along with a bamboo grove breathing in the humid Bình Dương provincial air. It could have been Cajun country.

The conventional narrative holds that Việt Minh sappers blew the middle section in 1947, during the First Indochina War. Hanoi had declared independence in 1945. France spent the next decade trying to reclaim its colony. The Sông Bé crossing had been a key artery for French supply lines into Vietnam and Cambodia.

Still, it's a mystery why the French left the bridge unrepaired for so many years. The story is incomplete.

In 1968, the Americans dropped a prefabricated Bailey Bridge into the gap blown by the Việt Minh, making the structure usable again. To prevent further sabotage, the U.S. Army cleared hundreds of yards of forest around the bridge. Supply convoys resumed, but this remained hostile territory.

ARVN troops manned the bridge, while an American platoon was stationed a hundred yards upstream. Firebase perimeters and landing zones dotted the surrounding area.

* * *

I turned my motorcycle off the road and wound on a narrow path through villages and farms. Some enterprising resident had opened a café by the bridge. I pulled in and spotted a table of young Vietnamese women—extravagantly styled, outliers in this corner of Bình Dương. Silently, they peered up from their iPhones as I strolled past.

Without warning, paparazzi surrounded me, phones out. They wanted to take portraits of me, and with me, a foreigner. So, we did, exchanging no words. After thirty or forty shots, I moved away, showing them my palm, at least in my world the universal movie star hand gesture for *No cameras. Please.* They took five or six more photos of me in mid-stride anyway, as I walked toward the bridge, no longer bothering to face their smartphones.

Perhaps this is what happens when rural Vietnamese, for the first time, encounter a Westerner who is not on a television screen; centuries of the Western Gaze are flipped. I once met a woman in rural Vietnam who showed me her phone and asked if I recognized the Western man in her wallpaper photo. She didn't know him at all. To her, he was just a random fellow from her social media feed. So, she copied and pasted his photo for her phone's backdrop. To my surprise, I did know him—he was a well-known middle-aged American businessman and longtime Saigon expat.

A rusting chain-link fence surrounded the Sông Bé Bridge to dissuade automobile and truck traffic from foolishly trying to use the bridge to cross the Bé River. Motorbikes can and do sneak through a gap in the fence. The implicit assumption is that one knows what they're doing and won't speed through the thirty yards of bridge ahead of the fence and ride straight off the cliff, as there's no fence at the precipice.

I noticed three motorbikes parked and three teenagers squatting at the end of the bridge, smoking cigarettes while staring down through the gap—probably a forty-foot drop to the meandering river below. At over ninety years old, the concrete Sông Bé Bridge has three elegant spans, though most of the middle span was destroyed. One of the bridge's pillars held a vintage rusted telephone box with wires and other mechanical bits still attached and dangling.

After I arrived, the teenagers looked up, and then went back to their business. They photographed each other while lighting cigarettes. After tearing through their cigarettes, they tossed the butts into the river and mounted their bikes, accelerating back to land much too quickly for the structure and its hazardous potholes, rebar twigs, and fencing.

The scene evoked "The Ledge," a flooded granite quarry that became an illegal swimming hole and lawless place in my hometown of Manchester, New Hampshire. In the 1970s and '80s, one would also find graffiti, teenagers, Budweiser, boomboxes cranking AC/DC, and Marlboro Reds at The Ledge. Spots like this seem to seduce people's recklessness.

Legend has it that some moron rode his Harley-Davidson off the 55-foot jump one Friday night at The Ledge in the late 1970s. He'd probably had too much to drink and was either showing off or rising to a challenge issued by one of his associates during an evening at The Zoo, Manchester's premier biker bar during that time period. His motorcycle would have sank the 120 feet to the bottom of the flooded quarry in seconds. Surely, the next morning he woke and instantly regretted the previous night's performance.

Teenagers still find their ledges. This one felt like a stage. The setting may change, but the choreography of bravado doesn't. Different continent, different generation, but the lure of danger, of showing off, felt familiar. There was something enticing about it.

There's little in the way of plaques or markers here. Just the ruined ends of the bridge, still clinging to the riverbank. The Vietnamese, ever pragmatic, didn't romanticize it. I wondered how many truckers crossing the new bridge even glance over at the old one. A supply route once worth defending with men and artillery is now just a half-ruined afterthought upriver.

Relics like this are rare. Cities have preserved prestige colonial façades. But to stumble across a rural bridge with its middle blown out in 1947 feels like uncovering something that wasn't meant to be found. After reunification, the government tidied up—removing what was unsightly, replacing it with a cleaner story. Still, some remnants escaped, hiding in plain sight.

Finding one of them feels like surreptitiously tapping the telephone wires of a secret conversation that Vietnamese history doesn't want me to hear. This was quieter, stranger, and more nuanced than the revolutionary narrative. It was eerie in this way, as though the bridge I was gazing at was a ghost that didn't quite want to be seen.

* * *

I returned to Highway 13 and took a break at a *bình dân* café. Truck drivers lounged in hammocks, and the café offered the usual range of juices and coffee. Two teenage boys were also lying in hammocks, and a teenage girl slouched behind the counter, with bleached hair and an orange T-shirt printed with the slogan *Armani Jeans Nothing Is Impossible to a Willing Hoa*. Like many counterintuitively superb English language T-shirt slogans in East and Southeast Asia, this one had no firm meaning. The husband-and-wife proprietors were also asleep, in separate hammocks.

The teenagers were discussing something as I rolled in, each uttering the phrase "đụ má" twice or thrice per sentence. This is a very naughty word that often infects the language of *cao bồi thôn*—"village cowboy," the elegant Vietnamese term for petty *bình dân* hustlers or those at the very bottom of an organized crime hierarchy—types who aspire to project country gangster grit. One strummed a flimsy acoustic guitar. I approached the girl and asked for an iced coffee. She froze, eyes wide—clearly not expecting a foreigner to roll in. Like the paparazzi at the bridge.

"Cà phê chồn nhé," she replied.

Cà phê chồn translates to "weasel coffee," made from coffee beans eaten, partially digested, and defecated by Asian palm civets. It is considered a delicacy; she was upselling me.

She poured four ounces of boiling water into a stainless *phin* filter perched on a glass of ice. Then she brought it over. Adorable yet inept *cà phê phin* contraptions filter water through coffee grounds into the cup below excruciatingly slowly, resulting in a concentrated and flavorful brew. The wait can be fifteen or twenty minutes.

Having spent the morning in the sun, I was feeling salty, but soon found myself inadvertently in the viewfinder of her phone. More photos. I was the exotic backdrop now. I unclenched. *All in the game*, I thought. Attention, selfies, and slack-jawed stares are the bearable price of admission for me to enter Vietnam's somewhat enigmatic rural world.

I wanted a bit of space and quiet. Sometimes, that's not to be. The girl hovered and asked me about myself, where I was from, and what I was doing at the Sông Bé River. I told her I was on a motorcycle trip, that I loved Vietnam, and that I was just wandering.

It felt like the startled curiosity of someone who rarely has to explain her world to anyone. Her bleached hair and slack posture suggested some boredom, but the upsell told me she had good instincts.

Then her mother woke up and peered out from her hammock. She rose without speaking. Makeup undisturbed. She came over like it was her shift.

It was more attention than I'd usually get in Saigon. And it was performative. What unfurled was countryside mixed-gender *làm quen* small talk in Vietnamese, some combination of chops-busting and coquetry, weighted to the gruffness. She asked me where I was from.

"I'm from the United States," I said.

She studied me for a moment, then decided: "No, you're not. You're from the Soviet Union."

"Negative," I said. "I'm American."

"You're ugly," she said, looking sour. "Look at you. Ugly guy." She pinched the hair on my arm, and from a distance measured my nose and tried to figure out the dimensions of my forehead.

Jaded, I fiddled with my *phin* coffee filter, willing the hot water to move through the grounds more quickly.

"Stop that," she said. "You have to be patient and wait. So, how tall are you?"

"Three meters," I replied.

"Stand up." I did, and so did she. "I'm 160 centimeters. There's no way you're three meters tall."

She was right.

Then they wanted to take another photo. I obliged, but the interrogation was satiating me. "You have blue eyes. Soviet Union. Bad people. All of you."

With weapons, food, and cash, the Soviet Union to a large extent underwrote Vietnam's war against the United States and helped rebuild the country after 1975. Soviet and Russian investment helped Vietnam develop its offshore oil industry in the 1980s and '90s. Most northern cadres from the war generation, now in their 60s, 70s, and 80s, treasure the Soviet Union, love speaking Russian, and delight in gathering at one of Hanoi's many Eastern European-style beer halls to reminisce about their years as students at Eastern Bloc universities.

Yet, among ordinary Vietnamese, especially southerners, Russians arouse some suspicion. I have some feel for the reason why, but when asked, a Russia-wary Vietnamese will usually dismiss the question with "because they're cheap." This is odd because, like most of the world's people, Vietnamese are also cheap. They're tough hagglers. They're savers. They live in a country with a fixed exchange rate designed to increase export production, not consumption. They review restaurant checks like they're commercial lease agreements. They invest in education and real estate. So, it's not clear why Vietnamese are suspicious of Russians because of their frugality, unless Russian people are light years cheaper than Vietnamese people. But I've not seen any evidence of that.

"I'm not Soviet. I'm American. Really. What do you think of Americans?" I replied to the café owner.

"They're OK. Just OK. Not much better than the Soviets. We put up with them."

I'd been around long enough to know that the goading would only escalate, so I pulled my notebook back out and signaled them that I wanted to hibernate with it for a while. I lifted the lid on my *phin* coffee filter again to evaluate progress. The water level had lowered about a fortieth of an inch.

"Just wait!" she said, seeing the opening to reengage and micromanage me, and then ordered her daughter back to the counter.

Mum loitered, looking at my phone and notebook from behind my shoulder, trying to glean any possible clues to explain the mystery of who I was and what I was up to. There had to be a deeper reason why I was in her roadside café. Soon, her daughter returned. Research and note-taking were not meant to be. I closed my notebook and turned over my phone.

"He looks like that guy from *Transporter*," she murmured to her daughter, perhaps assuming I couldn't hear her. *Christ,* I thought. Jason Statham again.

Then she turned to me and said, "You're quite an ugly fella. What do you think you're doing, anyway?"

She left and returned with a slice of watermelon, which was in season in this part of the country, as evidenced by the roadside floggers I saw everywhere hawking watermelons out of the cargo beds of Chinese three-wheeled "Pablo" rickshaws. She got back into her hammock and challenged, one hand holding the watermelon and the other pointing: "OK, fool, tell me what this is. Right now."

"Watermelon," I said. "Listen to me. If I were from the Soviet Union, I wouldn't be able to answer that question. They don't have watermelon in the Soviet Union." I gave this odd logic a shot.

"Hmm. I don't know about that. Do they have watermelon in the United States?" she asked.

"It's everywhere during certain times of the year."

"OK. You may be American, but you're still ugly," she smirked.

"Well, I think I've interrupted your day long enough. I should get going," I said, handing her money for the bill, before removing the stainless-steel single-cup *phin* coffee filter and downing a third of a cup of coffee on ice.

She sat up. "Where are you going now?"

I gave her a cryptic reply: "Certain questions have no answers."

* * *

The monkey. The rant against the USSR, Vietnam's Communist superpower ally that disintegrated three decades ago. The cursing village cowboys. It was a tableau of rural resilience, wary, half-asleep, but wired and surviving.

I smiled and lowered my motorcycle helmet back on my head. "Thank you for the coffee. Very delicious."

Tà Thiết

I was fifty miles from my day's goal of Lộc Ninh. But I had an abundance of time. About an hour after leaving the café at Sông Bé Bridge, I treated myself to a plate of spare ribs, rice, vegetables, broth, and iced tea at a *cơm bình dân* restaurant on Highway 13. This particular *cơm bình dân* was gentle and undemanding compared to others I've visited. Maybe it was the hour.

It was just before eleven. The floor sparkled. Staff stood around chatting, unhurried. The walls were washed in mint green paint and bare, save for grease stains, a 2014 wall calendar of women wearing *áo dài* (traditional long tunic with pants), and, oddly, two or three shoe heel prints at an altitude of about four feet from the floor.

One other early bird, an Electricity Việt Nam worker in a safety orange jumpsuit, sat quietly in the corner, sipping broth from a small bowl. He was engrossed in a copy of *Báo Công An* (Police Newspaper) spread across his aluminum table, the pages absorbing puddles of broth that accumulated from his distracted slurping.

Between bites, I plugged *di tích lịch sử*—historical relics—into my map app, a reliable keyword that sometimes turns up anything war-related. Not far to the northwest, over the line into Bình Phước, sat the Tà Thiết Base—officially, the Communist Regional Command national monument.

Well, now. Tà Thiết isn't exactly in *Lonely Planet Vietnam*. Before committing to the approximately 25-mile round-trip detour west from Highway 13 to a patch of forest on the Cambodian border, I looked at the Bình Phước provincial government website.

Following the Easter Offensive in April 1972, when the North Vietnamese Army tested the reach of its southern strategy, Hanoi moved its regional command post from Tây Ninh to Tà Thiết, fifty miles northeast of Saigon. The offensive had liberated and cleared this area of U.S. and ARVN troops. The plan was to take Saigon by way of Highway 13. That meant a nearby staging ground was essential.

Between 1972 and 1975, Tà Thiết was developed as a training and command center. The PAVN built downward: tunnels, trenches, workshops, classrooms, assembly halls, a canteen, and bunker living quarters for Party leadership. Conscripts slept in hammocks in the jungle. Tà Thiết Base grew under General Trần Văn Trà, the southern commander of all ground forces, and became the launchpad for the Ho Chi Minh Campaign, which ended the war on this very day in 1975. While Hanoi had the final call on the offensive, General Trà was the key architect.

According to the Bình Phước provincial government website, Tà Thiết also hosted the Third Congress of Heroes and Soldiers in March of 1973, the Central Military Conference in October of that same year, and the "conference to thoroughly study Resolution 21 of the Communist Party Central Committee for high-ranking cadres of the region and the provinces." Information that might only be remarkable to serious students of Party history. Today, the base has been restored as a museum of Vietnam's revolutionary past. Or, in the words of the online Bình Phước government portal:

Tà Thiết base zone is a revolutionary red address to introduce the tradition of fighting and improving the effectiveness of education of revolutionary value to cadres, soldiers and people of Bình Phước province in particular and the whole country in general.

Maybe a clunky description, but I'd be making the detour.

* * *

Thirty minutes later, I turned left off Highway 13 onto a country road heading west. The flat, dry landscape rolled on with me. I had the tarmac to myself. Until the howls of large-displacement motorcycles began closing in from behind. My side mirror flared with headlights. *Christ, they must be Harley-Davidsons*, I thought. They were.

They quickly overtook my Kawasaki—an honest-to-God motorcycle gang in Vietnam. In a hurry, they passed in ones, twos, and threes: big, fat, ostentatious American motorcycles: Road Kings, Road Glides, Sportsters, Fat Bobs, Fat Boys, Heritage Classics, Breakouts, and Ultra Limiteds. Many of these giant bikes flew titanic Vietnamese flags rigged to poles at their tail ends, straining and flapping against the rush of wind. The passengers on these bikes were savoring the ride, arms and fists extended skyward in triumph. As they passed, several commander-drivers in Oakley sunglasses and foam-ribbed bicycle helmets condescendingly stared at me, their gazes lingering for a few seconds. Our Vietnamese friends have learned something from the hubris of American Harley-Davidson riders.

Part of this swagger might have something to do with consumer prestige in Vietnam. New Harleys can range between $20,000 and $100,000 at the high end here, accounting for special consumption taxes and import duties. I've seen used Harleys selling for $75,000 on Craigslist. Considering that the GDP per capita in Vietnam is on the order of $4,000 per year, one arrives at a better sense of the demographic that rides these bikes. People who can afford this purchase—five to twenty times the average national salary—are relatively well-off, but more importantly, well-connected. These were city boys, not country *bình dân* guys.

Riding large displacement motorcycles makes sense neither financially nor physically in Vietnam. They are enormous, ten times the size of what a Vietnamese rides every day, a screwball choice for a country where the average man is around five feet six inches tall and 130 pounds. However, these bikes have caught on for some, particularly in Saigon, where conspicuous consumption is devotional. This is probably a legacy of the city's history as a commercial center and, to some extent, an inheritance from the American period.

In contrast, having survived collectivism and civil forfeitures during the revolution and still fearing public sector predation, most northerners prefer not to advertise how much money they have. This is why it's not unusual to see highly successful northern entrepreneurs dressing like farmers. Wealthy individuals in the south have developed a taste for expensive and flashy motorcycles, and wealth gives one a wholly different set of permissions and expectations in Vietnam. Like any self-conscious Harley rider, Vietnamese riders live by different laws.

* * *

Forgive me. But we need to go here.

Harleys are still aspirational in Vietnam. Harley-Davidson consumption in the U.S. has followed a clear demand curve, peaking with Baby Boomers. It's perhaps generational, as most of us born after the late 1960s have a love/hate relationship with these bikes. The whole thing became too exhausting at some point around thirty years ago. Most Baby Boomers in North America decided when they hit the age of forty-five that they *had* to have a Harley-Davidson, which timed well and did wonders for a company that had just finished modernizing its business and manufacturing processes in the mid-1980s.

American Baby Boomers took pride in their anti-establishment cred. They clung to it even after embracing capitalism in middle age. But they didn't bother trying to reconcile the incongruity, so it was painful to watch. The celebrated 1969 film *Easy Rider* probably offered an outlaw touchstone, and identifying with Peter Fonda and Dennis Hopper was tangible. So, they bought Harley-Davidsons, and the cruiser design for motorcycles exploded and took over the U.S. market. By the 1990s, the *Easy Rider* poetry of two lonely sages riding choppers while navigating an America that felt like a foreign country had been grossly debased.

Bloated cruiser motorcycles that were mere inches away from being compact cars—1200-cubic centimeter engines, radios, air conditioners, trailers, big cushioned seats for big bottoms, windjammers, helmets with headsets, and, in some cases, a "reverse" gear. And gear, lots of gear. Leather jackets, T-shirts, leather trousers, and motorcycle boots, all Harley-Davidson branded. Overweight riders in goatees, jeans, and white Reeboks suited up and took a spin, maybe once a month, to the lake with their spouse. Accountant by day, outlaw a few times a year.

Too old to ride, balance, or pick up 500 pounds of steel, most Baby Boomers have now aged out. And younger generations never inherited the *Easy Rider* romance or the Harley cult that came with it. Naturally, sales dropped. This might explain why I had such a hard time finding an English version of the Harley-Davidson Vietnam website, despite the thousands of expat motorcycle riders there: English-speaking expats aren't as passionate about these bikes as Vietnamese are. Maybe that's why the gazes felt reversed; mine skeptical, theirs defiant.

* * *

The parade rumbled past. I caught a few more contemptuous glances. One bike with a custom paint job on its windshield that read *TRƯỜNG SA HOÀNG SA LÀ CỦA VIỆT NAM*, or "The Spratly and Paracel Islands Are Vietnamese Territory." I started to piece together who these chaps might be.[1] They were Vietnamese nationalists who supported the Communist Party and identified with Vietnam as a strong, self-reliant nation capable of guarding its borders, particularly against China. Nothing wrong with those sentiments. But that day, the whole thing felt unusually cocky.

Vietnamese aren't usually the aggrieved patriots Americans can be. They don't lead with anti-China rants. But that edge is there. It's sensible to stay aware of it.

That was the vibe—a bit menacing. The dozen or so Harleys soon vanished into the horizon. I was happily on my own again.

* * *

Tà Thiết Base was close. A short distance later, I followed a sign onto a dirt road and searched for parking amid ten buses and thirty or so amassed Harley-Davidsons. Mystery solved: a nationalist Harley jamboree at Tà Thiết Base. I gave those still-hot leviathans a wide berth and parked in a different section of the lot.

Strolling down a trail to a meadow, I picked up the reverberations of a booming sound system and what I discerned was an amateur vocalist. Karaoke. In a small field in front of the ticket counter, a group of fifty men and a handful of women were relaxing on blue tarps on the lawn, some sleeping, others drinking beer, picnicking, and singing karaoke. I noticed familiar faces from the earlier meeting on the road, in workout gear and Oakley sunglasses, chugging cans of Bia Saigon. Their foam bicycle helmets, gloves, and motorcycle jackets lay scattered in the sun.

Two tour buses had driven onto the lawn and parked at odd-angled inclines, as though the drivers simply gave up. Their passenger doors remained open, and revelers dipped in and out of the buses for supplies pulled from large Styrofoam coolers. Empty cases of Tiger beer and crushed cans were already strewn across the meadow. I realized some in this crew were probably well-lubed, and the others were hurriedly catching up.

I purchased a ticket and entered. As I passed the revelers, some in the group spotted me, seemingly the only foreigner visiting Tà Thiết Base that day. They whispered to each other. Some men on blankets craned their necks to get a better look at me. There was an edge in the air, like something was being held back. Ironically, it felt a bit like the scene in *Easy Rider* where Wyatt, Billy, and George park their Harley-Davidsons and enter a southern café for a meal, keeping their cool as a group of local men at another table quietly snicker about their hippie appearance, with an underlying malice and tension.

Apart from the younger bikers, most of this group looked to be in their fifties and sixties, with a few appearing older and more delicate. About half wore the olive-drab quasi-uniforms sold everywhere in the country, the default attire for the war generation. Some wore green pith helmets with the PAVN insignia: a small red circle with a gold star in the middle, adorned with gold leaves and wheat stalks. A few were probably war veterans, while the bikers seemed there for the cosplay.

Probably 80 percent of the time, a crowd drinking beer in a public place like this in Vietnam will warmly but aggressively go out of their way to invite a stray foreigner to join them. Usually, it's because they've had a handful of jars, are feeling gregarious and friendly, and are seeking a little entertainment. Not these boys. The stares weren't threatening. Just firm. Like I'd wandered into a world that wasn't mine. Today was for Vietnamese only.

* * *

A banner hanging between the two buses caught my eye. I glanced and read *Đại Tướng Trần Văn Trà 01/01/18–20/04/96* in gold on a field of red, flanked by a gold hammer and sickle and a gold star. So that's what all the ruckus was about: it was the Saturday closest to the twenty-second anniversary of Ho Chi Minh Campaign Deputy Commander General Trần Văn Trà's death. I hadn't realized he inspired such adoration in southern Vietnam, despite his frictions with the Party after the war.

In 1982, Trà wrote a memoir critical of Hanoi's war strategy and the high death toll among southern Vietnamese. The book was heavily censored but went to publication anyway. Trà was excommunicated from the Party afterward.

Doubtless, April 20th is marked in some form at this place every year. Aging revolutionaries hop on tour buses to come to Tà Thiết Base to honor General Trà and mingle with young bikers.

Some war sites are memorialized; others are forgotten. Perhaps there's no formula for this, but it does have something to do with what happened there. I'd expected another relatively empty place earlier that day, but the General Trà wrinkle was welcome. Lai Khê had vanished into a rubber plantation; just a few bunkers left, unloved. Propelling the revolutionary narrative so effectively, Tà Thiết got a different treatment. It had staged the grand finale.

***

I joined a paved trail that led me into a thick jungle. At the entrance, I came to a large hut on wooden stilts and examined a bulletin board. A mounted poster printed in white all-caps Arial Narrow typeface on a blue backdrop shouted site regulations at me. Such signs are posted at just about every public place in Vietnam, and they bristle with rules. In this case, they included: no drinking, no smoking, stay on the trail, throw away garbage properly, wear long pants, use the restrooms instead of the forest, no climbing on the relics, leave by 4:00 p.m., respect those who served here, that sort of thing.

Lingering at the hut were a dozen visitors in business casual clothing, wearing large brimmed hats and fanning themselves with souvenir folding fans decorated with colorful dragons and mandarin men in robes. A tour guide in olive-drab slacks, a Khmer checkered scarf, and a pith helmet, was presenting on the martyrs and heroes of Tà Thiết. The heat was unbearable—over 100 degrees, humid. The kind that makes palm fronds sag.

Up the trail was a series of huts that replicated the original Tà Thiết Base. The trail darkened under thick jungle cover, a reminder that Vietnamese revolutionaries knew how to disappear. My first stop was an assembly hall. The clearing around the hut had been hacked back from the encroaching jungle; trees and long gnarly roots infiltrated the space. The assembly hall had a flat above-ground cement foundation into which beams were secured, ascending to a thatched roof. It was open-air, and inside were two rudimentary wooden tables and chairs. That was it.

Up ahead on the paved trail was another small blue-and-white sign on the left, reading *BOM B-52*. The sign was perched over a vast bomb crater, a pit carpeted in leaf litter, with thin young trees now reaching toward the canopy. I took in the undergrowth—there would have been hammocks strung up to all of these trees in 1973. The revolutionaries slept outdoors.

When I looked back, the crowd at the ticket desk had thinned out. I had Tà Thiết Base essentially to myself. I suppose most visitors out front strolled into the jungle, looked at the empty assembly hall, and returned to where the beer and karaoke machine awaited. The parking lot gets more foot traffic than the actual museum.

On the walk to General Trà's quarters, I passed a five-foot clay anthill—lopsided and cracked, with towers and sub-mounds swarming with swift red ants. His office was like the assembly hall: open-air, built of wood and cement, and tucked beneath the trees. Inside were more artifacts.

A photo of General Trà hung above a low wooden platform, serving as an altar. In front of it sat a large incense bowl, with several joss sticks still burning. Vietnamese pray to the deceased, especially family members and revered leaders, asking for luck, guidance, and protection. The rising smoke is believed to carry these prayers skyward. One wooden table, a pair of chairs, and behind them, a simple bed frame. A free bundle of incense rested on the table. I lit one and lingered, imagining what this place might have felt like fifty years ago.

***

Partly due to the bikers and revelers celebrating Trà, the site already felt like a highly charged nationalist space. Unlike Lai Khê, Tà Thiết had a tangible, living pulse: a crowd of people embodying the memory of the location. Yet, as would have been the case fifty years ago, I wasn't wanted here.

This wasn't one of the cinematic ones. No flicker in the ribs, no half-remembered frame from an old movie rising from the tree line. There were no American G.I.s in the mental reel, no soundtrack waiting to cue. Tà Thiết belonged to another story—one already spoken for. Reverent, official, loud. The jungle here didn't whisper. It had a PA system.

The reconstructed huts displayed black-and-white photographs of PAVN troops and volunteers, staged by Party cadres for propaganda. In every image, they smile as they work or fight, looking carefree. The leadership shots show General Trà and his commanders bent over battle maps on wooden tables, plotting their victory.

I studied them, but couldn't find a way in. I'd seen war photos all my life, but these didn't speak that same visual language. They weren't tragic or triumphant, just resolved. Already edited. I wasn't part of their audience.

Rarely do these Vietnamese photographs show revolutionaries in shock, wounded, or burdened with despair. Instead, they appear debonair and determined, adorned only with a passion for socialism and breaking history. The presentation suggests that the war was purely a revolution, devoid of personal animus against the Americans.

Yet, if the bikers I had met earlier were the biological and spiritual descendants of Vietnam's revolutionary generation, their bellicosity belied the propaganda. Fifty years ago, I might have been shot at for daring to ride into this forest. Today's reception wasn't all that different—unwelcoming, at minimum. Now, I was on the same land, baking in its dense, suffocating heat, trapped beneath a thick canopy that sealed the temperature in place.

* * *

I passed several more B-52 bomb craters on my way out. The party at the entrance had wound down. Seemingly, the goal among the revelers was to depart Saigon early, arrive at Tà Thiết, pay their respects, party hard for two hours, and then go home. One man broke down the karaoke system while several women crouched with white garbage bags, collecting empty beer cans. Others were saying goodbye for the year, suiting back up in their motorcycle gear.

Four or five older men lingered on the lawn, still drinking beer, smoking cigarettes, and telling stories. There's always time for one more. The Harley-Davidsons began to depart, flags fluttering behind them. I watched as motorbikes cruised down the paved walking trail in the jungle I had just come from. In Vietnam, no one is too concerned about where a motorbike does or doesn't belong—sidewalks, living rooms, and jungle trails all qualify.

I mounted the motorcycle and exited the park's westernmost gate. The Cambodian border was right there. I stopped at a *tạp hóa* for a glass of water and sat on a blue plastic stool in the shade. The shop felt more like a warehouse than a storefront, with towering stacks of fertilizer sacks and shelves lined with five-liter army-sized jugs of Nước La Vie, Vietnam's national mineral water brand.

The border region is scorched and dry in April. Dump trucks lumbered by on the road to the frontier gate, trailing clouds of red dust and hot sand. The dirt settled on the leaves of the roadside trees and bushes. It wasn't a pleasant place. But it wasn't unpleasant either. My time was up. I turned back to Highway 13 and rode north toward Lộc Ninh.

Lộc Ninh

The Easter Offensive of 1972 began with Lộc Ninh, the first town in Bình Phước (then called Bình Long) to fall. Three years earlier, President Richard Nixon started pulling U.S. troops out of Vietnam. This was part of the "Vietnamization" plan, which aimed to give South Vietnam control of daily combat and get the American troops home. From a peak of 540,000 in 1969, the number of Americans had dropped to fewer than 70,000 by March 1972, with most in support roles.

That same month, Hanoi tested this new equilibrium by launching the Easter Offensive. The North sent between 200,000 and 300,000 soldiers and more than 300 tanks toward three strategic targets: Quảng Trị near the DMZ, Kon Tum in the Central Highlands, and An Lộc. This marked the war's first large conventional PAVN operation, with fighting lasting until October.

It is estimated that the North Vietnamese Army lost 100,000 in the campaign, while South Vietnam suffered more than 50,000 casualties. Lộc Ninh was overrun in early April 1972, and from there, combat moved south as the North Vietnamese army besieged the town of An Lộc. Unsuccessful, the PAVN finally withdrew from An Lộc in July.

* * *

After spending some time with the veterans and patriots picnicking at Tà Thiết Base, I took Highway 13 into Lộc Ninh. The countryside had become lusher and cooler, and I'd probably gained some altitude. I rode under the town's welcome gate, a cheerful structure with beige pillars and a rectangular sign that read, *Huyện Lộc Ninh Xin Chào Quý Khách* (Lộc Ninh District Welcomes Cherished Guests). The banner included a red flag with a golden hammer and sickle on the left, Vietnam's national flag on the right, and an array of pink, blue, red, yellow, and lime-green flags flying above.

Seconds later, I arrived in the village center. I parked beside a middle-aged woman in a lavender leisure suit and a wide-brimmed fishing hat on my left, asleep in a folding chair beside a cart. Behind the cart's display case, an array of oranges, mangoes, avocados, and carrots were stacked neatly next to a blender. A bunch of ten or so coconuts still on the branch lurked on the sidewalk beside her.

Perched behind her on a small hill stood an official-looking building. Aged red plastic tables and stools clung to the sloped driveway at awkward angles. Next to the building, a UH-1 Huey helicopter from the war was on display.

I woke her. The coconut vendor was unfazed.

Sometimes I roll into villages and am ignored. Other times it's Sông Bé, and people make a fuss when they see a lone foreigner on a big motorcycle. Lộc Ninh doesn't get many visitors. Perhaps they're just a nonchalant lot.

That was fine by me. I pulled out my phone and searched for Lộc Ninh photos from 1972, as my coconut and straw arrived, just to get my bearings. The few that popped up were from the town's old airbase.

Back then, Lộc Ninh was a village of around four thousand people, mainly highland ethnic minorities. Situated so close to Cambodia's Fishhook region, the town was garrisoned with four thousand ARVN troops and seven American advisors in 1972. The base had first been laid down by Japanese forces during World War II—just one layer in the long, repurposed history of this terrain. Later, it served as an American Special Forces camp for reconnaissance into the Fishhook, eventually turned over to Saigon.

In December 1971, South Vietnamese intelligence began detecting large troop and armor movements just over the border in Cambodia. Something was coming. In the early stages of the Easter

Offensive, they found out: the North drove 25 Soviet tanks into the little town of Lộc Ninh. Much of the fighting was concentrated around the airfield.

Over three days, the PAVN attacked. American airstrikes pushed back the initial waves. During a dawn offensive on the third day, North Vietnam finally broke through, capturing the American advisors and three thousand South Vietnamese troops.

Only fifty ARVN soldiers managed to escape the net and worked their way south to An Lộc on foot, a 15-mile trek through PAVN lines. After Lộc Ninh fell, Hanoi declared it the capital of the Provisional Revolutionary Government. Their attention soon turned to An Lộc.

* * *

I emptied my coconut and rose from my red plastic stool, riding up the hill to where the UH-1 helicopter was. There was more up there: a small howitzer and a collection of rusted, defused shells and bombs behind a low iron fence. It was Lộc Ninh's town museum, shuttered behind a metal gate. The hill continued to rise, so I nudged the bike forward up the access road.

A broad plateau opened, marked by a bright green sign that read *Sân Bay Lộc Ninh* (Lộc Ninh Airport). It turned out I had been sipping on a fresh coconut just below where the battle of Lộc Ninh took place. On the plateau was what remained of the airfield and military complex, ground zero during the PAVN's three-day attack. The checkpoint was abandoned, so I rode through and surveyed what was left of the twenty- or thirty-acre installation.

The runway was intact, though cracks and gashes cut up the tarmac. Among the patches of weeds and dark-burgundy Bình Phước soil, traces of paint held—yellow arrows, guiding lines, faded white landing circles marked with an "H," undoubtedly for "helicopter." The paint was faded but legible, baked thin by decades of sun, rain, and roadside dust.

Opening up the throttle, I rode to the end of the runway. It was fenced in at the other side, and beyond the fence was a ten-foot wall that dropped down into a regular town road in contemporary Vietnam, unbothered by its past. A shirtless rider on a vintage green Honda Cub prowled past, one hand on the bars, the other managing a cigarette and occasionally steadying an air compressor strapped to the back seat.

I cut the engine, got off the bike, and walked the runway length, crouching to press my palm against the pavement. The heat radiated back. Tà Thiết had been celebratory, alive with motorbikes and voices; this place was empty, as if history had simply moved on. A berm rose on my left, so I drifted toward it. Cassava plants edged the fissured tarmac. Between them, the usual: Styrofoam clamshell takeout containers, rain-warped plywood furniture, the vestige of a couch set aflame and abandoned.

Lộc Ninh Airport felt used up—no plaques, markers, or indications that this place had once mattered. The victors and the vanquished had moved on. The dead had been buried. I stood alone, absorbing whatever there was to absorb, while somewhere, not far off, a truck rattled past, hauling scrap or furniture or something else no one wanted anymore.

I turned back toward the fence where I had stood earlier. This was the horizon PAVN soldiers must have fixed their gaze on in 1972, waiting for the order to advance. The same line where U.S. aircraft had unleashed their fire. Everything that was going to happen had already happened here. Now, there was only the heat, the wind, and the weeds and vines pushing up through the cracks.

The place didn't resist being looked at, but it seemed to want its privacy. No tricks, no overgrowth trying to hide the past. It just sat there—finished, maybe, but not erased. The stage was still set, even if no one was performing anymore.

At the runway's midpoint, the remains of a taxi area and the cement outlines of the foundations of former structures took shape. I wandered back into the adjacent field, recently tilled, the earth was broken and soft, dotted with young cassava shoots. A more mature area of woods walled this new section in, and I was likely walking through what used to be a patchwork of base facilities. I didn't need a plaque to tell me that this had been *something*. The land gives hints: the shapes don't feel accidental. A field that wants to be a grid, or a foundation that hasn't quite let go; nothing quite aligns.

A crude wooden shack sat at the edge of the old airfield, likely home to one of the farmers now working the land. Four simple men's olive-drab garments hung from a line in front of the house. A beat-up Chinese Honda Dream copy was parked out front.

I heard a small engine behind me, turned, and saw a man in a one-piece navy-blue jumpsuit on a slow-moving motorbike holding a long bamboo pole with his free hand. He led a cow and her three calves along the runway, channeling them away from the cassava and towards a fallow pasture ahead. Farther along, the traces of war surfaced. Dust leaked from fraying green sandbags, maybe first packed by ARVN soldiers in 1971. I came across the stubby white handles of the spoons that came with American Meal, Ready-to-Eat packets, or MREs, issued to G.I.s in the field. Where there were no cafeterias.

A bit farther on, I encountered a shard of clear glass—the base of what looked like a one-liter bottle. Stamped into it was "Evian," the French mineral water brand. Not exactly common in today's Vietnam, especially in glass. It may have come from a bottle seventy years old, one perhaps tipped back by a French colonial.

The sun dipped over a foothill leaning into a patch of countryside that had once made the front page of American newspapers—for a few days, anyway, in April 1972. Lộc Ninh had been only lightly touched since then, as much of the base had likely been destroyed in the fighting. The land gives hints, but here, it had been quiet for a long time. The town had let it rest and catch its breath.

* * *

I left the airfield area, returned to Highway 13, and began looking for a *nhà nghỉ* to lodge for the night. Hills began to appear on the landscape, marking the beginning of the Central Highlands. Twilight was descending. Up ahead on my left was Sunny Café & Gym, and I slowed. Two young men worked out under bright fluorescent lights at a weight station. Nearby, a group of teenagers gathered at a small aluminum table by the shop's front window, huddled around a smartphone, bubble teas in hands.

Next door stood a street-side bar, Quán Nhậu Bình Dân Bình, or "Mr. Bình's Proletariat Bar and Restaurant." Twenty dark-red plastic tables and at least eighty plastic chairs, loosely arranged, spilled across the sidewalk. The bar had a low roar to it, probably three-quarters full. Families and workers were out for a meal. By the looks of the towers of crushed Bia Saigon cans accumulating under some of the tables, a few were deep into their night already.

Vietnamese waitstaff don't normally remove empties during a drinking session. In a country lacking social or market trust, the accounting and bill at the end of the night need to be transparent—tallied in crushed cans, not memory—to avoid friction.

I swept for landmarks around the tavern to memorize the location for later. Three middle-aged men in forest-green jumpsuits arrested my attention. They were standing over a red table, downing full glasses of beer together.

The bar was at the road's intersection with an alley. Then, I saw it on the other side of the path: a half-constructed compound made of raw concrete, adjoined to a residence. There was a pile of sand, a cement mixer, a stack of bricks, and a shovel out front. And a sign: *Nhà nghỉ À. Tâm. Lịch sự. Phục Vụ 24/24, Thoáng Mát*, or "A. Tam's Guesthouse. Polite. 24 hour service. Cool."

Decision made. I turned and pulled in.

It wasn't a beautiful *nhà nghỉ*, but it had the right coordinates. Mr. Tâm led me to my room, and I dropped my bags. The room warmed as I flipped the switch. The fluorescent light flickered on, illuminating a royal blue plastic chair, like those at Mr. Bình's bar. A small color TV hung from the ceiling, and an inexpensive bed filled the space. Over the bed was a hyper-colored waterfall print that had survived a few studio enhancements before getting nailed to the wall. The restroom, entered through a hollow, thin, plastic beige door, was raised on a small concrete foundation. A spider the size of a tea saucer napped in the sink.

* * *

A half-hour later, I moseyed across the street to the *quán nhậu*. After a long day of travel from Lai Khê, I wanted to drink some cold beer for an hour, empty the tank, and climb into my bed at A. Tam's Guesthouse. The three middle-aged fellows in forest-green jumpsuits were still there, so I chose the vacant table beside them.

A waitress appeared and handed me a menu opened to the first page, with frog, sparrow, and other high-end *bình dân* restaurant specialties listed. Designed for an impulse purchase, no doubt, perhaps with a date peeking over my shoulder at the just-opened menu. Flipping further, I found what I wanted: grilled pork and perhaps a plate of *rau muống xào tỏi*.

I ordered a beer, and soon, two male wait staff approached my table with a two-liter clear plastic keg, its hollowed-out center filled with ice. The keg was on a platform, which made the contraption resemble a lava lamp. It was not what I expected, but I wasn't unpleasantly surprised. My dinner arrived about four minutes later, and I dug into the pork and sautéed morning glory.

Meanwhile, one of the men's wife and children showed up at the neighboring table and sat down. This would normally be a cooling point, where a husband might try to balance his attention with drifts toward his family. The point in the script where the tempo eases. Not with these boys. On with the show.

War Horse cigarettes lit just as the last one burned out, Bia Saigon vanishing on contact. His wife didn't seem the least bit bothered. The kids settled in with coloring books, quietly, like they'd done this before.

This kind of utopian roadhouse indulgence, unimpeded even by a spouse's arrival, would have a few of my friends in Hanoi and Saigon rethinking their life choices. They would be wide-eyed and wistful, marveling at a marital arrangement that seemed to defy gravity.

They ordered another keg as I reviewed some of my photographs from the day on my phone. Sated, I gently lowered my chopsticks onto a plate slick with residue from the sautéed morning glory and garlic.

* * *

"Hello!" one of the men said.

That was what I'd been waiting for.

I filled my glass and clinked with each of them. I told them I was on a motorcycle ride through Bình Phước province and interested in seeing a few war sites. They waved off my elevator speech and doubled down on the joy.

They'd been at the *quán nhậu* for three hours, fresh off their shift. As one man leaned into the keg for a fresh pour, his wife wore a composed, public-facing smile—the kind reserved for dinner parties and long stories told by the head of the table. One of the children glanced up, briefly curious, then returned to coloring.

They effusively told me about themselves and their routine. All were employed with Electricity Việt Nam, one of the country's largest state-owned enterprises. Most days were spent in a truck, crawling through Bình Phước to patch and upgrade the power grid.

"We are proud Lộc Ninh," one of them remarked. "This is a good place. We meet here every day at 4:00 p.m. Drinking every day. This is our quán nhậu. That's Hiền's family."

We had another. And another. By then, any theories I'd had earlier that their vigorous drinking session marked a special occasion had dissolved. This was the reg.

We were sitting curbside, and off in the distance rose a tall hill outside of town. It was bushy at dusk, the color of old parsley. The mountain was symmetrical, capped with a radio tower and antenna. Hiền (gentle, virtuous) indulged me for a moment. He pointed to the top.

"That's Vietnamese Army. They watch Cambodia from up there," he said, squinting towards the summit. Then he gestured down toward the valley below.

"Americans were up there too. The base was down there."

"LZ Buttons," I replied.

He turned and made eye contact. "That's right....do you have a family yet?"

That's about all he knew or wanted to discuss. It was abrupt, but I wasn't sensing a deep interest in war history at my table. That was fine; I wasn't a trained researcher here for a formal interview. I was game to keep things light.

I know historians in Vietnam who specialize in the revolution and resulting wars. Many have successfully delved into personal stories of trauma and sacrifice through interviews, and they all say the same thing: an extraordinary level of interpersonal trust must be earned before anyone shares more than the revolutionary narrative. There's a lot of undiagnosed post-traumatic stress disorder in Vietnam. But there are also layers of intergenerational reinforcement—vocabulary learned in school, talking points passed down in families or among peers, the language and priorities of state propaganda, and a hundred other subtler cues shaping how people talk about the country's monumental twentieth century.

This isn't unique to Vietnam by any stretch. The United States has its own forms of social choreography, unspoken cues that shape how we talk about our history, to ourselves and to others. Our narratives cover the spectrum, from patriotic to shameful. There is usually a kind of consensus, looser perhaps, but still present, about how we frame the past and ourselves. In Vietnam, it often takes three or four long conversations, one researcher told me, before someone begins to share authentic human stories. And when they do, the telling can feel like a discovery process, like they are encountering their memories for the first time.

* * *

"Đến Cà Mau!" one of my new friends exclaimed as he handed me a full glass of beer.

Back to immediate business; these fellows had other interests. The phrase translates to "to Cà Mau," Vietnam's southernmost province, at the tip of the Mekong Delta. It's an old favorite. The analogy between a glass or bottle and the country's vertical shape came about because some Vietnamese beer drinkers consume entire glasses in one gulp.

We can surmise what their motives were, and over time, it became a shorthand. If a full glass represents Hanoi, at the top of the country, a completely drunk glass stands for Cà Mau, at the bottom. Knowing the code allows for negotiations—a trip to Huế, the imperial capital, equidistant between the two extremes, can be a counter-offer.

"Not Huế again," one of them groaned. "Go halfway, then come back."

Eh, the hell with it, I thought, and raised my glass. Over the next ninety minutes, the north-south travel continued. They were ravenous, and I was slowing down. One of the men grabbed my phone, opened the camera, and went to work.

"TRANSPORTER!" he cried out as he dropped his thumb on the shutter button.

His wife's attention shifted to her own phone, fingers tapping idly across the screen as if shutting out the noise around her. The kids, unbothered by the unfolding performance, drifted away from their table. They weaved through stools and knees like they were regulars, pausing to chat with a waitress crouched beside a cooler.

After dozens of photos, we sat back down. The boys shouted over each other as they poured more beer and lit another round of War Horse cigarettes. After a final negotiated trip to Huế, I'd had enough. It had been a busy sixty minutes. I stood.

"No, no. Not possible." one of the men remarked, as he palmed my forearm.

"True. This is happening," I replied.

They were puzzled by the sight of a man standing up before 9:00 p.m. to go home after drinking in a bar. After some negotiation, they let me go. We said our farewells, exchanged phone numbers, and I stumbled back to my guesthouse across the street. It was probably 8:30.

***

I woke the next day to the sound of multiple motorbike horns blaring as they passed in front of the guesthouse. I didn't feel too clever. They'd poured a fair bit of alcohol into me the night before. I slowly pulled on my riding gear, packed, and checked out of the *nhà nghỉ*.

I took a *bánh mì* sandwich from a sidewalk stand and headed to an outdoor coffee shop across the street. I ordered a fresh coconut and an iced coffee. As I grazed and loitered, I realized that, unlike in the U.S., it's not gauche to bring takeout food to a café in Vietnam and eat there. In a country with so much competition, so much service industry *supply*, they're happy to have your business, if only for beverages.

Over breakfast, I scrolled through the forty or so photos from the night before at Mr. Bình's *quán nhậu bình dân*. All four of us were in various group hugs, me in civilian clothes, and the three in dark green jumpsuits. Theirs were wide and effortless smiles, savoring a moment they never wanted to end. Yet it never did end. That was the reg.

As I swiped through the burst mode roll, I saw my expression gradually change from inebriated joy to growing concern as I inched my way toward the photographer, freeze-frames of my hand reaching to him. To take my phone back. Forty photographs was enough.

I finished up and groggily rode under the gate from the previous day, but from the other side. The sign read *Hẹn Gặp Lại!*—"See You Again!"—with *District Lộc Ninh* scripted underneath. I was sorry to leave this little party town. But I was on my way to An Lộc.

An Lộc

Between Lộc Ninh and An Lộc was another site I wanted to visit in Bình Phước province—on behalf of an old friend who had served with the United States Agency for International Development (USAID) at the agency's provincial development office adjacent to Quần Lợi Base Camp, a.k.a. Landing Zone Andy, in 1967.

Sam Oglesby remembers the absurdity of his work with USAID at Quần Lợi. It was impossible to get anything done, as the Americans had no support from local officials or citizens. In essence, he was operating in Việt Cộng territory: there were some intricate, hidden dynamics at play. He remembered the camaraderie of his Vietnamese coworkers, sharing jokes over tea. But beneath it lay a sense of distance, an understanding that, despite a year in Vietnam, he had remained an outsider. Their intentions, it seemed, were in conflict.

Corruption was pervasive. South Vietnamese provincial officials often sold USAID goods on the black market or pocketed a cut of American aid money. By all accounts, most of Sam's superiors spent more time in the area's red-light district than in the office.

Sam's experience at Quần Lợi captured the complexity of the area's past. The U.S. Army established LZ Andy in 1966 by seizing sections of the sprawling Terres Rouges rubber plantation. Operated by the French and guarded by Legionnaires, it was worked by Vietnamese peasants and included a grand estate and swimming pool for the owners and their entourage.

Sam said his French neighbors lived easily. They woke at 5:00 a.m., inspected the rubber trees, oversaw the Vietnamese workers in the field, and usually returned to the estate by noon. Then, they would swim in the pool and sit down to a grand boozy lunch prepared by servants. Followed by long naps. Yet, it was an open secret that the NVA operated freely at Terres Rouges, sanctioned by a quiet agreement with the owners that included protection payments to the Việt Cộng. Terres Rouges is still an active rubber plantation, though now under Vietnamese ownership.

The U.S. Army stationed elements of the First Infantry Division at LZ Andy, a key post along South Vietnam's western edge. Like most bases in Saigon's hinterlands, Quần Lợi was a node in a vast, tenuous line meant to stem the flow of Communist troops and supplies from Cambodia and protect the capital. The base sprawled across parts of Terres Rouges. Onto the expropriated land, the Americans superimposed bunkers, an artillery battery, an airstrip, and improbably, a golf course. Despite daily patrols, high-tech hardware, and textbook counterinsurgency doctrine, they never managed to locate the Communist units, who had been operating throughout the plantation the entire time.

The PAVN knew these forests better. Camped just beyond the base perimeter, they moved silently under the canopy, tucked into the treeline. In 1969, they attacked LZ Andy. A year later, U.S. and ARVN forces from Quần Lợi rolled west into Cambodia as part of one of the largest ground incursions of the war. Over 50,000 troops crossed the border to dismantle the sanctuaries that had long given the North Vietnamese both protection and strategic depth. It was a last audacious attempt to tip the balance.

In 1972, Quần Lợi passed to the South Vietnamese Army. Within months, the North took it back and used it to launch the siege of An Lộc. A base that once symbolized American firepower had become a pressure point against the very system it was built to defend.

* * *

The Quần Lợi soil, as promised, was deep red. It was iron-rich and thick, the kind that collects on boots and fatigues. The airstrip is gradually disappearing. Its tarmac was cracked and misaligned, overtaken by fifty or so rainy seasons and hardy rubber trees that had pushed through the seams. The jungle is patient.

The People's Army of Việt Nam now controls part of LZ Andy, its perimeter upgraded. Over a wall on one side of the runway, authorities built life-size cement models of bunkers and tanks, training props for the sons and grandsons of the revolution.

I rode the runway slowly, weaving through the overgrowth, hoping not to draw attention and cross paths with the personnel stationed here now. At the edge of the base, I paused by a cement wall. Beyond it, barefoot soldiers, shirtless in the heat, were playing soccer under a cloudless sky. From my distance, they might have been figures from another era, temporarily at ease in a place shaped by war. The air was thick with humidity; their banter light, easy. A hint of the old plantation leisure lingers in Quần Lợi.

I thought of Sam Oglesby, who'd served near here decades earlier but never made it back. He spoke of Quần Lợi when I asked, but he kept his distance. There was some ambivalence.

Like many American veterans, Sam returned disillusioned. He joined the United Nations Development Program after leaving Vietnam and moved back overseas. Today, he's retired; a proud Communist in the South Bronx.

I eased out onto a narrow road, dust curling behind my tires. A decrepit Honda Cub, retooled into a country delivery truck, puttered down the lane ahead of me. I fell in line and followed it toward An Lộc.

* * *

Or so I thought. Despite being a provincial town about five miles from Quần Lợi, it took me about an hour to get to An Lộc. Somehow, I circled the same six-way country intersection several times, retracing my steps, checking the map, pulling over, trying again. The heat pressed down—100 degrees, maybe more. I was stuck in the loop, and I was tired.

On my last pass, just after finding the correct exit portal, I swerved to avoid a large Hyundai truck that had moments before lost control and flipped onto its side, dumping its contents in the road. About twenty thousand loose sweet potatoes blocked travel on the pavement. The driver wasn't badly hurt, and thirty villagers were helping him gather the sweet potatoes, by the handful. A tow truck had arrived, and the driver stood by, smoking cigarettes as the volunteers cleaned up the mess. Everyone was in for a long evening.

* * *

As I rode west, dodging speeding trucks while passing country stores, dry rice fields, irrigation ditches, and construction sites, I closed in on An Lộc. I approached the town from the south, passing through the sections of Highway 13 that were the scene of weeks of inch-by-inch fighting between an ARVN division trying to relieve the besieged town and PAVN defenders during the Easter Offensive.

Three North Vietnamese Army divisions surrounded and attacked An Lộc in April 1972, leading to a siege that lasted sixty-six days. Hanoi never took the town, in large part because, despite the withdrawal of ground troops under Vietnamization, the U.S. Air Force and the U.S. Navy were still committed to South Vietnam at that stage.

The United States and South Vietnam launched hundreds of air strikes on the North Vietnamese, decimating the hamlet's periphery, while the PAVN launched an estimated 80,000 artillery shells and rockets on central An Lộc during the siege. The airspace over An Lộc was jammed with American aircraft for months, some bombing the fringes while others waited for their turn, in holding patterns at higher altitudes.

Any photograph from April to July 1972 will show a nebula of smoke and haze hovering above An Lộc. The PAVN tried to overrun it several times, but with each attempt, American aircraft stopped them. In early June, the ARVN 21st Division finally broke through the siege, and the North Vietnamese Army withdrew.

The PAVN suffered nearly ten thousand casualties, and the ARVN sustained 5,400. An Lộc was shell-shocked; it was a wasteland of rubble, destroyed houses, bomb craters, dead and wounded civilians and soldiers, hulks of scorched military vehicles, downed trees, broken glass, concrete, and steel. One American advisor compared it to the appearance of Berlin in 1945, after years of massive Allied bombing campaigns.

* * *

Today, An Lộc is a municipality of ten to twelve thousand people, with houses and infrastructure huddled together on a modest slope. Up close, it's pure Vietnam, with a cacophonous array of shophouses, motorbikes riding the wrong way on one-way streets, loud signs, and sidewalk food stalls.

Not much evidence remains of the horrible two-month battle. The hills that ring the settlement look the same, as does An Lộc's signature hilltop radio antenna, which can usually be spotted in battle photos from 1972. Lined with shophouses and other small businesses, churches, and temples, the town looks prosperous now. Most were built after 1972, the year the city was flattened.

But the siege finally surfaced. As I motorcycled through, it caught me in an unexpected way. I rode past a Socialist Realist monument in the center and stopped. It was a raised mound of lawn framed by a white concrete structure. A sign in front read, *Mộ 3.000 Đồng Bào Tại An Lộc*, or "Tomb of 3,000 Compatriots in An Lộc."

This was a mass grave from the siege, when the scale of the fighting made evacuation impossible and even medical supplies couldn't reach An Lộc. Nearby, a tall, white circular sculpture and shrine stood at the end of a plaza behind the grave. A smaller sign bore a stark phrase: *3,000 People Destroyed by American Bombs in the Summer of 1972.*

Standing over the remains of three thousand people, the population of a village now buried beneath a small patch of earth, I was jolted at the realization. It was a brief feeling of primordial anxiety in the pit of my stomach, a feeling that sank low and wouldn't rise. The atmosphere crackled with an unseen current, carrying something beneath the surface, a low hum. This was more than I'd expected.

I considered what it must be like to live in An Lộc, to pass by a mass grave every day. It evoked the two years I spent in Rwanda, where mass graves are woven into the landscape and the 1994 genocide is inescapable in the country's self-identity. In Rwanda, the genocide is not just history—it is a spiritual weight, omnipresent in conversation, in the media, in daily life. It's part of who they are. Rwandans, in my experience, are an optimistic people, but this sorrow vibrates beneath everything, palpable and inescapable.

Only passing through An Lộc for a day, it was unlikely I'd understand how the siege and this monument impact life here. With such a physical symbol of loss, this history can't be smoothed. The people below me weren't reburied; they were left there together. Standing over the mass grave, I felt a dissonance between An Lộc's vibrancy and the sadness buried beneath my feet.

Feeling foggy, I looked around. The memorial complex was empty apart from me and one young man, oddly wearing a vinyl motorcycle jacket in the heat, leaning on his Honda Wave, parked on the sidewalk. His neck was craned downward, facing his phone. I silently passed him as I returned to my motorcycle.

* * *

I toured a city center bizarrely dominated by dental and optometry practices. Signs like *Nha Khoa Sài Gòn* and *Mắt Kính Sài Gòn* abounded, the association with Saigon implying service quality. Dental practices had sound systems plugged into extension cords, booming dance music on the curb in front of the shop. Others had rotating red emergency lights hooked to automobile batteries, all in an effort to market and attract new customers. In a town of about twelve thousand, I counted seven dental practices and eleven optometrists within two blocks.

Hanoi tried to quash private enterprise after the war, but markets and entrepreneurship are in Vietnam's DNA. The *Đổi Mới* reforms of 1986 suggested that this post-1975 experiment had failed, in less than a decade. Business clusters reappeared immediately.

Now, most people juggle one or more jobs mixed with side gigs or micro-enterprises. On main roads, most homeowners run a shophouse business: cafés, *cơm bình dân*, taverns, general stores, mattress shops, clothing and shoe stores, restaurants, copper dealers, and more. Some put up multiple signs or cover entire facades, often with the requisite neon lights and loud music spilling onto the street. This chaotic entrepreneurship is quintessentially Vietnamese.[2]

A case study fit for an MBA curriculum, Lạc Thạnh restaurant in Huế thrived as Vietnam opened to tourism in the 1990s. A local entrepreneur, who was deaf, launched a shoestring-budget restaurant catering to backpackers and hired a staff of deaf workers—not just for novelty, but more likely as a way to provide income opportunities in a labor market where persons with disabilities struggle. Fiercely unpretentious yet welcoming, with good food and friendly service, Lạc Thạnh became a favorite among travelers.

When I first visited in 1998, the menus were in English, the prices low, and the specialties distinctly Huế, along with obligatory gap-year banana pancakes. The restaurant made it into an early edition of *Lonely Planet Vietnam*, and backpackers began stopping there. But by my return in 2003, a competitor, Lạc Thiện, had set up shop across the street. Its name was nearly identical, its menu was a photocopy, and its staff were also deaf. The corporate espionage was blatant. At that point, the word was that yet another competitor, the Lạc Thôn, was about to open in the same neighborhood.

This wasn't just Huế. It is the whole country from the *Đổi Mới* era onward. Vietnam thrives on reinvention, adaptation, and openness. And commerce always finds a way. An Lộc was no different.

Standing over the mass grave earlier, I'd already felt a dissonance between the town's vibrancy and the history buried beneath my feet. I'd felt less of it after a ride through the central business district. The mass grave murmured of the war's horrors, but its storefronts shouted of endurance. The past lingered, but so did the living.

Survival and rebuilding here weren't poetic or heavily reflective; they were practical. A destroyed town center became a business district, personal tragedies turned into business plans. Decades later—hyper-competitive, messy, relentless Vietnam: this was what resilience and recovery looked like.

* * *

I decided to find lodging and drop my bags. I discovered a *nhà nghỉ* in an alley near the center of An Lộc. The owner furrowed her brow as I rode through the gate. A proprietor hesitant to rent a room to a solo foreign traveler. Still, after a few minutes of *làm quen* small talk, during which I complimented the plastic Santa Claus standing on the reception desk, she handed me the key to the motel's VIP Room. She informed me that the room was about $12 a night.

"VIP" is a term the Vietnamese often use in marketing, but at the end of the day, it doesn't usually mean much. The VIP Room was a concrete, windowless box with an uninspiring restroom filled with cobwebs and a tough mattress. There was, however, a laminated poster on the wall facing the bed, depicting a nude couple embracing, with their private bits blurred. The room also had a remote-controlled air conditioner bolted to the wall, probably elevating it to VIP status and premium pricing.

The sun was going down, and I figured the splurge was warranted. I showered and prepared for a feast in An Lộc.

I asked the woman about restaurants, hoping to find a local marvel. She recommended a few noodle places, which was disappointing but expected. Most small-town restaurants will be noodle shops: *phở, bún bò Huế, mì Quảng*, etc. Country people don't go to restaurants for grand dinners all that often. These places are reliable, but at the same time noodle shops are eat-and-run places with a big pot of boiling broth always ready. Dishes are served seconds after ordering. Customers down the bowl as quickly as possible and return to their lives. Good for lunch. But after a day in the saddle, I wanted more than a bowl of broth at a stool on the sidewalk.

* * *

I managed to find a restaurant called Nhà Hàng Phổ Biến—Popular Restaurant—on the map, which I'd hoped might be a mellower Mr. Bình's place from the previous night. I walked down a dark road lined with crowded outdoor cafés, people dressed up and strolling about. Couples lingered over fruit juices, a pastime Vietnamese savor, chatting as they did.

The air was thick with smoke from the surrounding farmland; it was the burning season. Farmers set fire to rice field chaff in preparation for the next planting. Dozens of blazes flared, stinging my eyes and tasting of ash.

I arrived at Nhà Hàng Phổ Biến and heard the "Một hai ba dô!" before I saw them. The phrase translates to "One, two, three bottoms up!" and is often ambient noise in the evening in Vietnam. Hearing it indicates that a drinking session happening nearby has found its sixth gear.

I made eye contact with a ruddy-faced seated man who swayed and lurched while I drifted by his table. He was dining with a clientele of fifteen, most just as flush as he was.

He slurred to me in rough English, "Oi...Hello! What's...what's your name?" followed by group cackling.

Eyeing the tabletop, I estimated sixty empty cans of Tiger beer, twenty dirty plates and bowls, a bottle of rice wine, and scattered buckets of ice and tongs for their room-temperature-served beer.

It was a raucous *bình dân* restaurant. Yet these weren't the happy Electricity Việt Nam boys from the previous night, and the scenario hinted at an ominously different outcome. Sometimes, one encounters a group of half-cut fellows motivated by a wish to see what a foreigner's consumption and debauchery limits are. For the pleasure of it.

Similar to the night before, I might have joined them and introduced myself. Like the previous night, the pacing would have accelerated rapidly as my hosts shifted to drinking *trăm phần trăm* (100%), entire cans of beer in one gulp, with them. Many forthcoming lagers would have been consumed according to the same protocol. But the vibe would be different, more insistent, closer to a hostage situation.

They'd try to muscle me into taking bamboo bong *thuốc lào* hits, a potent variety of tobacco with such a high concentration of nicotine in its leaves that it's used to make pesticides. Eventually, one of the men would have produced a one-liter green Sprite bottle filled with bathtub rice wine, and the group would double down on its commitment to accelerated crapulence. I've found myself out-of-my-mind intoxicated after thirty minutes with new Vietnamese friends like these.

I wasn't going to play these odds and stagger back to the hotel at 7:00 p.m., waking the following day to the sound of my phone ringing at 7:00 a.m., as I realized I was blessed with an apocalyptic hangover and an aggressive case of diarrhea. I might haphazardly pick up that phone call to find that one of my new friends from the previous night was calling to invite me to drink coffee and then play soccer for a couple of hours with the same group, followed by a late-morning drinking session. Christ. I'm a fully grown man.

I've been on the other side of evenings like that, and I'll decline the offer and instead commit myself to a thirty-six-hour recovery, replete with drawn curtains, infinite trips to the restroom, pepperoni pizzas, phone on silent, and screenings of *Rocky III*, *Rocky IV*, *Magnum Force*, *Dirty Harry*, *Every Which Way but Loose*, and *Any Which Way You Can*. That's all I'm usually capable of doing. Accepting these invitations is rarely worth the pain.

* * *

More cackling. *Nah*, I thought to myself, tuning them out and resolutely rambling forward. I found an isolated table in a corner, a semi-concealed village-style hut designed for atmospheric dinners, and sat. Minutes later, I had a plate of fried chicken in front of me. I then limped home, sore from the motorcycle ride, along the same road I'd walked earlier.

An hour had passed. The cafés were still humming. Many of the same couples hadn't moved an inch, their juice glasses now half-empty and frothy. Evidence of deliberate and restrained sipping. Most days, Vietnam blurs with motion. But not tonight. Credit to these temperate souls for stretching out a simpler kind of evening, luxuriating in the carefree passage of time.

Fire Support Base Burt

The morning cracked open at six with the blast of an impact wrench. An auto shop next door was already awake, rotating tires. So loud that the operation seemed to be set up outside my door.

I rose and dressed, picking up a *bánh mì* sandwich from a cart in the central business district on my way out of An Lộc. Soon, I was riding through dense rubber plantations again. The road proceeded through a plantation, with dirt tracks extending into the forest from either side. Each trunk was barely twelve inches wide, the trees rose fast and narrow, their posture oddly graceful. Nearly universally, they bowed as they rose skyward. The roads resembled a tunnel, as the tops of the trees on either side bent toward each other, blocking the sunlight and the sun's heat.

Today, I would ride from An Lộc to Tây Ninh city, over 50 miles, and between the two try to find Fire Support Base Burt, where a battle took place in 1968 and inspired the film *Platoon*, one of the most well-known works of the Vietnam reexamination era in 1980s America. Additionally, I would hunt out a Special Forces camp in a village called Ka Tum. My time on Thunder Road, Highway 13, ended as I turned west and traveled Road 752, which weaved its way below the Fishhook and along the Cambodian border.

Despite only having ridden for two or three days, my body was beginning to reject the demands I was making: as soon as I mounted my motorcycle that morning, it felt like a cutlass had pierced my bottom. This unpleasant sensation hung with me for the rest of the day.

* * *

After thirty minutes of rubber forest, I pulled over at a café next to a rural gas station to eat the takeaway *bánh mì* with a glass of *mía đá,* or sugarcane stalks crushed into juice with ice. I was the only customer on that warm morning, and the shop owners, a young husband and wife, were asleep in lawn chairs out front.

The café was unpretentious: a lean-to roof, a couple of red chairs, and the smell of petrol. The owners roused. I sat down, and the gent hand-cranked out a glass of *mía đá* for me by rolling sugarcane stalks through his machine. I took a sip, and the earthy taste was familiar: sugar water and soil, cut with a few drops from a squeezed lime. I unwrapped the *bánh mì* and heard a high-volume Vietnamese pop ballad closing in on me from behind.

A small Hyundai cargo truck pulled up. The driver turned off the ignition but left the car stereo playing, the cassette player running on the truck's battery. I craned my neck.

Their arrival was cinematic: two men climbed out; the driver looked thirty-five and the passenger probably sixty-five, both in aviator sunglasses and oversized slacks with oversized Chinese vinyl belts whose tails flapped loosely beyond their buckles. Both wore the faded yellow rubber *dép tổ ong* honeycomb sandals beloved by blue-collar Vietnamese everywhere, backlit by a soundtrack of a young man playing piano, delicately whispering a chorus of "vì anh thương em..." ("because I love you").

Without speaking, the younger man began unloading coconuts and sugarcane, like it was muscle memory. The café owner hovered over the unloading, asking him to place the coconuts into a bin adjacent to the *mía đá* machine and stack the sugarcane against a fence a few feet away. The older man sat with me after the café owner said, "He speaks some Vietnamese."

Intrigued, he began with some softball questions, the kind that every foreigner in this country has heard. "Vietnam's cheap, isn't it?" Standard ice-breaker, especially from older men.

"Mía đá only 10,000 đồng! Jet Cigarettes only 10,000 đồng!" (40 cents). Jet cigarettes are a mainstay bottom-shelf brand; War

Horse carries more swagger. He showed me his pack of Jets. "You must love it here."

"Yes, I do love it here. Vietnam is a wonderful country."

"You can meet a girl at the café and take her to a love hotel cheaply," he said.

"Well, what if I have a wife?" I asked.

He thought about it for a moment. "Well, take your wife along."

I closed the topic by tilting my head and exhaling, "Eh...."

The other man finished unloading the truck, which contained an order of probably thirty coconuts and a few bundles of sugarcane stalks. This delivery probably happened every morning.

With the bill due, the café owner then began trying to renegotiate. "Look at these old coconuts you brought me. You don't have fresh ones this time?" He counted the coconuts again, and again, to confirm the numbers were correct. He reweighed the sugarcane stalks. "This is light!" he said.

"No, it's not," the other man replied, and more unnecessary dialogue followed. Haggling is all performance.

This discourse, with all its friction, probably happened every morning.

Finally, they settled, with the owner handing over 70,000 đồng ($3) in cash to the man sitting with me. That seemed like an exceptional deal for the café owner. The elder rolled up the two bills and held them, lethargically gazing at my motorcycle.

Soon, all four of us shared the red plastic table and chairs, the three watching me unhurriedly sip my *mía dá*. The elder's eyes circled the bike, my helmet, and my knee pads. I knew what was coming: the *audit*, designed to help the man stealthily gain an understanding of my salary and net worth in the most precise terms possible. He didn't disappoint.

"How much did that helmet cost?"

"$100," I said.

"How much were those knee pads?"

"$75," I replied.

"Are you renting that bike, or do you own it? How much did it cost?"

"$4,000," I said.

Then, a pause.

"How much money do you earn here? What's your monthly salary?" he asked.

Vietnamese are generally more comfortable talking about money than Westerners, even when those conversations highlight major, but often admired, income gaps. It's not judgment—it's bookkeeping. They just want the *number*, whatever it is.

This monthly salary question always comes up, and inquisitors often deploy a similar strategy that begins by making the foreigner comfortable with interrogations about how much they paid at the market for everyday items in Vietnam: an orange or a shirt, for example. The goal is to make the foreigner think they're conversing about "foreigner prices," which tend to be jacked up, artfully enabling the Vietnamese to exude authority due to advanced market intelligence.

Most foreigners are happy to concede this, as the cost differences tend to be negligible when accounting for exchange rates and the foreigner's buying capacity. Once the foreigner's guard is down as they might be quietly feeling smug about the minuscule numbers, the Vietnamese will reframe and spring the real question and conversation on them: "What is your monthly income?"

Another Machiavellian subplot to this approach is that most foreigners think in terms of annual salary, while Vietnamese tend to discuss monthly wage. The number is deceptively smaller, but the math is effortlessly done.

It's gauche to broach the topic among Westerners. We think it leads to pissing matches about salary, status, and achievement. I suppose it can, but some take the ban on this conversation too far. I had my motorcycle repaired some time ago in Saigon, and my mechanic from the U.K. gave me a loaner bike while mine was in his shop. It was a weathered, thirty-year-old 125-cc Suzuki, but it had some charm.

When I returned it, I told him I liked it. It was probably a $300 motorcycle, and he maybe did $100 of upgrades on it. "How much did this bike cost?" I asked him, knowing he knew this was a standard question in Vietnam. "*Mate...*" he replied with a disingenuous smile. "C'mon." You'd have thought I was asking him to open the accounting books of his business. I knew that the "c'mon" meant for me to show a little class.

* * *

"Enough to eat and drink," I finally replied to the man at the café, ready with a canned reply to his canned question. Nobody wants to sit in a café and reveal their income is fifty times greater than the host's, and disclaimers about purchasing power tend not to help.

He didn't acknowledge my answer, sitting there and staring into space, enjoying the banter. He still had the 50,000 and 20,000 đồng bills loosely rolled up in his hand. It was a quiet display, casual but unmistakable. I'd seen this move before. For some reason, especially countryside fellows or street hustlers, when they receive money, sometimes they don't put it in their wallet immediately. They hold the bills, roll them, fondle them, etc. Holding or flashing cash for longer than most people would do is, in my experience, a *cao bồi thôn* power move.

Street peddlers, shop owners, or gas station attendants will have a wad of đồng in their pockets folded over with an elastic band. When a customer makes a purchase and needs change, it gives them a chance to pull out the wad, flip it open, and fish through it for your bills. People seem to love the feel of cash and the visual message that a fellow with money in his hands sends.

I recall riding a motorbike through a Hanoi neighborhood one evening and coming across a senior citizen in boxer shorts and a tank top, in the middle of an alley. He was demonstrably intoxicated, stumbling and waving a fistful of đồng around, angrily yelling in half-sentences at some men across the alley. Some of the bills fell onto the street. This was pure alpha choreography, and he radiated intense energy that he wasn't someone to be messed with. It's easily something my French-Canadian factory worker grandfather might have done.

The elder's deputy was sitting across from me. He hadn't said anything but made a lot of eye contact. He was sizing me up for some reason. Everyone was enjoying the air on this desolate road as more delicate love songs flowed from the truck's stereo. I broke the ice and told the older man I was visiting historical sites from the war. He seemed interested.

"This part of the country saw a lot of combat in the old days, and the Americans were everywhere," he replied.

He let this summary sit. As a man in his mid-sixties, he would have been of conscription age in the early 1970s. If he were from this area, which was likely, he would have, at minimum, grown up around that combat, American soldiers, South Vietnamese soldiers, military convoys, jets flying overhead, and gunfire in the distance. And if he had been in the South Vietnamese Army, there probably wouldn't have been too many postwar opportunities beyond coconut and sugarcane distribution. And silence.

As I was about to spring the real question on him and ask him if he was in the army, he suddenly dropped his cigarette, crushing it with his *dép tô ong* sandal into the gravel below. That pair of PVC sandal soles had probably extinguished thousands of Jet cigarettes, melting and cooling, leaving the undersides riddled with black scars.

He rose and motioned to his partner that they were getting back on the road. A boy walked from the gas station to the café and asked for a *bò*, or "cow." Red Bull. The café owner rose to retrieve one.

As I downed the last drops of my *mía đá*, I congratulated myself for following every word of an argument about coconuts and sugarcane and not rising to the bait about my net worth. Before I learned much Vietnamese, these *làm quen* moments were rougher—more miming, more penis jokes, more awkwardness. I realized, though, they're still not terribly complex once we're all speaking the same language.

* * *

After an hour of riding the Cambodian border-hugging Provincial Road 752 and turning onto a dirt path, I was back in the jungle. I was a mile or two directly south of the Fishhook, looking for Fire Support Base Burt, following coordinates I'd found on an online directory of U.S. bases in Vietnam.

A Fire Support Base was usually a small temporary artillery outpost whose role was to shell anything that reconnaissance patrols made contact with nearby. Foot soldiers would be deployed to these bases for anywhere from a few days to a few weeks, and spend the majority of their time coming and going from days-long interdiction sweeps against PAVN or Việt Cộng troops and supplies moving through the adjacent jungle, calling in artillery coordinates when needed. Fire Support Bases were normally primitive: apart from tents, sandbags, and barbed wire, there would have been neither much infrastructure nor poured concrete at an installation like Burt. Thus, the jungle quickly reclaimed many of these former sites.

As I prowled the path on my motorcycle, a small altar on the side of the road suggested I may have found FSB Burt. Altars like this don't appear at random. The land gives quiet signals—ghosts often linger where the blood once fell.

In Vietnamese folk belief, ghosts are not to be trifled with, and battlefields are full of them. Altars are there as an offering, to keep wandering spirits calm. Shaped like a miniature house, the altar sat atop a three-foot pole, holding a bowl of long-burned-out joss sticks and four empty, dirty sake cups on a shelf. Inebriate the spirits with the occasional cup of rice wine, and they'll relax, the logic goes.

I dismounted and lit three joss sticks. The sun was intense, and the temperature was near 100 degrees. I realized it would be easy to get lost and dehydrated, and it was a fair distance to civilization. I had a period photograph of FSB Burt on my phone, but it was hard to get a sense of the original layout amid the thick jungle around me. I didn't know where I was going, but I knew if I found anything, such as a shard of a sandbag, weird ditches in the middle of the jungle, or any fifty-year-old garbage half-submerged in the soil, I was probably in the right place. Given the heat, I gave myself thirty minutes. If I came up empty, I'd evacuate. I entered the woods.

Once past the forest wall and off the road, the air thickened with the drone of cicadas. Lurking somewhere, I assumed, were lethal snakes. Craters and odd lumps dotted the ground, their shapes suggesting old firing positions or foxholes, though I couldn't be sure. The heat was stifling, and the dense vegetation left me disoriented and drenched in sweat. Only occasional clearings broke the monotony of the forest, their unnatural emptiness offering no respite from the sweltering midday air. It felt more like dusk, far from any village; I was entirely alone.

I checked the forest floor for remnants of the 1968 battle but found nothing. Doubt crept in. Then, I stumbled on a vast crater, about 65 square yards. Too large to be a simple bomb crater, it was a complex feature—forests don't usually form depressions like this, naturally. I followed the slope down. Young trees had already claimed the crater's unblemished floor. I circled. If the land gave a signal, I missed it.

I climbed back up, puzzled, and took one last look at the hole in the earth from the ridge. Sweat trickled down my neck and back. After that thirty minutes, I lost my bearings. I felt off, a disorienting haze settling in, like nitrogen narcosis. It was probably time to head back, but it took another ten or fifteen minutes of stumbling through the thick jungle before I found my way out. When I reached the dirt road, I swept the horizon: there was my motorcycle, parked about 200 yards away, next to the altar. I'd unwittingly covered more ground than I'd meant to. Sometimes the jungle and heat have a way of rearranging everything.

* * *

Firebase Burt was the site of the Battle of Suối Cụt (Cụt Stream) on January 1, 1968, which inspired the second half of the 1986 movie *Platoon*. In late 1967, Pope Paul VI persuaded the Americans and South Vietnamese to observe a ceasefire on January 1, 1968, which the Việt Cộng also endorsed. Roughly two thousand American soldiers spent New Year's Day 1968 alternating between perimeter duty and enjoying the ceasefire's brief interlude.

Six hours before the end of the ceasefire, 2,500 NVA and Việt Cộng troops surrounded and attacked Burt in what turned into a brief but fierce battle. Several Communist human wave attacks broke the perimeter, leading to hand-to-hand combat. After consecutive American air strikes, the Communists finally withdrew at five o'clock the following morning.

Having enlisted a year earlier, 21-year-old Oliver Stone was one of the 25th Infantry Division defenders at the base. He later directed *Platoon* and several other films about the Vietnam War. Another Suối Cụt veteran was Larry Heinemann, who went on to write four books shaped by his time in combat.

By sunrise, nearly 350 Vietnamese and 23 Americans had been killed. The two sides fought in such close quarters that bodies piled up around the base's foxholes and trenches. The next day, the Americans bulldozed the North Vietnamese dead into a mass grave, then evacuated Burt. This burial by bulldozer was recreated in the final scene of *Platoon*.

* * *

Later that day, someone in my network, who assists the Vietnamese government in locating the remains of fallen soldiers, confirmed that the crater I'd climbed into was indeed the former mass grave at Suối Cụt. About ten years ago, the government had removed and reburied the bodies. My contact, who knew the site well, said the crater had no other explanation. The rest of the area remained undisturbed. I realized I'd been climbing the contours of that grave. I hadn't known. But I should've. The land gives quiet signals.

I'd watched *Platoon* when I was a teenager, long before I knew where Suối Cụt was. It was one of the more gripping war movies I'd seen—mud, dread, elegy, adrenaline. The slow-motion flares, the psychedelia, the disassociation, the jungle—beautiful and brutal, like a ritual you weren't supposed to watch. I didn't know then that some of it had happened here, in this spot. I didn't know I'd someday climb into the crater where the bodies were bulldozed. Part of me still sees it through that lens. That's the part I've never quite shaken.

Sometimes, I tell myself there is value in walking these forgotten places, filled with ghosts from both sides. It's a way of remembering, and I've never met a veteran who opposed my doing so. Sometimes, I tell myself these visits matter. But this one felt different.

As I rolled out, I glanced back. The altar was still there, just beyond the trees. The air shimmered with heat.

Ka Tum

Naive to what I'd just seen at FSB Burt, I rode out and felt a breeze slip into my helmet and jacket, finally cooling off. I got back onto Provincial Road 752, and feeling peckish, I looked for a *cơm bình dân*, but was rewarded with a restaurant called Cơm Tấm Sài Gòn instead.

Though more common in southern cities than in the countryside, *cơm tấm* translates as "broken rice"—grains whose market value plummets due to their damaged state, usually the scraps left behind during milling. Once scorned by classy society, broken rice carved out its own place as a beloved comfort food among farmers and patrons of *bình dân* street restaurants, especially in the south. That's changed. Today, *cơm tấm* dishes like *sườn ốp la* (grilled pork chop on broken rice, topped with a fried egg) appear on the menus of posh bistros in Saigon.

Three Hyundai long-haul trucks were parked out front, alongside a family of chickens pecking the dirt—both good signs that lunch would probably be excellent. I dismounted and stepped through a chain-link gate into the open-air restaurant and walked into a faceoff between two truckers in baseball hats, squared off in aggressive stances, pointing and shouting at each other, lit cigarettes still burning in their mouths.

Behind the grill, the chef-maestro barked, "THÔI THÔI, ĐỦ RỒI" ("Stop, enough already!") over the sizzle of pork barbecuing. It worked. The two men paused and sat at their respective tables, cigarettes still dangling.

I ordered *sườn ốp la*, and by the time I'd settled into a far table and peeled off my jacket, the plate arrived: pork, iced tea, bitter melon broth, and a bowl of *mắm chấm*. A staple at any Vietnamese table, *mắm chấm* is a dipping sauce made from fish sauce, lime juice, garlic, chili, and sugar—meant to balance salty, sour, sweet, and spicy flavors. It's so delectable I could drink it by the pint.

I bathed my pork chop, egg, and rice in *mắm chấm* and immediately asked for a second bowl for dipping. Only then did I get to work. Jesus Christ. No one on the planet barbecues pork better than a Vietnamese *cơm tấm* grillmaster.

* * *

Fifteen minutes later, I was back on 752, crossing into Tây Ninh province and riding near the Cambodian frontier for another 20 miles to a town called Ka Tum. It had once hosted a small American Green Beret forward base and airstrip. These small Special Forces teams operated from remote border outposts, tasked with reconnoitering Ho Chi Minh Trail activity and training local militias to resist Communist influence in the countryside.

The highly secret Special Operations Group was a volunteer Green Beret unit that actually—and unofficially—crossed these borders into Laos and Cambodia to map the Trail network, gather intelligence, rescue downed American and South Vietnamese airmen, and direct air strikes. In prowling those jungles, thick with North Vietnamese troops and weapons, SOG volunteers took on some of the war's most daring missions. Several were launched from Ka Tum.

* * *

While rural Vietnamese are generally a friendly lot, the atmosphere shifts near international borders. Throughout history, Vietnam has had its share of trouble on its periphery, and outsiders in border areas have often brought negative harbingers. Whether it's the many times China has sent troops across the northern frontier to pacify Vietnam during a thousand-year occupation, or the burden of Western missionaries evangelizing among Central Highlands Montagnards—well undermining the goal of state oversight over organized religion—there's good reason for the paranoia.

More recently, in 1977 and 1978, Khmer Rouge troops raided border villages in the Mekong Delta, followed by a Chinese invasion from the north. In places like this, outsiders receive more scrutiny. Ka Tum is just four miles from the border.

As I neared the outskirts, I noticed a one-story, yellow, official-looking building along Provincial Road 752. I did a double-take—it had two partially underground bunkers on its front lawn. The setup was clearly pre-1975; the concrete was old and weathered. Each bunker had narrow rifle slits and faced the road.

I pulled over and was immediately approached by a gent on a dilapidated Chinese "Hongda" Dream—Hongda Dream in name only. Its fairings were gone, its fate sealed as an exhausted rural workhorse. The gent was shirtless, sinewy, and soiled from manual labor, probably in his mid-forties. He rode with one hand, smoking a cigarette and balancing a large shovel on his shoulder with the other.

"What are you doing?" he asked.

"Nothing. Just taking a photo."

"Nope. No photo."

He got off the bike, shovel in hand, keeping hard eye contact as he dropped his cigarette to the dirt. Whatever swagger had made me stop and poke around a border war relic evaporated. He wasn't going to swing the shovel. But he didn't need to.

"Why don't you get out of here? Right now," he said.

"Yep, I can do that," I replied, repressing a sudden urge to defecate in my trousers. I retreated to Provincial Road 752.

Vietnam's border areas don't show its buoyant or frivolous side the way well-trodden tourist spots do. There's more state apparatus out here: more military, more police, jet-black sedans with red plates, and more paranoia.

Ten minutes later, I entered the village and began searching for the old Special Forces camp. A Swedish friend who unofficially oversees our network of Vietnam War-era base and landing zone explorers had earlier said the camp's airstrip still ran through town, along with a one-acre plot where tents and bunkers once stood. According to him, the base is now abandoned land, but I would be able to make out the pentagon shape that once housed the administrative center.

I wandered Ka Tum's country lanes, trying to follow my map, drawing cold, puzzled stares from villagers. I pulled over at a roadside café near my coordinates, ordered a coffee, and asked.

"I'm looking for the site of an old American army base near here. Do you know what I'm talking about?"

The café owner shook his head and suggested I check out some museums in Saigon for that sort of thing. He might genuinely not have known. But given that the remains of the old base sit in the center of town, that seemed unlikely. To him, my question was probably unorthodox, maybe even risky. A foreigner on a motorcycle in any frontier village doesn't go unnoticed.

After the war ended in 1975, Vietnam modernized its domestic security apparatus with help from the East German Ministry for State Security, or Stasi, once experts in surveillance and citizen-informant networks. The government hasn't looked back. To say that internal security is vital to the Vietnamese government would be an understatement; citizens are well-practiced in engaging with authorities over perceived threats.

During my visit to Ka Tum, I was undoubtedly watched. Nobody wanted to be summoned to explain why they'd helped a foreigner asking about an old Special Forces camp. Chances are, just pointing me in the right direction could lead to that kind of appointment. Local police might associate anyone who spoke with me *with me*, interrogate them about who I was, how they knew me, and what my purpose could have been. With border areas and abandoned American bases, if the government isn't aware of or orchestrating the visit, well, it's suspicious.

* * *

I finished my coffee and looked at the map again. As far as I could tell, I'd been drinking coffee right on top of the old Special Forces base. Curious, I wandered into a shady wooded area behind the café to see if anything in the land might hint at what had once been here—odd clearings, strange rises, bomb craters.

I moved slowly through the trees, past chickens and dogs, and came across some ditches that looked like old craters. At a creek behind the café, I introduced myself to a middle-aged man fishing in the shade of a conifer tree. Another man lay nearby, on his back, dozing. The fisherman squatted on his haunches, like he was hiding. I'd spooked him.

I asked him if he knew anything about the old American base at Ka Tum. He opened his eyes wide, raised his fingers skyward, and quickly swiveled his open palm side to side at the wrist, facing me the entire time. It's a Vietnamese gesture that can mean "no," but also, in context: *I don't know. Leave me alone.* He turned his head back to the creek. Ka Tum looked like a bust.

I was starting to see the rhythm of these places: arrive, ask, get nowhere, leave. They didn't explain themselves. They didn't need to. If anything, they resisted being pinned down. Maybe it was never about uncovering something. Maybe it was about understanding the choreography—the land, the people, the silences, all moving in ways I hadn't quite learned to read.

I sulked back to my motorcycle and withdrew from the paranoid café, easing onto a dirt path at about seven miles per hour. A middle-aged woman in floral pajamas and a *nón lá* conical hat pulled alongside me on a Honda Chaly motorbike. On my other side, a teenager on a bicycle appeared, also keeping pace. The woman stared straight ahead, scolding at full volume, her voice sharp and steady. This performance was directed at me.

The teenager had some courage, he pulled in closer than he needed to.

"Where are you from?" he asked in practiced English.

"I'm American," I said.

"Where are you going?"

"I'm just going around on my motorcycle. Tourism."

He paused, then tried again. "Really. What are you doing? Where do you go next?"

Meanwhile, the woman hung on, still railing in her deep Tây Ninh accent. I turned to her. "What's the problem?" She looked at me and continued. I couldn't make out her words, but I got the message.

I told the boy I was riding my motorcycle, and to piss off. He turned right. Finally, the woman accelerated away.

The dialogue felt like the opening salvo of an interrogation. He was asking all the right questions. If this young man found himself with a mandatory invitation to meet with a local official to answer questions about the foreigner who passed through on his motorcycle, he'd have bland answers.

* * *

Ten years before my Ka Tum visit, I'd been on a motorcycle trip near the China border in northeastern Vietnam with some friends. Our destination was the Bản Giốc Waterfall, a minor tourist attraction on a river marking the frontier. It was gorgeous, and completely isolated.

Back then, visitors to frontier areas had to register for a frontier pass and pay a fee to local authorities, a substantial easing of the previous total ban on access. The permits let officials track foreign visitors, and the extra revenue didn't hurt either. Given that the pass took weeks to process, we took our chances without one.

We left Bản Giốc, following a quiet country road flanked by karst formations and the Quây Sơn River tracing the border. A faded sign for a historic border monument caught our eye, so we turned. There it was: a weathered stone slab inscribed with Chinese and Vietnamese characters. Around it, men sat on rocks, staring at their phones, each guarding a pile of black garbage bags—smugglers, presumably, waiting to trade cartons of Vinataba cigarettes for cash.

Across the meadow, a young border guard in uniform called out, smiling. His English was hesitant but eager.

"Where are you from?" he asked.

We told him: one from England, one from France, one from the U.S.

Then came the real icebreaker: Premier League football—Manchester United, Chelsea, Arsenal. The global teams Vietnamese love. His post seemed lonely. The interruption in his day was a cause for joy.

After an indulgent detour into English football, we asked if we could see the border marker. He lit up and commanded several more minutes, explaining the border's history and his job. He was in fine spirits. "You are my guests here," he said, waving us toward the stone.

We explored the marker, and the guard even took a group photo of us before returning to his post over the border. After a moment, we turned to leave and "re-enter" Vietnam.

Crossing back, the mood shifted. Switching to Vietnamese, his tone hardened.

"You are now entering the Socialist Republic of Vietnam from the People's Republic of China. This is a restricted frontier zone. All travelers must present valid identification and authorized entry documents. Passports, please."

We tried to jog his memory. "Buddy. We were just talking about the football, remember?"

He didn't.

"Passports, please."

He examined them. "Where are your Frontier Passes?" he demanded. We explained we didn't have any. His voice rose. "You cannot visit this area without a pass. *Do you understand?*"

I asked, "These Frontier Passes...can we register for them here and now?" He hesitated, then sighed. "Yes. The fee is 40,000 đồng."

About two dollars.

I handed him a 100,000 đồng note and hurried back to my bike. My English friend followed. Fumbling for the deficit, a twenty, our French companion dropped a wad of 500,000 đồng bills. We didn't ask what happened next.

* * *

In Ka Tum, I ran out of leads, so I messaged my friend in Sweden who knew the town. From his desk in Stockholm, he directed me to the airstrip, now one of the town's two main roads. Spilling with plastic goods, tools, fruit, and budget apparel, a dry market sprawled over the old runway.

Success.

For posterity, I motored the road, tracing its straight path back and forth. Fifty yards away, the faded outlines of a Special Forces camp—a clearing amid homes behind the market—still showed its pentagonal shape. The land was mostly fallow, and I could see the outlines of spots where tents and other infrastructure sat in the early 1970s. The center of the camp, now a soccer field, seemed unchanged—trails cut through the pentagon, direct routes between houses. Two dogs cautiously approached, barking at me.

The choreography was becoming familiar: approach a forgotten site, walk the perimeter, listen for the dog. Something historical happened here, but neither the land nor the people wanted to say what. The terrain gave no speeches—just heat, brush, and the occasional plaque that tells us little.

The dogs chased me off. Ka Tum, in the end, wasn't terribly hospitable. I departed and merged onto Provincial Highway 792. It was 2:00 p.m. Tây Ninh city, the provincial capital, was just an hour away. Pulling over and pulling up *di tích lịch sử* (historical relics) on my phone, I wondered if anything along the way would catch my interest. It wouldn't have shown up on any map in 1968, but today it was there: the Central Office for South Vietnam (COSVN), a historical site just a few miles away. COSVN had been the North's elusive, always-moving political and military HQ, its mission clear: liberate the South and dismantle the American-backed Saigon regime. The Americans called it "The Bamboo Pentagon." It was worth the diversion.

* * *

Founded by North Vietnam in 1962, COSVN emerged after the North decided on reunification, concluding that the U.S. and South Vietnamese governments had no intention of ever upholding the 1954 Geneva Accords which committed all sides to free elections to reunify Vietnam. Hidden deep in the jungles of northern Tây Ninh province, COSVN became the secret Communist command center, perpetually on the move. The U.S. and South Vietnam spent vast amounts of resources hunting it down, but every time they got close—or bombs fell—COSVN would relocate, sometimes across the border into Cambodia, sometimes to another part of Tây Ninh or Bình Phước. More recently, the replica of COSVN had been built at one of these sites to attract tourists.

I turned off Highway 792, expecting more of what I'd seen at Tà Thiết two days earlier: concrete flooring and cement columns, rebuilt huts, altars, black-and-white portraits of revolutionaries, manicured trails, and thatched roofs in the jungle. There would be little in the way of unburied war trash there—just the occasional B-52 bomb crater and a historically reverberating forest. This would be a stage set with a small museum, not a ruin. That was fine; at least my presence there wouldn't alarm any locals. The COSVN replica sat deep in rural Tây Ninh, hugging the Cambodian frontier. It probably didn't get many visitors. A desolate but lush one-lane country road—devoid of *tạp hoá* stores or motorbikes—led me to the Central Office parking lot.

A man in a green military uniform, balancing on the rear legs of a wooden chair and scrolling his smartphone, gave me a wave. I dismounted and saw a young woman in Việt Cộng attire—a museum staffer in a light black cotton pantsuit, checkered scarf, and *nón lá* conical hat—gleefully smiling.

I wasn't in Ka Tum anymore.

The jungle canopy pressed the heat and humidity down like a heavy, soggy blanket. The air was thick and unmoving. My motorcycle jacket clung to my skin, soaked with sweat, and I trudged forward, looking for the paved trail that ran into the jungle from the parking lot.

Walking, I passed re-created huts, kitchens, and assembly halls, reconstructed from palm fronds and timber. An orchestra of cicadas rose in unison, welcoming the visitor. The trenches, reinforced with concrete, slithered between the structures, and scattered B-52 bomb craters dotted the jungle—evidence of American near-misses on this hidden outpost. Visibility was poor; the forest thick and unyielding.

I imagined the place in its prime—hundreds, maybe thousands of North Vietnamese soldiers moving through it with Kalashnikovs over their shoulders, squatting over meals, dozing in hammocks, ferrying orders from one hut to the next.

Walking through the COSVN restoration felt like entering Vietnam's revolutionary pantheon. I paused at the hut residence of

Nguyễn Văn Linh, the young revolutionary who later became the Communist Party General Secretary who launched the country's Đổi Mới economic reforms in the 1980s.

The altar inside his hut displayed a photo of comrade Linh, an old radio, some folded newspapers, and a pair of eyeglasses in a glass box, all curated for a visitor like me. The war's nerve center, now a monument to its triumph, was mine to wander through alone. Beams of sunlight filtered through the jungle's layers, dappling the forest floor. The air felt alive, as a jungle can—palms flitted with the slightest breeze while others stood motionless in the oppressive heat, resigned and resistant.

This place, a flat jungle straddling Cambodia, was heroic and optimistic, warmer than the other battlefields I'd visited. As though it had escaped tragedy. But COSVN had been restored, celebrated, polished. It wasn't Ka Tum. There was confidence here, the confidence of victory, and I was invited to witness it. The war was behind the country now, and this was its wartime secret, feat, and legacy.

As I circled back to my motorcycle, this equilibrium fractured—intentionally. I came upon an old ARVN M-41 tank and a battered M-113 armored personnel carrier, half-split open from a rocket-propelled grenade. These relics hadn't died here. They'd been placed here. Part of the postwar artifact tourism circuit, they were curated for effect.

The government had scattered the remnants of American military might across towns, museums, and memorials. These tanks, like the restored COSVN, were meant to be seen. They were meant to demonstrate the violence of the war, yes—but also its triumph. The two were inseparable. Victory and violence, both monumentally preserved.

* * *

After my walk, I approached the museum, passing a different security guard—seated at attention in a red plastic chair with a Kalashnikov on his lap. He was fast asleep.

The one-room exhibition held more black-and-white photographs in glass cases; most were stock images from Party Congresses spanning nearly ninety years of organizational history. I surveyed the photos, reliving the trauma of all the dry Ho Chi Minh biographies I've tried to finish over the years.

Histories of anything related to the Communist Party of Vietnam tend to accentuate the action of organization: how Party cells were organized, how the Party was split and reformed along new organizational lines for long-term planning purposes, how demonstrations and worker actions were planned, Leninism and its organizational traits, how communications and propaganda arms were coordinated and the organizational units that planned them, how the Central Committee was organized, how the Party's military wing was organized, and so forth. An awful lot of process.

Organization and planning are still hardwired into the Party's DNA. Leadership will sometimes launch sweeping restructurings: administrative units are split, merged, or expanded. These shifts ripple down into local bureaucracies, redrawing maps and job descriptions alike.

To an outsider, it sometimes looks like it might be reorganization and planning for the sake of reorganization and planning. But like the frequent home renovations ordinary Vietnamese often undertake, organization may be its own form of joy and fulfillment.

Take this excerpt from a national newspaper's top story on a day in 2019:

Vietnam has streamlined four districts and 539 communes for the 2019-2021 plan, said the Ministry of Home Affairs, adding that the achievements are based on the data of 61 provinces, not including Ho

Chi Minh City and Cần Thơ City. The number of districts in the streamlining plan is 20, and two northern provinces of Cao Bằng and Hoa Binh have completed the progress for four districts. The number of localities joining this task is 13. The number of communes in the streamlining plan is 1,026 in 42 localities, and the reorganization has streamlined 539 units.

I once asked a Vietnamese friend what all this frequent bureaucratic churn delivers. He just sighed.

* * *

Triggered, I slid out past the sleeping guard.

COSVN felt curated for visitors, inviting us to stroll quietly through history as the victors wrote it. Walking among neatly reconstructed huts and tidy trenches, I caught myself enjoying it. This wasn't the guilty thrill of a ruin or abandoned battlefield. It was different: a sense of permitted trespass, of historical voyeurism politely sanctioned. Maybe that made it easier. Or maybe it made me uneasy in a quieter way—a discomfort I preferred not to name.

I surveyed COSVN once more and ruminated. Hell, I even knew what COSVN was when I was a teenager, having read about it in *America in Vietnam*, the classic 1980 book with the green-and-orange cover featuring a photograph of a CH-47 Chinook.

Today, I had done what the U.S. Army never could: stumble onto COSVN, take a pleasant walk through its scorching jungle, understand the layout of its secret headquarters, and greet some cheerful Việt Cộng guerrillas and a slumbering security guard.

I gathered my things, returned to my motorcycle, and pointed toward Tây Ninh city.

Núi Bà Đen

It took me more than an hour to reach Tây Ninh city from the leafy, ultra-clandestine grounds of the Central Office for South Vietnam—about 25 miles. Fifty miles north of Saigon, Tây Ninh is a small city by Vietnamese standards, with a population of around 150,000. It's a center of rural commerce and home to the flashy Holy See of Vietnam's indigenous Cao Đài religion, which somehow manages to syncretize major worldwide faiths.

The city is low-rise and spreads along the Vàm Cỏ Tây River. As I entered its outskirts and crossed a bridge, I came to a traffic circle anchored by a 60-foot-tall concrete monument: a worker, a soldier, and a white-collar professional standing in unity, celebrating the Communist Party, victory, and reunification. Most towns have one, though some are grander than others—a reminder of how we got here.

Soon, I was riding through a familiar type of neighborhood, the faded mid-century modern quarter: crowded, buzzing, layered with shophouses, street food stalls, pedestrians, loiterers, and restaurants. When I'm on a motorcycle trip, I gravitate toward these districts. They offer atmosphere, as well as the luxury of parking the bike and walking to a *quán nhậu*.

After riding in the heat and visiting four war sites that day, I was wiped out. First order of business: find a *nhà nghỉ* and then a restaurant where I could decompress and dine on some rice.

Then I saw it: *Nhà Nghỉ Hải Âu* (Seagull Rest House)—a very trendy hotel name in Vietnam about fifteen years ago. A tiny neon sign pointed down a narrow alley. I turned and threaded my way through a tight, residential labyrinth. It was pure southern Vietnam, where everything is left open: doors, windows, gates, curtains. Passersby can see exactly what residents are doing. And the residents are unbothered.

One woman was reading a book beside a window. Two shirtless men were fixing a motorbike at the next house. A man in pajamas was watering flowers at the one after that.

Northerners complain about the southern lifestyle—too public, too exposed. But southerners seem unfazed; they go about their business, used to having people around. It's too hot to close doors and windows.

One northern friend described her move into a Saigon apartment complex decades ago. Her neighbors kept their doors wide open, as they might have in an alley or a single-family shophouse. Every time she came home, she saw it all: uncleared dishes, laundry, men dawdling around in their briefs. Part of it, she figured, was to encourage air circulation. But I've also heard Southerners just like having people around them.

Sometimes her neighbor would look up, spot her coming off the stairs, and wave, welcoming her home.

I pulled up at the *nhà nghỉ*. The owner came out, probably expecting a more conventional guest—but instead, it was me, a foreigner.

"Không, không," he waved me off. "Hết rồi" (Full.)

"I know you're not full," I said. "There aren't any motorbikes here. Where is everyone?"

"Well, they're all coming back later," he parried.

He was unsure of my boundaries, my habits. *Was this grotesque man going to use drugs in the room? Come back late and make noise? Invite a police visit?* I was an unknown quantity.

"C'mon, buddy. I'm tired. Can I rent a room tonight?"

He compromised. "Fine."

He'd built a rectangular addition onto his three-bedroom home, laid out like a miniaturized American mid-century motel. Eight windowless rooms stood side by side, like outhouses at an outdoor concert.

I opened my door and switched on the light, noticing the large laminated boudoir photo of a busty blonde woman with a voluminous hairstyle in black lingerie taped to the wall over the bed. Similar to many Communist and post-Communist countries in transition, the grip of late-Cold War Western aesthetics on Vietnam has been very slow to loosen.

The proprietor inspected my muddy motorcycle and asked me to roll it into my tiny room.

I imagine he wanted to spare couples and other guests the optics of something grimy and unpleasant parked outside before spending amorous time together in the neighboring rooms.

"I'm not going to do that," I said.

"Fine," he replied.

* * *

After a shower, I set out on foot in search of food. I was lodged in what I took to be friendly *quán nhậu* territory—but I felt a creeping anxiety about the odds.

On my way in, I'd mostly passed noodle shops and cafés. It was hard to believe there wasn't a single *quán nhậu* in the area. This neighborhood, with all the right indicators, turned out to be a hostile *quán nhậu* desert. Something didn't add up. So, I expanded my search radius, reconnoitering beyond my area of operations.

I passed two noodle shops, an electronics store, a dessert café, and a sidewalk juice stall. Within my radius was a *phở* place, and across the street, a brightly lit, air-conditioned Korean barbecue restaurant with its door closed and windows sealed tight. Inside, an idle battalion of waitstaff stood at attention in their white shirts and black pants, frozen beneath a grid of clinical fluorescent lights.

As with most Korean places, a deficit of Vietnamese charm.

A few blocks later, I checked the map. I spotted Quán Ăn Phổ Biến—Popular Restaurant—not far off. The name sounded aspirational and familiar, but at least it was unmistakably Vietnamese.

It probably wasn't the *quán nhậu* I needed: the noisy southern outdoor institution where beer flows freely and red plastic tables stand defiant above a carpet of chicken bones, wet napkins, spilled lager, cigarette butts, and the occasional stray boiled vegetable.

But it was 7:00 p.m., and I was getting desperate. I picked up my pace.

When one pulls a joker in a food desert like Tây Ninh city, one ends up eating alone at 7:00 p.m. at Popular Restaurant—an empty, three-hundred-seat, semi-outdoor hybrid of wedding venue, sports bar, and office banquet hall.

Popular Restaurant had no other customers that evening. It had capacity. Forty or fifty aluminum tables were already set for a surge of guests, each with bowls, wet towels, glasses, chopsticks, and entire rolls of toilet paper tucked into neon pink plastic holders. In reserve, folded aluminum tables and stacks of low plastic stools waited in the corner.

On second glance, a decent start. Quán Ăn Phở Biến had other strengths. It was decidedly *bình dân*: an outdoor dining room on a concrete slab, surrounded by chain-link fencing. From the inside, it did feel a bit VIP. The parking area extended under the corrugated metal roof, where the owner's sedan was parked beside a table set for twelve. Hundreds of red plastic stools—the especially short kind, often mistaken by Westerners for children's furniture—Vietnamese like *low*. It signaled promise: good staples might be on the menu. As with any place where the owner parks an automobile in the dining room, that was another good sign.

At the front of the dining room stood a low stage, decorated with a large artificial Christmas tree and a life-size Santa Claus statue holding a saxophone. Beside them, a vinyl banner displayed a photo collage of the national soccer team. Piled in front of the stage were extra tables, stacked chairs, and a karaoke machine—ready, but dormant.

I gambled—and this time, I won. The anxiety lifted.

Three young waiters descended. One handed me a forty-page menu. I handed it back and asked if they had *đậu sốt cà chu*a (tofu in tomato sauce) and maybe some barbecued pork ribs. Even if not on the menu, any respectable Vietnamese kitchen should be able to deliver both dishes.

"Right away," one said. I asked for a bottle of Bia Saigon.

"We don't have Saigon. We've got Tiger and Heineken."

"You don't have Vietnamese beer?"

"Well, Tiger..."

That poked at my pedantic side. "Tiger is Singaporean beer. Just because it's brewed in Vietnam doesn't make it Vietnamese. They brew Heineken here too, but no one tries to pass that off."

Some places try to sneak Tiger under the radar. I hadn't been there for four minutes, and there was already friction with the waiter. Sigh. I didn't come to Tây Ninh to prosecute the case of what constitutes Vietnamese beer. But the defense presented Tiger.

* * *

Tiger and Heineken are, like "Hotel California" in karaoke, default choices—supremely middle of the road. They're everywhere. People drink Tiger and Heineken in Vietnam, but part of me thinks they do it because they have to. I suspect a clause in many of Heineken's distribution contracts mandates that bars and restaurants carry only Heineken and Tiger, since Heineken owns both.

Vietnam has fine domestic beers, though admittedly, they all taste like they came from the same keg: run-of-the-mill Asian pilsners, but certainly good enough.

There's also the satisfaction of drinking legacy brands. You see them in old photos of American and South Vietnamese soldiers:

333, Saigon, Larue. And the logos haven't changed much since then—I'm sold on that point alone.

Vietnamese beer has always been about place. Bia Hanoi in the north. Bia Saigon in the south. Bia Dung Quất brewed near the oil refinery in Quảng Ngãi. Bia Trúc Bạch sold near Trúc Bạch Lake, where John McCain parachuted in 1967 after being shot down over Hanoi. Some of these breweries are still state-owned, so drinking Bia Saigon is a way of supporting Vietnam.

But somehow, Heineken, or 'Ken, as it's called in Vietnam, has convinced the country's growing middle class that it's the cooler and, more importantly, the *safer* tipple. Unlike Vietnamese brands, Heineken allegedly contains no formaldehyde, which, *ahem*, might still be used as a preservative in some local beers.

The marketing lands. 'Ken and Tiger are now Vietnam's go-to session beers—default choices for football-watching. Vietnam is becoming more global in this regard. And maybe, just a touch blander.

At least Budweiser knew when to dial it back before doing too much damage. Another staple for American personnel during the war, Budweiser reentered the Vietnamese market in 2008. The buzz at the time was that it would disrupt the domestic beer market. Vietnam would finally have a national brand, albeit an American one.

To my delight, Budweiser never really caught on. A few years in, the brand quietly repositioned itself in the "luxury" category, meaning there was no longer any expectation that it might become an everyday consumer product. It's still around, but thankfully, it never captivated anyone.

McDonald's followed a similar arc. When the chain launched in Vietnam in 2014, it was ambitious, projecting hundreds of franchises within a year or two. The logic, at the time, was that

Vietnam was finally ready to "join the world" and consume things the way other countries did.

It hasn't quite played out that way. Turns out, Vietnamese don't care much for McDonald's hamburgers. They prefer noodle dishes and *bánh mì* sandwiches for fast food. Given the choice, I stayed in-region and ordered a Tiger.

* * *

I poured the bottle into a glass and calmed down. Quán Ăn Phở Biến was mighty peaceful that evening. Crickets chirped; a motorbike passed now and then. From the house next door, I could hear someone washing dishes and singing to himself.

Three minutes later, my food arrived—in mammoth portions.

Most Vietnamese restaurants serve family-style plates for sharing, and cooks don't downsize when it's a solo diner in a three-hundred-seat empty restaurant. I figured I wouldn't finish either dish. Maybe the family guard dogs would inherit the rest.

But I surprised myself. I ate about four pounds of tofu and tomatoes and a dozen miniature deep-fried pork ribs marinated in sugar, lime, and fish sauce.

Thank Christ they forgot to bring the rice.

I limped back to my *nhà nghỉ* and passed out by 8:15, serenaded by a bicycle prowling the country lane out front, amplifier rigged to the handlebars, the stern middle-aged male voice dreamily chanting the "bánh mì... bánh giò!" lullaby on loop, the sound fading gently into the night as the bicycle rolled down the lane.

* * *

The next morning, I awoke at dawn. I planned to visit Núi Bà Đen, a 3,000-foot mountain overlooking Tây Ninh city. I hoped it might simply be an abandoned hilltop position from the war—still holding some physical remnants or war detritus to reward a resolute debutant archaeologist like myself.

The most common English translation is "Black Virgin Mountain," which adds something the original Vietnamese seems to neither imply nor require. *Núi* means "mountain," *Đen* is the color black, and *Bà* means "older woman," usually in a respectful context.

So: Grandmother Black Mountain.

Núi Bà Đen was strategic—the only substantial topographical feature between the Central Highlands and the Mekong Delta coast. It once hosted a U.S. Army communications station and about 150 G.I.s. Việt Cộng guerrillas controlled everything below the summit—much of the mountain itself and most of the surrounding paddies. The Americans, stranded above, had to be resupplied by chopper.

American and South Vietnamese forces launched repeated efforts to flush out Việt Cộng units hiding in the mountain's cave network. In early 1975, the North Vietnamese Army finally captured Núi Bà Đen, laying siege to the South Vietnamese garrison on the summit for a full month.

* * *

I purchased a take-out *bánh mì* on my way out of central Tây Ninh and looked for somewhere quiet to eat. I found a bench beside an irrigation canal, with a clear view of the mountain in the distance.

It was 7:00 a.m., and the suburbs were already turning hot and humid; a haze floated over the rice paddies.

In the old snapshots I've found online of soldiers stationed in Tây Ninh during the war, Núi Bà Đen is almost always in the background. It was iconic to those who served at the many bases that once ringed the city.

That morning, the brown mountain looked like it was levitating above the smog and dust. Somehow, it felt celestial.

As I sat with my sandwich, an elderly woman passed by on a bicycle. "Ah. I see you're eating a sandwich," she said.

"Yes, grandmother. I am eating a sandwich." She rode on.

In Vietnam, I find that people sometimes observe something observable and just verbalize it. For instance, I might be sitting in my underwear, reading *Bóng Đá* newspaper with my apartment door open, and see my neighbor arrive home in office clothes. While he's unlocking his door, I might say, "Returning home from work, eh?" "That's right," he'd reply. The more demonstrably obvious the observation, the more natural the exchange.

I motorcycled through a few miles of flat paddy fields, watching Núi Bà Đen grow steadily larger. Soon, I passed under a white gate with the words KHU DU LỊCH NÚI BÀ ĐEN printed in blue all-caps Arial Narrow font. I hadn't expected a *KHU DU LỊCH*, or "tourist zone," the overly bureaucratic term for a theme park.

I kept going another mile until I reached a massive parking lot, five percent full, with just a few dozen motorbikes scattered in rows meant for thousands. I dismounted and followed the signs toward the entry ticket counter, a 700-yard walk from the parking lot.

On the saleswoman's recommendation, I bought the "VIP Package," which included two gate passes, a round-trip gondola ticket, and shuttle bus transport. My purchase gave me seven or eight fragile paper tickets to manage, which quickly became soggy in my sweating hands.

The gondola station was about a mile away. I boarded the shuttle and passed colorful cement animals—elephants, giraffes, and others—along with Party monuments and war veteran memorials.

And rows of empty, but open, *cơm bình dân* restaurants. It was 7:30 in the morning. Each probably had seating for two hundred, with managers and waitstaff idling, their heads tilted toward televisions bolted to the ceiling corners.

I stepped off the shuttle at a small cluster of souvenir shops and cafés, brushing off a young man's offer to shine my army boots.

There was no queue at the gondola station. In minutes, I was alone in a private gondola, the cabin gliding silently upward. Below, dense jungle burst from volcanic rock as Núi Bà Đen loomed. To my left, an unexpected "slideway"—a waterslide-like track for wheeled go-carts—twisted down the mountain, passing through what had once been Việt Cộng arms caches and cave hospitals.

After four minutes of silence, I leaned back, enjoying the view. I had expected a twenty-minute ride, but moments later, the gondola slowed to a halt. I'd barely begun. It turned out the gondola only takes tourists partway up the mountain. The gondola terminus sat next to a temple complex still under construction, at the halfway point.

For centuries, the mountain has been home to shrines and temples linked to a local legend. Long ago, a young woman climbed to the summit to pray. There, she was confronted by men who intended to kidnap her. Rather than be taken, she threw herself from the peak.

Later, her spirit appeared in a vision to a monk, who shared her story with villagers. Over time, she came to be revered as *Bà Đen,* the mountain's grandmother.

The new complex—two bold, colorful temples—was meant to reimagine these ancient shrines for the modern era. In front of them, a grand terrace stretched out, offering a sweeping view of Tây Ninh and Bình Dương provinces below. Just beyond the temples sprawled a construction site. A six-story building was being carved directly into the mountainside. It could have been anything, maybe a lavish hotel with a casino, maybe a rudimentary dormitory for monks.

Three rough *cơm bình dân* canteens dotted the terrace nearby, along with a café tucked behind a large gate, where a banner read *An Toàn Là Hạnh Phúc Gia Đình* (Safety Means Family

Happiness)—all nods to construction workers, not tourists. Beside them stood a compound of about twenty side-by-side outdoor showers, flanked by twenty mobile men's restrooms. Facilities at this scale, built for laborers, were a clear sign: something grand was coming to Khu Du Lịch Núi Bà Đen.

I could've hiked another 1,500 feet to the summit, but decided against it. The costs and benefits didn't quite align. I wandered around the half-summit instead, passing cement mixers, extension cords, stacks of tile, putty knives, and brick hammers.

Laborers in cement-stained orange vests and hardhats moved between tourists in business casual or pastel dresses, snapping selfies at the edge of the balcony. It was mid-morning, and I had plans to visit a town called Dầu Tiếng on my way back to Saigon. Better to cash out here and reinvest the time.

Núi Bà Đen didn't offer resistance or revelation. It didn't even pretend to. History had been vanished, reimagined as amusement. People come here now to ride gondolas, snap selfies, eat snacks in cafés, or watch construction workers build something new. There was no choreography to decode, no careful silence to read. There were no hints for the land to give: the mountain had become something else entirely. I'd arrived a decade too late.

* * *

I made my way back to the gondola for the return trip. This time, I had company. A construction worker in his mid-thirties wedged himself in as the doors were closing, slipping through as the cabin lurched into motion.

We sat on opposite sides, glancing at each other, then out at the unfolding view of Núi Bà Đen and Tây Ninh province below.

He broke the silence and, unexpectedly, started in Vietnamese. *Worth a shot*, he probably thought.

"Are you married?" he asked.

"Yes, I am," I replied. "I have one son."

He let that sit for a moment, then asked if I'd hiked the mountain today. When I said no, that I wasn't interested, he looked surprised.

"Really?" He tilted his head, as though assuming that's just the kind of thing that Western tourists always did.

It was already hot. Vietnamese trails are often perfectly vertical and steep—no switchbacks. I'd done enough that morning. Still, he seemed to be projecting, as though a spontaneous hike straight up a brown, sooty, rocky, medium-sized mountain in 100-degree heat was somehow self-evident to someone like me.

That assumption isn't uncommon. I wondered if perhaps he'd been exposed to some local tourist industry marketing materials in his time. Though interest in outdoor pursuits is gradually rising, most Vietnamese don't hike for fun terribly often. Nor are they a people known for extreme sports and outdoor recreation much beyond, say, light impact activities such as strolling or passing time at cafés in scenic places. So, Westerners are often the vehicle for industry advertising, which serves the additional purpose of marketing to curious Vietnamese the legendary party they're missing.

Sometimes the brochure photograph is of six young wide-eyed Westerners in matching bikinis and life jackets being towed while seated on an inflatable plastic banana in Hạ Long Bay, screaming with delight as if they've entered Nirvana. Or a sunburned backpacker riding passenger on the back of an Easy Riders Vietnam motorbike, arms outstretched, eyes closed, drifting through Central Highlands rice fields, wearing the beatific glow of someone jacked up on MDMA and communicating with God.

Don't get me wrong: Vietnam's fun and beautiful. But the industry has a way of overstating things. Sightseeing there isn't quite the transcendent religious experience they'd have us believe it is.

Westerners are generally less dim and more low-key than the marketing suggests. The imagery is rather well done: I can only conclude it's a piss-take. Touché.

"Are you married?" I asked.

He was. Two kids. He worked as a laborer on the temple and hotel complex at the gondola terminus. He didn't live on the mountain—he stayed in a barracks at its base with about a hundred other workers, commuting home to Bình Dương province on weekends to visit his family.

I brought up the history: there had once been an American and South Vietnamese base on the summit. "Have you ever seen any relics of that time up there?"

"I don't have any idea about that," he said.

"Well, in the old days, there were many soldiers here," I added.

"Yeah, I've heard. I don't know about that," he answered. He changed the subject and asked where I was from.

I realized I wouldn't get any historical nuggets out of this lad who spends his days on Núi Bà Đen and, had he been looking, would've stumbled across war garbage or crumbling structures up there. He wanted *làm quen*, not a discussion on the war. Fair enough. Vietnamese people are normal in that way—they're not obsessed with the minutiae of their country's history. Like anyone else, they just want to shoot the breeze sometimes.

The gondola ride was ending, and we debarked. "Where do you live?" he asked. I told him I lived and worked in Saigon. We exited the station and quietly walked across the parking lot, passing idling shoeshine salesmen. Before we parted, he drew out his phone and asked for my number.

"Uh, sure," I said, and recited it. He immediately dialed. When my phone rang, I glanced down. Unknown number.

He pointed and said, "That's me calling."

It was an old-school move I don't see so much anymore. Fifteen or twenty years ago, when inexpensive mobile phones began flooding the country, Vietnamese men collected phone numbers. I've had men request my number after giving me street directions—ten-second encounters. Usually, I'd never hear from them again. Maybe they simply liked the status of having a bulging contacts list, or maybe they decided it wasn't worth the effort to befriend a foreigner.

But sometimes, they would follow up and call—often later that night, or the next day. They'd want to meet at a café for *làm quen* conversation. Since Vietnamese people can spend a fair bit of time at the café, that meeting could last an hour or two. And if some time had passed since the first encounter, I'd sometimes answer the phone without any idea who it was. I simply couldn't recall meeting the fellow—forgetting a Vietnamese person's name is a fundamental breach of etiquette, even if the initial encounter lasted thirty seconds and happened three weeks earlier.

I found my motorcycle and suited up to depart Núi Bà Đen. As I motored out of the parking lot, I noticed one uniformed attendant sitting in a plastic chair in a booth at the gate, leaning the chair back on its bowed rear legs, balancing with his feet braced on the desk top. One hand was behind his head, massaging his scalp. He was video chatting with some shirtless fellow who looked like he could've been his brother.

The guy I met on the gondola still hasn't called me a second time.

Dầu Tiếng

With Núi Bà Đen behind me, I pointed my motorcycle east, toward Dầu Tiếng. The road cut through some of Tây Ninh's most contested terrain of the war: the Michelin and Bến Củi rubber plantations. These French-owned estates, spanning a combined 30,000 acres, had anchored the colonial extraction economy, where Vietnamese workers labored under conditions not far from slavery.

In the 1920s and '30s, the Communist Party staged some of its first mass actions here—strikes, occupations, and violence against French managers. The terrain, dense and shadowed, was ideal for guerrilla operations. Later, the Việt Cộng moved in, coexisting with the French in a delicate arrangement of payment and protection. The U.S. and South Vietnamese Armies swept the area regularly, and fighting at Michelin and Bến Củi remained relentless.

By the early 1970s, falling global rubber prices, widespread Agent Orange defoliation, and escalating violence pushed many French overseers to abandon their holdings. They repatriated, leaving the plantations in suspense. The industry, slow to recover, began to stabilize in the decade after 1975, when newly formed state-owned enterprises assumed control. Today, Vietnam is once again one of the world's top rubber producers.

The road I followed that afternoon had surely once carried American and South Vietnamese convoys. Aside from the occasional dirt track plunging inward, the dense forest concealed more than it revealed. Those convoy passengers would have swept the roadsides for signs of movement in the shadows—anything beyond the workers quietly slicing trees and collecting latex.

* * *

I was riding to Dầu Tiếng to see a swimming pool. Camp Rainier, built in 1966 and abandoned in 1975, had once been a major U.S. Army installation on the town's outskirts, near both the Michelin plantation and the Saigon River. It featured a runway for large supply aircraft, artillery, and a fleet of UH-1 Huey helicopters for air cavalry operations in Bình Dương and Tây Ninh provinces.

In the 1960s, the base spanned much of what is now a prosperous town set on a flat plain, surrounded by rubber forests. Ordinary Vietnamese weren't permitted inside its walls. Outside the perimeter, though, shantytowns sprang up—offering GIs the usual comforts: beer, haircuts, cigarettes, and massages.

Inside the base, there was a swimming pool. Built by the Michelin Rubber Plantation around 1930—likely as a luxury for the French management team—it had fallen into disrepair by 1967.

American soldiers, few of whom knew such amenities in Vietnam, renovated it. They installed ten showers underneath the raised structure, patched damage from a grenade blast, and added a fresh coat of paint. They set up a high-dive platform with a board rigged from a Huey helicopter propeller, built a hi-fi system, and even painted a Playboy bunny on the pool floor.

The pool became a cause célèbre, with a 1967 article in the 25th Infantry Division newsletter *Tropic Lightning News* calling it the "greatest morale booster at Camp Rainier since Armed Forces Television began airing *Batman*."

* * *

As I rode out of the rubber forests, the landscape shifted, as rows of shophouses began spilling onto the road. Dầu Tiếng was bustling. Motorbikes crowded the streets, and I navigated around groups of riders pulled over at the roadside, negotiating and buying live river fish from market women. Money changed hands, and the sellers cradled flopping catfish from plastic tubs into shopping bags, hooking the bags to the fairings of passing motorbikes—as everyone here does.

Traffic thickened as I rolled into the center of town, beneath a red-and-gold banner strung across the main road: *Huyện Dầu Tiếng Kính Chào Quý Khách*—Welcome Our Dear Visitors to Dầu Tiếng District. Heady vibes already.

Passing a municipal park, I clocked its ration of leftover war hardware—tanks, helicopters, jeeps, and defused bombs, all neatly lined up at the entrance. One stood out: a Willys Jeep with *QDND VIỆT NAM* stenciled on the hood, short for Quân Đội Nhân Dân, the People's Army of Việt Nam.

This Ohio-manufactured Willys Jeep served both sides. It was first used by either the Americans or the South Vietnamese Army, then adopted by the PAVN, which repurposed abandoned military vehicles after the American withdrawal and South Vietnam's fall. It likely passed to the Dầu Tiếng People's Committee at some point—but no one changed the designation. So now it's displayed as a captured North Vietnamese Willys Jeep.

Vintage U.S. Army airstrips are not difficult to find in Vietnam. Sometimes they've been repaved and upgraded, now serving as ordinary roads. In other cases, airstrips in towns that once hosted bases remain largely abandoned. Surprisingly, these sites and their wide perimeters are often left untouched in a country as densely populated and land-hungry as Vietnam.

Rather than being developed, many of these old runways sit idle, neither claimed nor truly abandoned, serving as wide, cracked pavement shortcuts between regular roads, dotted with oddly situated bushes, young trees, and dust. Though they remain unofficial, they are used by the local community.

The old Camp Rainier airstrip runs perpendicular to the town's main road. Its dimensions remain mostly intact, though the surrounding land has found new uses. On either side are backyards and an informal market, where women in conical hats and pajamas crouch over tubs of live shrimp and vegetables.

I continued down the runway, past a group of men assembling carnival rides—two-seater rocket ships, mechanical arms, and bumper cars lying in neat disarray on the cracked pavement and red earth. This airstrip would host a carnival of some kind. A pair of stray dogs meandered through, glanced at the activity, then padded off. Debris—weathered lumber, rusted fencing, sagging furniture—lined the edges of the runway like afterthoughts.

* * *

Several decades ago, Dầu Tiếng stood at the edge of a very different map. The Michelin Rubber Plantation reached into the town itself. Once the Việt Cộng and then North Vietnamese troops began operating in the forests, the U.S. positioned bases around the Iron Triangle to enable rapid helicopter insertions against Communist forces. Camp Rainier, just outside town, became a linchpin in that network. During the Tet Offensive of January 1968, it was nearly overrun.

Launched during the Lunar New Year in January 1968, the Tet Offensive marked a psychological turning point in the war. More than 85,000 North Vietnamese and Việt Cộng forces attacked over one hundred cities and military installations across South Vietnam. Militarily, the offensive was a failure—but it shattered the perception that the U.S. was on the brink of victory. In its wake, public support in the U.S. eroded sharply.

Camp Rainier came under siege again in February 1969. North Vietnamese battalions nearly breached the perimeter; rockets and mortar fire shredded the airstrip, while smaller squads slipped into bunkers and defensive lines. After days of brutal fighting, the Americans forced them back with armored vehicles and chopper sorties. As they retreated, the attackers scattered propaganda leaflets for the Americans to find. One of them read:

The Vietnamese people have no hate for the American people. We are fighting for the independence and freedom of our people, just like the U.S. people did in the 18th century. We have sympathized, supported, and welcomed the U.S. anti-war men who love peace and refuse to die for the weapon-dealers in the White House and Pentagon. Don't fold your arms to yield to death! For the future and happiness of your family, refuse to go out to the field. Demand withdrawal. If forced, lay down your arms. You will receive humane and lenient treatment.

This wasn't just psychological warfare. It was empathy, of a sort—urgency and reassurance aimed at a soldier unsure whether to keep going. They reached for an imagined G.I. on the verge of doubt: sympathy laced with pressure, bundled into a final pitch for defection.

It was 1969, and the tone of the war had shifted. The Tet Offensive had revealed deep fractures: an anti-war movement had taken root at home, public trust in the U.S. government was eroding, and the troops at Camp Rainier were likely wrestling with those contradictions, too. The North Vietnamese understood this—their leaflet aimed squarely at those doubts.

I stopped my motorcycle at the end of the airstrip. I'd traced enough perimeters by now to recognize when I was performing for myself—showing up, pacing slowly, nudging at rust and rubble for signals I wasn't even sure I'd recognize. Maybe the ritual's glue had loosened, or maybe I'd become less dazzled with my own choreography. Or maybe I just needed a beer.

***

The sun was slipping low, so I peeled off the old airstrip and began hunting for a *nhà nghỉ*. A hundred yards on, two sirens beckoned—one on the main road, the other down a shaded slope lined with banana and coconut trees. I picked the quieter of the two. Rhododendrons and frangipani bloomed in red clay. The place was walled and gated, the paved courtyard moonlighting as a front yard.

A middle-aged woman in pajamas emerged and waved me away. "Hết phòng rồi," she said. "Không nhận Tây Ba Lô đâu." No rooms left. No backpackers.

Tây Ba Lô, or "Western backpack," is the crisp slang term that needs no translation for hoteliers and *bia hơi* waitresses across Vietnam. It refers to the young, often wide-eyed, often Caucasian shoestring traveler: part gap year, part Instagram travel diary, living cheap, here for *adventure*. The nickname isn't especially hostile, but it's never reverent. Just a label that's come to stand for a certain posture—equal parts awe and obliviousness. For the Vietnamese, that posture is instantly identified by the giant travel backpack, longhair, Teva sandals, cargo shorts, graphic t-shirts, and body aroma.

It's the same tableau—and the same target demographic—recycled in tourism brochures: wide-eyed Westerners on budget motorbike or inflatable banana float tours. An ecstasy sold back to them as validation of their instincts against a quiet life.

Behind the smiles, there's an unspoken caveat: not someone you'd trust with the keys. They'll be gone in a few weeks, back to their Western lives.

To be fair, most *Tây Ba Lô* are fine—earnest, curious, trying their best to see the world and grow as people. But a sizable minority lean hard into the country's permissiveness. Vietnam is cheap. Foreigners generally have to cross a high bad behavior threshold before finding an audience with the police. Most locals are easygoing. So *Tây Ba Lô* drink too much, push too far, and rent under-powered Honda Wins for legendary self-guided tours through the countryside, without helmets or licenses. To many, the country is an unsupervised playground. A sizable majority of Vietnamese working in the service industry has seen the pattern at some point: pillage disguised as tourism—mounds of empty beer cans, hotel rooms trashed, tempers flared, streets kept awake.

Tây Ba Lô corral themselves in certain districts. *Cao bồi thôn* follow them. On Bùi Viện Street in Saigon and Tạ Hiện Street in Hanoi, a whole economy sprang up to serve—hostels, bars, tour agents, and massage parlors packed shoulder-to-shoulder, each undercutting the next. The competition is zero-sum, the services priced accordingly. Streets of loud bars that never close, neon haze, and a sonic assault of trashy Southeast Asian dance music, where everything's nearly free and nothing is remembered. Petty theft, drugs, pavement brawls, shakedowns, prostitution. Especially in Saigon, the mafia is here, always watching.

Long-termers give these streets a wide berth. They've seen the sun rise over the casualty *Tây Ba Lô* curled up on the sidewalk, cheek pressed to the tile, 100 beers deep, hair matted with spilled Long Island Iced Tea, roused and offered knockoff Ray-Bans by a kid on a bicycle, as Vietnamese families sweep the *phở* restaurant frontage around him and prep the day's broth.

This was the *Tây Ba Lô* threat her vigilance had been wired for: it was a primordial survival algorithm.

I wasn't a *Tây Ba Lô*, but it wasn't the first time I'd been called one. She couldn't have known. In my day, it was any Westerner riding a Minsk in Hanoi's Old Quarter.

I ignored her and dismounted. I had to convince her I wasn't a *Tây Ba Lô*, and usually, a "hello, older sister" in Vietnamese is enough.

She blinked, then called inside to her daughter. "Lấy phòng cho Ông Tây." Come give a room to Mr. West.

Ông Tây. The well-mannered older brother to the unruly *Tây Ba Lô*. *Ông Tây* has a respectable job and haircut, speaks a little Vietnamese, follows the rules, and earns the honorific.

* * *

This *nhà nghỉ* had all the attributes. A *tạp hóa* next door sold everything I could possibly need. Across the street, Quán 555—a seductive *quán nhậu bình dân*—radiated the warmth of a country backyard barbecue.

I stepped into the two-story Vietnamese house. A side addition held a row of single rooms, each with a wooden door and a padlock. At the front desk, another woman in pajamas sat cross-legged on a collapsing black plastic conference chair, one that had long since lost the tensile strength in its springs. The back leaned lazily at a 170-degree angle, still partially sheathed in showroom cellophane, some of it peeling like dry skin. She was watching the 7:00 p.m. Vietnam Television News. I followed her to the first door in the row.

"I'll take it," I said as she brought the key to the lock.

The room was magnificent. A 12-inch television was bolted high on the concrete wall, cobwebs dangling above it from the peeling ceiling. The bed sheets bore cigarette burns. So did the windowpanes. More had melted into the lacquered surface of the wooden desk, as if these walls had seen a few too many secret romances over the years. On the plastic shelf above the sink sat a bright green drinking mug—its cartoon duck faded—filled with toothbrush kits and condoms. More cobwebs gathered in the upper corners of the restroom.

I plugged in the refrigerator. The little engine sputtered to life. It was empty. I called the front desk and ordered a beer from room service, but feeling impatient, I went and fetched it myself. It was a Bia Saigon that had probably been sitting in the sun most of the day.

Heritage brands are usually served hot; they don't pander. I took a long, ice-cold shower and got ready for an evening out at Quán 555.

* * *

Dầu Tiếng is a numbers town. It has a robust, organic lottery infrastructure: closed-captioned television monitors broadcasting results were everywhere. One near the *nhà nghỉ* front desk was bolted to the ceiling, a vivid 6-by-30 matrix of numbers blinking across it. Vietnamese tend to be animated by the lottery—and all forms of gambling, for that matter. But Dầu Tiếng felt different. The lottery here ran deeper.

Senior citizens and children often serve their communities as lottery agents, weaving through tight alleyways and narrow streets, peddling stacks of tickets to anyone loitering curbside over a coffee or glass of beer. The tickets are hard to miss—about the size of two business cards placed end to end, each printed with bold lotus blossoms in lucky reds and golds. The number sits in the center of each ticket in the stack, waiting to be chosen.

The agents are quick to sell and eager to move on, but lottery luck isn't taken lightly in a country where numerology holds a gentle grip. Buyers sift through the stack, searching for a particular *số đẹp*, a "beautiful number," lucky by birth date, symmetry, or superstition. Most tickets cost about 10,000 đồng, roughly 40 cents, and I wonder about the agent's margins. If they sell thirty to fifty a day, there's likely at minimum a glass of *nước chanh* limeade waiting for them at the end of the shift.

To an outsider, the whole system is opaque. You might find the winning numbers buried in *Công An* (Police) or *Bóng Đá* (Soccer) newspapers. They're probably announced on television, too—but with eighty-plus provincial channels included in the most basic of cable packages, even that's a black box. The payout? Usually the equivalent of $15 or $20.

***

The sun was slipping away as I wandered across the road to Quán 555, where two more television monitors flashed the same lottery results, one near the men's room and the other in the outdoor patio area. The tavern, inconspicuously attached to a modest single-family home, seemed to thrive in the absence of zoning regulations—a reality in rural Vietnam where commercial, residential, and agricultural spaces often bleed into each other—it's all *one* zone.

I ambled up a steep, partially paved driveway into the dim interior of the restaurant. Laughter echoed from a table where a group of men shared drinks, while a few private tables—tucked away hidden refuges—lined the driveway. These gazebos, made from bamboo and banana leaves, glowed under low-wattage bulbs that dangled from above. I slipped into one of the secluded corners, ready to take in the atmosphere. I ordered a plate of tofu in tomato sauce, which soon arrived. I dug in.

Moments later and feeling well-fed, I glanced over the bamboo wall of my gazebo. The dining area was little more than blue plastic tables and red plastic chairs—the pragmatic furniture of rural Vietnam. A young woman knelt between tables, washing dishes in a large plastic basin. Suds overflowed, trickling down the uneven concrete floor, past the tables, and into a shallow gutter that carried the water toward the country lane out front.

I moved through the open double door to the attached house, looking for the restroom. I spotted one of those hulking, famously uncomfortable Vietnamese cushionless rosewood sofa sets—glossy, hand-carved, and seemingly designed to punish the seated—beside a family altar and a television. Hanging beside the altar was a plastic commemorative plate bearing a photo of Võ Nguyên Giáp, the revered general who led Vietnam to victory at Điện Biên Phủ in

1954, in uniform. It was an emblem of national pride, a quiet reminder of the revolution's continued presence.

Outside the double door, three plastic tables formed a grand setup, with a one-burner portable gas cooking stove at the center of one. Colorful plastic dishes lay scattered with bits of tofu, vegetables, pickled greens, and herbs for *lẩu*, or hotpot. The scene was chaotic but contented; the six or seven men drinking rice wine together now gazed dreamily at the empty pot they had just destroyed. Cooked noodles and soggy cabbage still dangled over its rim.

It's claimed that *lẩu* traces back to the Mongolian invasions of the thirteenth century. Nomadic Mongols, it's said, camped out on the steppe and liked their meat boiled communally—dropping a pan over coals, heating water, and adding meat and vegetables. The Vietnamese adopted the dish, but today, *lẩu* is more than nourishment. It's festivity. It's often what's ordered when a group of Vietnamese people get together. Everyone is a chef, everyone eats. Part of the fun is the busyness: everyone reaching their chopsticks in, no one quite agreeing on how long anything takes to cook.

The problem for foreigners is that, unless you're out with a Vietnamese group for a dedicated *lẩu* night—a somewhat rare scenario for most expats—you're more likely to encounter it as the final course of a ten-plus-course work-related dinner. By then, you're already bursting with rice, beer, and everything else.

"How do they have room for *lẩu*?" one might ask. Good question. It's not comfort food for most Westerners, and in this setting, *lẩu* can feel like a bit of a chore, especially when dining with partners or government officials. You're already full of shrimp, vegetables, pork, spring rolls, noodles, and rice pancakes. The good stuff. You're sleepy.

And then the *lẩu* arrives: a tabletop burner, a giant pot of boiling water, and mountains of raw meat, noodles, and vegetables to cook yourself. It's the equivalent of digging deep and finding room for a big bowl of beef stew after two helpings of Thanksgiving dinner.

*　*　*

I stepped up to their table. "Excuse me, gents. May I join you?" I asked, interrupting their comas.

They straightened, blinking. "Uh ... sure. Sure. Please."

These fellows actually didn't want me to join them. I'd passed their table earlier, and as we've seen, a table of half-cut country squires might usually extend the nightcap invitation. But not this crew. I was the interloper. Still, the die had been cast. At this point, it was incumbent upon me to commit and try to entertain them.

All were in their mid-forties, all from Dầu Tiếng. Some ran businesses; others were town or provincial officials. One was an architect. The quiet one at the head of the table owned both the house and Quán 555, his side business. His wife was grilling brochettes; his daughter was squatting over the basin washing dishes; his son, maybe seven, galloped through the dining room. This was their nightly ritual, a wind-down after ten or eleven-hour workdays.

The man picked up a bottle of Sprite, one that'd probably been in circulation in its new role for a year or two, from the ground near his chair. The lime green plastic was hazy. Sprite it was not—it was a jug of homemade *rượu*, or rice wine. In this case, moonshine. Another man handed me a thimble-sized glass. We raised our cups. One burning gulp, clean and sharp.

I figured I might as well explain why I was there, so I volunteered that I was on a motorcycle trip to see old bases and battle sites from the war.

"Well, you're in the right place," said the architect beside me. His name was Đức (virtuous). Like the others, he wore an unobjectionable polo, shorts, and sandals. His black hair was parted with precision. "All of this town was once a big American base.

Vietnamese people weren't allowed inside the perimeter back then. Did you see the runway?"

"I visited it today. Looks like they're setting up for a carnival."

"That's right," Đức nodded.

"I'm also looking for a swimming pool from the French period."

"It's still here. You didn't find it?"

"No."

The host refilled our glasses. Đức said, "I'll take you there tomorrow."

Around us, the evening was winding down. The men patted their bellies and stirred a few remaining pickles in their bowls with chopsticks, their eyes growing heavy.

"He's fat," one man said, leaning toward his neighbor and eyeing me.

"Ah, yes," I said. "Had a similar conversation with two women near Sông Bé Bridge two days ago. But yes, I'm a fat guy. I've been lucky in life."

The retort landed, and the gossiping stopped. In this part of the world, plumpness can be a by-product of good fortune, wealth, or prosperity. The men nodded. Another round of moonshine was poured.

Since we were now talking health and lifestyle, I leaned toward Đức. "What time do you wake up in the morning?"

Perfectly normal question to a stranger in Vietnam. People delight in sharing their eating, drinking, sleeping, exercise routines, and wellness secrets, which, ironically, aren't really secrets. The national regimen, more or less: sleep by ten, up at six, three meals a day, some exercise in between. Đức, it turned out, was a bit of a renegade.

"I wake up at five," he said, without hesitation. "I'm in the office twelve hours a day—seven to seven. I exercise after work. Then we come here to eat and drink, every night. Then go home to do more work."

He patted his belly. He was forty-five, unmarried, no children. He could run his schedule how he liked.

"Wow," I said. "How many hours do you sleep at night?"

"About three," he replied. Punishing schedule.

"Why on earth would you only sleep three hours per night?" I asked.

"Making money," he said. "I'm an architect. I have my own firm. Always working for success."

"Christ. What about your health?"

He patted his forearm. "No problem."

A practiced reply, no doubt. One he'd grown accustomed to giving his mother and neighbors, who had probably admonished him for a lifestyle that was well out of balance.

Our host poured one final round, emptying the Sprite bottle, and gave the closing nod. It was close to ten.

"I'll call you at 5:45 tomorrow morning, and we'll visit the swimming pool together," he said. The appointment was a bit early for my liking, but it's rare that a local offers to guide you to a war site.

I waved for the bill. The host frowned. "No, no, no. You're my guest here."

But I had invited myself to their table, not the other way around. I took out my wallet. He pushed back, I pushed harder, and eventually, I won. He was extremely hospitable, but I paid for my tofu and beer.

I crossed the lane toward my *nhà nghỉ*, the familiar blue flicker of VTV news casting its glow behind the front desk in the unlit reception area. I slipped past and headed for my room.

* * *

I awoke to the sound of my telephone ringing. It was precisely 5:45.

"I'm in front of your hotel. Let's go," Đức said—and hung up.

Then I heard the town's public address system stir to life. A government broadcast.

These open-air speakers, mounted to telephone poles, are increasingly rare in Vietnam. But during the war and postwar subsidized period—the 1970s through the '90s, when radios and televisions weren't abundant—they were essential. The People's Committee used them to warn of incoming bombers or deliver news from the front. Later, cadres read from state-run newspapers, folding in slogans about socialism, health, and community-building.

Messages usually ended with: "Remember to exercise today, for..." or "Let's work together to build..."

In the parts of the country where these public address systems are still used, most Vietnamese probably tune out the broadcasts. But I've always loved this odd, loud soundscape. It's like a postcard from the past, tinged with static and slogans—spoken in dense, bureaucratic Vietnamese by speakers of a certain vintage. Sometimes the announcements are grand. Often they're mundane: reminders to brush your teeth, or tend your garden.

I scrambled around the room, buckling my saddlebags and gearing up. Ten minutes later, after paying the concierge, I stepped out into the morning and met Đức.

"Ready?" he asked.

I followed him along windy country roads until it became clear we were circling back to the park I'd visited the day before. The same community center lawn, lined with dozens of U.S. bombs, an M-41 tank, a UH-1 Huey helicopter, and a Willys Jeep once used by both sides.

Next to it, partially obscured by brush and signage, was the swimming pool. I had missed it.

Đức stopped and extended his hand. It was 6:00 a.m., and he was eager to be in the office. I thanked him, and we parted ways.

The pool was a two-level white concrete block, maybe a hundred feet long and fifteen feet tall. Stairs led to the top, where the basin sat above the locker rooms and equipment spaces below. But the staircase was gated and locked. Pity. It wouldn't open for another two hours.

I tried to peer over the edge to see if the black Playboy Bunny logo American soldiers had painted on the pool's floor was still there, but the angle was wrong.

Still, I could picture it: concrete and chlorine atop a bunker-like structure, surrounded by jungle and artillery. The rubber forests just beyond might well have hidden North Vietnamese scouts, quietly surveilling the swimmers. And yet, in the late '60s, it would've been the envy of any G.I. serving elsewhere in Vietnam.

I stepped back and imagined American soldiers blasting Tommy James and the Shondells on the poolside stereo. Vietnam War films from the '80s and '90s often go with the Rolling Stones, Jefferson Airplane, or the Doors, but I've always found that a bit suspect. Most conscripts weren't of Haight-Ashbury, Venice Beach, Greenwich Village, or Laurel Canyon. They came from working towns, military families, barbershops, union halls, and church pews—not the heaviest of counterculture enclaves. That whole soundtrack feels retrofitted, filtered through the lens of the Reagan years, when those archetypes were cemented. More likely, in the day it was Marvin Gaye, Buck Owens, the Miracles, or Creedence Clearwater Revival.

They'd have been living it up in Dầu Tiếng, under a brutal sun—splashing each other, doing cannonballs, pushing friends off inner tubes, all while floating above a Playboy Bunny logo. Drinking Budweiser and letting the moment stretch out like late summer, forgetting, just briefly, that it would end with a helicopter ride back to war.

I gave the pool a final look and swung onto my motorcycle. It was forty miles to Saigon. Breakfast awaited.

CENTRAL HIGHLANDS

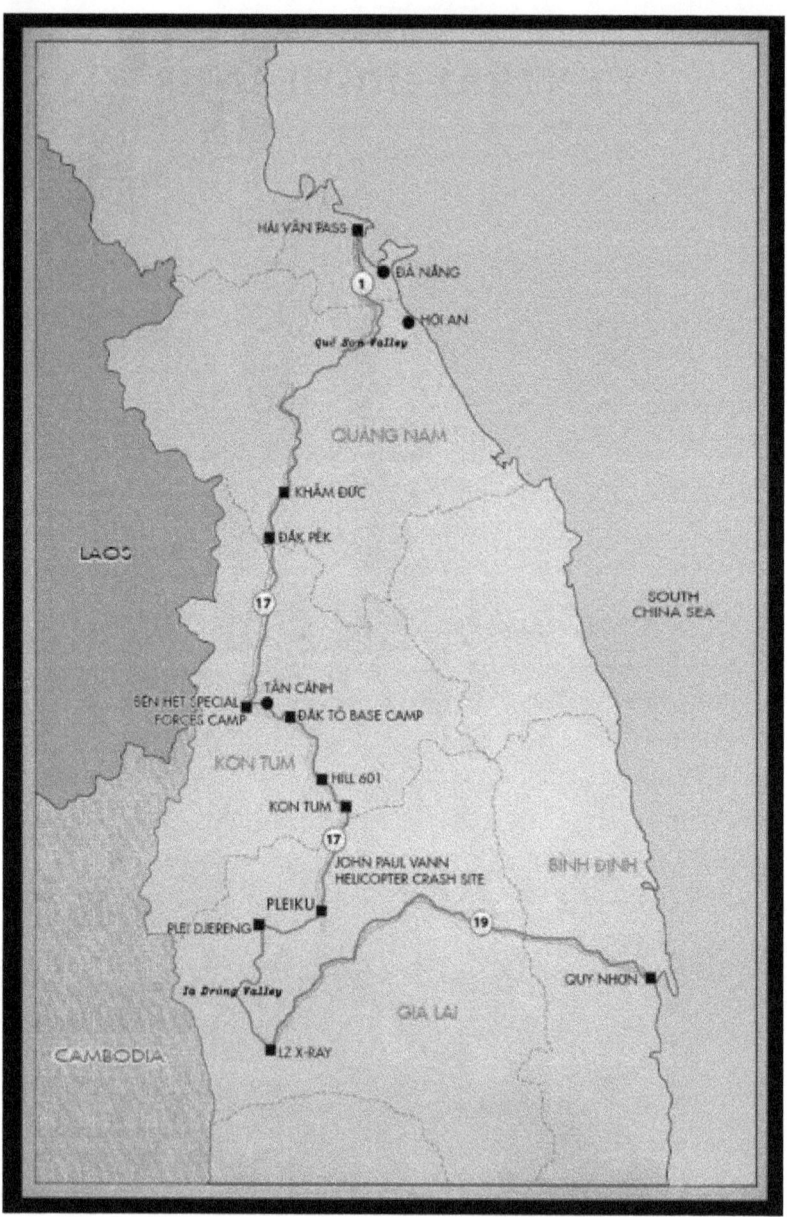

MAP: CENTRAL HIGHLANDS

Ia Drăng

I returned to Saigon to begin the next leg: a ride into the Central Highlands to visit former military bases and battlefields. My motorcycle traveled north by train, and I flew to pick it up in the coastal city of Quy Nhơn. From there, Highway 19 led inland to Pleiku, then north on the lush, mountainous Ho Chi Minh Highway toward Kon Tum, tracing the contours of the Cambodian and Lao borders.

Đường Hồ Chí Minh is a 750-mile, two-lane road that links Saigon and Hanoi via sections of the original Ho Chi Minh Trail in mountainous western Vietnam. Built in the early 2000s to relieve congestion on Vietnam's busy coastal spine—it follows stretches of the original wartime trail. Still, it remains sparsely used, remote from where most Vietnamese actually live. The vast majority of the population, markets, and distribution centers are clustered along the east coast, so most of the logistics traffic stuck to Highway 1. A rider who chooses it over Highway 1 gets the Central Highlands largely to themselves.

After Kon Tum, I would swing east to the lowlands of Quảng Nam, then follow the war's imprint north through Quảng Trị—once the heart of the DMZ—accompanied by Vũ, a local guide who takes American veterans back to battlefields for a living. Eventually, I'd cross into Quảng Bình, the former southern tip of North Vietnam, to meet an Australian friend and rejoin the Trail. The route wouldn't mirror any tidy chronology. It was a patchwork, each region holding its own time, its own story.

* * *

I flew one of the country's budget airlines, VietJet Air, to Quy Nhơn. The launch of this carrier years ago marked a watershed moment. The domestic tourism industry took off in the mid-to-late 2000s, fueled by two decades of rapid economic growth. Budget airlines slashed the unaffordable ticket prices once set by the state-owned carrier, juicing the hospitality sector and sparking a boom that continues today.

I recall taking domestic flights in 2008 with passengers who were undoubtedly flying for the first time. Little things gave them away: people wearing motorbike helmets in-flight; fidgety men cross-legged in window seats, snapping the window blind open and shut every few seconds throughout a two-hour trip; others staring intently at their boarding passes the entire flight, as though memorizing them. Some shouted conversations over their shoulders to relatives ten or fifteen rows back.

I've heard stories of people trying to board with live chickens or bulk produce in their carry-on luggage. And those stories are certainly believable. But that was a long time ago, in the scheme of things. These days, middle-class tourism tropes—package tours, theme parks, tour bus parades, matching baseball hats, overcrowded breakfast buffets, and guide flags—are just as commonplace here as anywhere else.

As we taxied along the runway after landing in Quy Nhơn, the passenger address system hissed, then played "Hello Vietnam," a 2007 pop ballad by Belgian singer Phạm Quỳnh Anh. VietJet plays the tune during every landing, meaning its flight crews collectively hear it hundreds of times a day.

The song expresses Quỳnh Anh's longing to visit her ancestral homeland and understand who she is, having grown up in Europe and knowing Vietnam mostly through Western pop culture. A second-generation diaspora expression of the southern story. She sings *All I know of you is the sights of war / A film by Coppola, the helicopter's roar*. The song was a hit among both Vietnamese and the overseas Vietnamese community. The title was, I suspect, a nod to Lionel Richie. I will forever associate it with VietJet Air.

As the aircraft slowed and the passenger bridge came into view, a silent signal seemed to transmit through the cabin. Within seconds, passengers were on their feet, jostling for space, even as the plane was still taxiing. The aisle clogged with people climbing over each other, yanking suitcases from overhead bins. Others surged forward in a human wave, squeezing past senior citizens and children alike.

As the mosh pit cleared, Quỳnh Anh continued: *One day I'll finally know your soul / One day I'll come to you / To say hello Vietnam.* I filed out with the others, stepping over a carpet of VietJet-branded wooden chopsticks, Styrofoam clamshell take-out containers, and coffee cups, with bits of sticky rice, grilled meat, shrimp tails, and crumbled rice crackers strewn across the seats and floor.

I took a taxi to Quy Nhơn's Diêu Trì train station. It was just before 7:00 a.m., and the cargo office hadn't opened yet. The sun was still low, but the neighborhood around the station had already been humming for hours. Market women in *nón lá* conical hats had laid tarps across the parking lot, marketing pyramids of tropical fruit and snacks for train passengers hustling inside.

A gentleman in a sky-blue Vietnam Railways uniform gradually drifted closer to where I was waiting, keeping silent company. He was fishing for a *làm quen* exchange—with a bit of subtlety—and I rose to the bait.

"Chào Anh. Anh có gia đình chưa?" I asked, turning to him. He was married, of course, with two children in their late twenties. In his sixties now, he also had several grandchildren. Originally from Nghệ An province in north-central Vietnam, he'd lived in Quy Nhơn for thirty years. I offered him my version of the story, and he gently followed up with a few questions—what I was doing in Vietnam, how my family was getting along back home.

When I first moved to Hanoi in 2002, I didn't quite understand how *làm quen* worked. To amuse myself, I told people I was from the Soviet Union. That didn't last, as every second or third *làm quen* partner would switch to *làm quen* in Russian and I'd lose all credibility. Since then, I've come to appreciate it for what it is: a way to build connection and find footing in this country.

I remember visiting my former in-laws in northern Vietnam once, drifting through a family conversation I couldn't follow. Noticing I was left out, my then-mother-in-law leaned over and asked, "So... how much do you weigh?" I smiled and gave her my best estimate.

Still, being a foreigner who can manage a *làm quen* session can sometimes attract attention. A young university student materialized and cut off the Vietnam Railways worker, speaking English to me. "You speak beautiful Vietnamese! Where did you learn? Are you fluent? What's your name? Where are you from?"

Easy, fella, I thought. The dark side of *làm quen* is getting buttered up by a wildly enthusiastic college student—in English. My Vietnamese isn't beautiful, but that didn't matter. Even if I'd been fluent, he would've pushed for English anyway.

These outgoing, twentysomething, globalized types are everywhere in Saigon. With relatively high exposure to the world beyond Vietnam, they're ravenous for integration and English-language conversation. When visitors gush about how dynamic and modern Saigon is, this is often the crew they're referencing. They're usually situated somewhere in the breathless press dispatches we *still* see about Vietnam's remarkable postwar evolution framed by a discussion on *Đổi Mới*—the 1986 reform still treated like breaking news—inevitably titled *Good Morning, Vietnam.*

Sure, they embrace global culture: they're Ed Sheeran fans, have read Jeff Bezos biographies, and dig the Marvel Cinematic Universe.

Middle-of-the-road stuff that this curmudgeon doesn't get too excited about. Maybe it's generational. But Vietnam already has so much charisma—historical, cultural, human—that I get nervous when young people seem too eager to overhaul the future. Of course, that's not my call.

More often than not, conversations with these young urbanites prompt me to hold court about myself or the United States. I represent a popular culture leviathan, and they want more globalization in their lives. That's fine. But there's enough American frivolity in the world already.

The gent in the sky-blue uniform was now physically blocked, edged out of a chat that had just pivoted to English. I thought: *Not happening; you're not hijacking my làm quen session with my new friend.*

"No. I'm not fluent," I replied. "Thanks for the compliment."

I turned and reached out to the older man, shaking his hand. The student drifted away and produced his iPhone. That ended the audition.

* * *

I found the cargo office, and the crew uncrated my bike. The day before, the manager had called to confirm its arrival in Quy Nhơn, casually noting, "There's a *cash* fee of 100,000 đồng ($4) to unpack your motorcycle. Can you manage that?" I gladly handed it over. No sense getting precious about informal payments on the first morning of a long trip.

Reunited with my motorcycle, I wound my way out of Diêu Trì train station and headed west, the sun at my back, the road wide open ahead.

Those first moments on a motorcycle at the beginning of a trip are intoxicating. I like to start early, and Vietnamese are morning people. Countryside mornings can feel like late afternoons here:

things move more slowly before 8:00 a.m. People linger over their coffees at country shack cafés. Proprietors work their businesses; women in silk pantsuits sweep floors and heat steamy vats of soup broth over open fires while old men in white tank tops and boxer shorts dally, grilling pork with copies of *Công An* (Police) newspaper rolled up under their arms.

It's easy to be lured by country mornings and scenes like this—drawn into squatting on a 10-inch-high red plastic stool, nursing a street-side coffee for ninety minutes—only to find yourself hitting the road at 10:00 a.m., when half of Vietnam's day is already done. That temptation ought to be resisted, but the atmosphere is hard to leave.

I did notice the heat—it was already there by 7:30 a.m.—but that didn't worry me. This is Vietnam, after all. It was damn hot, and no Vietnam War story would be complete without gratuitous descriptions of the heat.

Pleiku was about 100 miles west on Highway 19. On Pleiku's periphery was my day's destination: the Ia Đrăng Valley, home of Landing Zone X-Ray and the site of one of the war's earliest major battles between the North Vietnamese Army and the United States, in 1965 near the Cambodian frontier. Given road conditions and topography, I figured it would take a few hours to reach LZ X-Ray.

* * *

The lowland landscape as I motored out of Quy Nhơn was chiefly asparagus-colored scrub, growing from soil so white it looked like the sun had baked the moisture out of it. The sky was big, vast, and cloudless. The sun scorched.

Elevation gradually rose as I crossed into Gia Lai province and ascended to the plateaus leading to the foothills of the Trường Sơn mountain range, which stretches over 650 miles through central Vietnam and Laos. I began to see more cultivation: yard-high cassava trees, rows of them stretching to a horizon of distant foothills several miles away.

The towns I passed through still followed the spatial layout, clustering, and architecture found throughout lowland Vietnam. It was clear we hadn't fully entered the highlands yet. The highlands are looser—less organized—with wooden houses and shacks speckling the land, and plots divided haphazardly. Unlike the lowlands, there's space.

I rode around giant Socialist Realism monuments anchoring town traffic rotaries, heroic sculptures of Vietnamese men and women rushing into combat. I passed beneath street-width red-and-gold banners that exhorted rural Vietnamese to plant trees, remember Ho Chi Minh, and develop the Central Highlands together.

I knew I'd finally crossed an informal border when two Jarai men in tattered army-green fatigues overtook me on their Sufat Win motorbike. A woven shoulder bag, patterned in deep reds and blacks, was slung across the passenger's chest, his free hand resting on the machete laid across the top. Their smiles glittered as they passed—like they'd just swallowed a chocolate cake.

Puzzled but game, I nodded. They broke away, then slowed, matching my speed, eyes fixed on me. The operator glanced forward occasionally, just enough to avoid a crash. After a charged minute, I pulled ahead. They loosened the tension with a military salute. I smiled. A few minutes later, they overtook me again—two more salutes. I returned the gesture. They slowed. I passed. More salutes.

Welcome to the Friendly Central Highlands.

* * *

Vietnam is 85 percent ethnic Kinh. The rest belong to fifty-four officially recognized ethnic groups, most of them highlanders—known, still, by the lingering French term

Montagnards. The Jarai, numbering about four hundred thousand, are one of those ethnic groups. Not so long ago, fifteen, maybe twenty years, whole stretches of the Central Highlands were off-limits to visitors. It's a region long marked by uneasy loyalties, contested identity, and a wary relationship with the state. For Hanoi, it has always been a place that doesn't quite fall in line.

The United Front for the Liberation of Oppressed Races, or FULRO, exemplified Hanoi's unease. A fragmented, non-aligned alliance of minority groups, FULRO pushed for autonomy across Indochina. Between 1964 and 1992, its fighters launched insurgencies against South Vietnam, North Vietnam, the United States, and the Việt Cộng, sometimes all in the same year. In the 1980s, the group renewed its guerrilla campaign against a reunified Vietnam, with support in the form of arms, cash, and encouragement from the country's longtime adversary, China. At its peak, FULRO fielded an estimated seven thousand combatants.

The highland minority groups of Vietnam continue to maintain distinct identities, languages, and customs—despite decades of government efforts at cultural assimilation. Throughout the twentieth century, their political allegiances were often complex, with some groups aligning tactically in pursuit of postwar autonomy. French missionaries found converts here, and Christianity spread widely across the Central Highlands. Communism and Christianity don't mix well, though. Even today, American visitors will occasionally be arrested in Gia Lai for traveling with suitcases full of Bibles. Deportation usually follows.

U.S. Special Forces began deploying to the Central Highlands early in the war to help defend the region from incursions along the Ho Chi Minh Trail, which threaded through Laos and Cambodia. They camped near Montagnard villages, training roughly forty thousand locals in combat, distributing cash and weapons to build alliances. In return, Montagnards served as guides and fighters, helping American Rangers navigate the terrain and the war.

Around two hundred thousand Montagnards died, and 85 percent of highland villages were either destroyed or abandoned during the conflict. After the war, thousands fled across the border into Cambodia. The U.S. military evacuated and resettled about two thousand in the United States—some of whom later regrouped and attempted to stage an armed return to the Central Highlands.

The postwar Vietnamese government worked to pacify the Central Highlands by shifting its demographics. With incentives to relocate, lowlanders flooded the region's New Economic Zones. Tens of thousands of ethnic Vietnamese moved to the underdeveloped but resource-rich highlands, chasing prosperity. A century ago, the Central Highlands was 95 percent Montagnard. Today, it's closer to 25 percent. One hears a lot of northern accents in these parts.

As I pulled away from my companions with the machete, the roadsides gradually filled with other Jarai on foot, tending to their business. I passed beneath a long red banner that proclaimed: *Tất Cả Vì Dân Giàu, Nước Mạnh, Xã Hội Công Bằng, Dân Chủ, Văn Minh* (All People United for a Rich and Strong Country, and a Fair, Democratic, and Civilized Society). Propaganda is ubiquitous in the Central Highlands, and here, it feels insistent.

Beneath the flashes of ceremonial color, olive-drab and camouflage clothing are the default in Jarai villages. Most people here get up in the morning and put on army pants. I passed more Jarai pedestrians—machetes in hand, chickens dangling upside down by their ankles, sooty fertilizer sacks bulging with blocks of cooking charcoal. From afar, they were always climbing or descending a hill. They do this every day, in the heat and the rain.

* * *

An hour later, I was approaching LZ X-Ray. This former battlefield lies in one of the most remote corners of the country—the Ia Đrăng Valley, about two miles from the Cambodian border. It was here, in November 1965, that the United States and the North Vietnamese Army faced off in their first major engagement—what would become the opening round of a war that dragged on for ten more years. Ia Đrăng dominated U.S. headlines that month and gained lasting recognition through *We Were Soldiers Once ... And Young*, a book by Lt. Gen. Hal Moore, who commanded the First Battalion, Seventh Cavalry. Moore is played by Mel Gibson in the 2002 film of the same name.

By 1964, Hanoi had concluded that guerrilla campaigns in the South wouldn't be enough to achieve reunification. The decision was made to send regular North Vietnamese troops down the Ho Chi Minh Trail to reinforce the Việt Cộng. It must have felt like an open window: the U.S. military presence in Vietnam was still relatively small—just sixteen thousand troops, mostly advisors and Special Forces units stationed along the Cambodian and Laotian borders. These teams trained Montagnard troops under the Civilian Irregular Defense Group (CIDG) program and conducted reconnaissance along the Trail.

Then came the August 1964 Gulf of Tonkin Incident, which triggered a rapid American buildup: bombing campaigns, major base construction, and finally, the arrival of ground troops in May 1965. By year's end, over 180,000 American soldiers were in Vietnam.

North Vietnam rolled the dice. In October, the PAVN crossed into Vietnam from Cambodia and laid siege to Plei Mei, a Special Forces camp roughly six miles from the site of what would later become LZ X-Ray. Their strategy: probe Gia Lai province, hit Pleiku, and, if successful, push to the coast—splitting the Republic of Vietnam in half with a horizontal wedge of PAVN forces.

American air strikes and South Vietnamese troops broke the siege after a week of fighting, forcing the attackers west into the jungle near Cambodia. U.S. intelligence believed about twenty-five hundred northern troops had retreated into the Ia Đrăng Valley, somewhere near a 450-foot hill on the Chu Pong Massif.

The assault at LZ X-Ray began on the morning of November 14, as nearly two thousand U.S. Army and ARVN troops landed in waves of Hueys at the foot of the Chu Pong Massif. Almost immediately, the first units to disembark came under fire from the base of the hill. Soon, LZ X-Ray was being hit from three directions, even as helicopters continued ferrying in the rest of the force. The chosen landing zone was, in effect, the middle of a North Vietnamese Army camp.

Over the next three days, the two sides traded probes, charges, artillery, air strikes, and hand-to-hand combat. On day two, with American ground forces surrounded, they issued the "Broken Arrow" distress call—code for imminent collapse—and summoned all available air assets in South Vietnam to bomb the perimeter. The Chu Pong Massif was pounded by B-52s and attack aircraft for forty-eight hours, raising a mushroom cloud that lingered for days. The North Vietnamese eventually withdrew into Cambodia. The U.S. and South Vietnam suffered about nine hundred casualties; the North Vietnamese, around a thousand.

* * *

As I neared the site, the road deteriorated—deep ruts and buckling earth carved by rainy season floods. I turned left onto an even rougher track and slowed, realizing I was passing the lonely People's Army of Việt Nam base marked on my map, just beside LZ X-Ray. Being an American in a sensitive border zone near a military installation, the correct move was to keep a very low profile. I rolled my motorcycle into some bushes, dismounted, and eased down a footpath away from the road.

And there it was: the Chu Pong Massif. Unmistakable. I'd seen the film, read the book, studied the photos. It rose in a staggered row of low peaks, collated like pages from a copy machine—mounds of dark green fleece from a distance. I kept walking and found myself in a meadow of wild grass, waist-high in places, leading toward the hills. The trail forked, one branch continuing into a strand of young rubber trees that stretched to the horizon.

LZ X-Ray was a name I'd known long before I arrived—from the movie and the book. I'd imagined those scenes, drawn by something I couldn't fully name. Standing there now, squinting into the quiet heat of the real valley, it felt familiar—as if I'd crossed a threshold I'd been quietly approaching for years. Calling it history gave the whole thing shape. It was just another battlefield, another perimeter to walk. But that wasn't entirely true. It never had been.

There was no trace of the Battle of Ia Đrăng here. Then again, there was no sign of anyone passing through recently. LZ X-Ray was perfectly silent that afternoon. The chaos, intensity, and emotion of those three days had gone dormant, overtaken by an audible breeze running down the Chu Pong Massif and spilling into the meadow, as if retracing the steps of North Vietnamese soldiers descending on huddled Americans and South Vietnamese in the landing zone. It felt lighter than I'd expected, as though the land had healed and moved on from the horrors of November 1965.

Strolling through scattered cassava, I kept my eyes on the ground, combing for any war garbage, bomb craters, or aged foxholes—but realized I'd have to settle for the distinctive panorama before me. I committed myself to the heady feeling of having this isolated historical place to myself, pausing for long deliberate gazes at the hills. I'd remember it. After an hour, I returned to my stashed motorcycle and prepared for the slow ride to Pleiku, through 35 miles of jungle roads. Twilight had begun. The sun retreated west, backlighting the Chu Pong Massif and bathing LZ X-Ray in an orange radiance.

* * *

I rode into Pleiku two hours later. I'd been to Pleiku before, and it's not my favorite Vietnamese city. Atmospherically, it underwhelms. Pleiku seems to have gone through a growth spurt after the war; its functional and spiritless 1990s architecture sprawls in an omnidirectional way, rendering it a weird metropolis dropped onto an otherwise empty plateau. The streets lack the hustle and raucousness that greet in every other hamlet, town, and city in Vietnam. It's more of an ordered, doors-closed, shades-drawn community.

Pleiku is a company town. Hoàng Anh Gia Lai (HAGL), Vietnam's second-largest conglomerate after Vingroup, is headquartered here. A *Đổi Mới*-era capitalist success story, the company started out making furniture in 1990 and now has its hands in real estate, rubber, sugar, mining, and power generation. Then came football: HAGL owns one of Vietnam's more famous V League 1 clubs, which plays its matches in town.

The company holds a billion dollars in assets in Laos, hundreds of millions more in Cambodia and Myanmar, and significant investments in Thailand. Its founder, Đoàn Nguyên Đức—a coastal lowlander and now one of Vietnam's wealthiest men—owns most of Pleiku. His company's name is emblazoned on the central hotel and the city's only skyscraper. Maybe that's why Pleiku feels so straitlaced: one man's will to impose order and decorum on this Central Highlands outpost.

I rode several loops around the central business district, searching vainly for a magnetic *nhà nghỉ*. I passed the skyscraper and imagined Đức and some classy friends in the Executive Board Room, celebrating a business deal with over-practiced restraint. They'd be drinking fancy European red wine rationed in tablespoon-sized servings from goblets big enough to hold a bottle, handling the glasses reverently and performatively, sniffing more than sipping. Like rich Vietnamese do; the unspoken message being *this is very expensive*.

Finally, I gave up and pulled into the brightly lit Khách Sạn Thành Công (Success Hotel). It looked a bit ominous; blinking LED signs advertised a karaoke studio and nightclub, which can make for an unlucky stay on the wrong night.

A security guard directed me to park my bike around the back. I motored on and found the lot. As I approached, I noticed a middle-aged man glaring at me from inside the attendant's booth. I parked beside his shack and slowly dismounted, working out the kinks in my bottom and lower back. The man hollered and motioned for me to park in one of the lot's far corners.

They always wait until you're off the bike and standing before they start grumbling.

It turned out I had parked in a spot reserved for automobiles. I acknowledged him, got back on the bike, restarted it, and moved. He shook his head. There was nothing ostentatious about my parking job, but he objected anyway.

"Hey. Move your motorbike. This way," he said, sweeping both arms like an airport tarmac marshal. I'd parked perpendicular, and he wanted me to park parallel. The parking lot was empty. I've dealt with obsessive-compulsive, cantankerous parking lot attendants in Vietnam before; something about this dull profession brings it out of them.

There are a lot of lousy vocations in Vietnam: ditch digger, *bia hơi* waitress, mid-level manager at a Korean or Chinese foreign direct-invested export-oriented manufacturing enterprise, street nail clipper salesman, motorbike delivery for bricks or rebar, restroom attendant, *cao bồi thôn*. But for me, the most tedious profession imaginable is that of a parking lot attendant. Parking lots are small, and motorbikes are numerous.

Rarely does the "Parking Lot Full" sign appear, even when the lot is bursting with motorbikes. For revenue's sake in this low-margin business, they never turn a bike away, and the burden of making the parking lot function falls to the attendant. Accordingly, a ten-hour day in this profession involves the endless repositioning of bulky machinery—squeezing bikes into tight spaces, pivoting them on their kickstands, and shoving or dragging them out at impossible angles.

For example, I'll fetch my motorcycle after spending an hour in a supermarket. The parking lot will be so densely full that the attendant will have to move eight or ten motorbikes to retrieve it, executing a ballet of 21-point turns, nudging the other bikes into slivers of space to free mine. Foot pegs will catch foot pegs, and each blocking bike will have to be tilted up and away to enable the target bike to pass below the foot pegs. After doing so, he will have to move the ten bikes back into their previous spots, again navigating the foot pegs and angles, only to find that he just buried the motorcycle of the next shopper, who turns up with a ticket in hand, ready to go home.

Parking lot attendants are chess players and outsourcers at heart, anticipating all of the maneuvers ahead of time and thus demanding millimeter-scale changes to one's parking work, knowing that the 21-point turns are coming.

The Thành Công was generating a cranky vibe. I refused the parking lot attendant's request: "Nope. It's fine where it is. I'm not moving it."

He let the matter go. They always do.

* * *

I returned to the entrance and passed through the tiled lobby. In very comprehensible Vietnamese, I approached the desk and asked the receptionist if a room was available. The question should have been anticipated, really. She frowned, tilted her head, and curtly asked me to repeat the opener of perhaps the most fundamental of guest-concierge dialogues at a hotel. She made me repeat the question two more times. Finally, I mimed the inquiry, and she gave in, handing me my key and returning to her smartphone.

Behind her was a taxidermied steer's head. It felt out of place, and with a different receptionist, I might have asked for the backstory. I escorted myself to the elevator, up to a clean white concrete room with security bars on its one window, which seemed strange for the fifth floor of a seven-story hotel with no exterior features to scale.

Hoping to rustle up some *quán nhậu bình dân* cuisine, I descended and took a walk. To my surprise, there weren't any taverns in the neighborhood—not even a *tạp hóa* corner store of any repute in the first 300 yards.

I entered and inspected the first one I came across, but they didn't sell cold beer or nuts. The shelves were stocked with pens, diapers, baby formula, super glue, toilet paper, and dried noodles. I continued walking, passing closed shops with copper pipes, plumbing equipment, wedding dresses, and sheet metal in their display windows. I passed a clock dealer with a shirtless geezer sitting out front in a lawn chair, in front of an electric fan, gazing at the pavement. I passed a porridge restaurant.

Vietnamese towns and cities without *quán nhậu* taverns and colorful *tạp hóa* shops are the equivalent of listening to a solo Sonny Bono record: something important is missing.

* * *

It can't be fun to live in Pleiku. I called off my search, found a *phở* stand, inhaled a bowl of Vietnamese beef noodle soup in seven minutes, and meandered back to the Thành Công.

It took a funeral to add life to this Pleiku neighborhood.

A few doors down from my hotel was a one-story house with a courtyard that hugged the sidewalk, lined with rented aluminum tables and chairs. Small groups of people clustered around these tables, chatting while eating catered food together. Family members making the rounds to visit with these guests wore white funeral scarves tied around their foreheads.

Several spectators and I stopped before the house to listen to a three-piece band playing piano, drums, and saxophone.

Unlike the more melancholic traditional music typically played at funerals, this band was playing a sort of Vietnamese jazz. The music was bright and somehow walked the line between celebration and sorrow; the most likely scenario was that the deceased liked jazz music.

Like much of this country's soundtrack, funeral music is usually played loudly. This band had some volume, too.

Some fellows passing by caught my eye and plugged their ears, grinning—a small performance, clearly for me.

The strains were silvery, so I left mine open.

* * *

Vietnamese people are quite tolerant of noise. The men with their fingers in their ear canals evoked a different motorcycle trip to Bình Phước province, ten years earlier.

My friend and I spent a night at a *nhà nghỉ* that doubled as a *quán nhậu*, with a large roadside concrete terrace. There, a barbecue grilled meat beside a cooler loaded with Bia Saigon and durian.

Three generations of family ran the compound. The senior in a tank top and underpants ran the grill, while we rolled dice, drank beer, and played *Michael McDonald's Greatest Hits* on loop through a portable speaker we'd brought. As the night unfolded, our volume increased. Our dice matches became more animated and louder, even by our standards. See *Tây Ba Lô* discussion, previous chapter.

By 9:00 p.m., the restaurant had closed and emptied, but we carried on until ten, which is late in the countryside.

The grillmaster, ever vigilant, kept replenishing our empties so smoothly that I recall going to bed thinking I'd only had *one* can of Bia Saigon that day. The number was probably closer to seventy.

No one complained, reprimanded, or sent us to our rooms.

At 6:00 a.m. the next day, we emerged hungover and stumbled back to our cement table from the previous night. My mouth tasted like a locker room, and I had a pounding headache. Massive eighteen-wheelers barreled by on the village's two-lane country road, honking their steroidal horns to clear the congestion of motorbikes, pedestrians, and bicycles. Next door, at a mechanic shop, a motorbike revved at 8,000 RPM, and the client and mechanic were shouting to each other over the engine's wail. On the other side of the *nhà nghỉ*, someone was running an electric saw through steel sheets.

Without prompt, an eighty-something woman arrived with two bowls of *bún bò Huế* (central Vietnamese beef noodle soup), screaming "BÚN BÒ HUẾ!" in my ear as she pointed to the bowl of soup. Then she repeated herself, "BÚN BÒ HUẾ!" and pointed again.

We'd shared the previous day that we were riding to Khe Sanh, 600 miles north.

The same grillmaster screeched, "YOU'LL NEVER MAKE IT TO KHE SANH. JUST GO BACK TO SAIGON!"

It was a deafening breakfast, but it was never not charming. Either they were upset about our rowdiness the night before, and this drubbing was payback, or they weren't fazed by volume. More likely, the latter.

***

After loitering at the wake for a few moments, I headed back to the Thành Công, took the elevator to the fifth floor, and entered my room. Nursing a can of piping hot Bia Saigon, I reflected on the next leg of my journey—a two-day tour with a guide, recommended by a friend, to explore sites around Pleiku and then venture north to Kon Tum, a town I consider Pleiku's more carefree sibling.

The region, much less developed than the sprawling suburbs of Saigon, promised to reveal more of the war's lingering presence, with the war still clinging to the bits of concrete and war garbage I would probably encounter.

But as the music of the funeral band floated through my window, it carried Vietnam's rural magnetism with it. A reminder that this place had enduring personality despite its scars. I lay in bed, groggily listening to the performance, and the band finally knocked off at around 11:00 p.m.

Having been around Vietnamese funerals before, I knew they'd be right back in their spots at dawn tomorrow.

Plei Djereng

I woke in a panic the following morning, jarred by the *boom* of a man evacuating his bowels with absolute urgency. I could hear a shower running in the background. Seconds later, the toilet flushed, followed by the one-second-long explosive rush of water hitting the surface of a low-grade porcelain sink.

The sound from the sink punctuated the air again. And again. The soundtrack confused me; it felt like I'd fallen asleep and woken up in a restroom. I roused myself and oriented my thoughts.

The walls of the Thành Công Hotel were mighty thin, it turned out, and it seemed I had a front-row seat for a dramatic toilet performance, the kind of highly engineered and intense morning routines Vietnamese men are famous for.

The shower powered down, and I heard the distinct clap of a dropping toilet seat. I pieced together that there was a second chap in the same washroom: he had exited the shower, commandeered the bog, and defecated with the same fury—an unorthodox sequence, in my opinion.

No words were exchanged. Standing next to his seated friend, the first man angrily brushed his teeth over the sink: five seconds of aggressive brushing, followed by an aggrieved and loud spit, punctuated by a guttural noise for effect. Five more seconds and another spit. Then, another toilet flush, followed by the blasts of water in the sink.

What on earth has gotten into these guys? I wondered as I lay in bed. I checked the time: 5:07 a.m.

This three-minute symphony finally arrived at its coda when the entry door to the hotel room beside mine slammed. I heard an elevator chime, and their room fell silent.

As my heart rate slowed, I thought of the hotel staff. I've seen recently vacated hotel rooms in Vietnam before, as housekeepers attempt to resuscitate them: the washrooms are always trashed, and inevitably, three or four towels are on the floor, absorbing gallons of water.

Down below, the funeral jazz band stirred and began tuning their instruments.

* * *

A committee met me in the hotel lobby two hours later. Knowing that the roads ahead would cut through wild country near Vietnam's borders with Cambodia and Laos, I realized a guide familiar with the local terrain—and police—would be invaluable. Recommended by a friend, I hired a man named Xuân (born in the spring) and his driver, but unexpectedly, there was also a woman alongside them. I introduced myself and learned her name was Trang (serious, intelligent), and she was from Pleiku.

I asked her if, by chance, she was from the Provincial Department of Public Security, thinking she might be a minder. She smiled and said no; she would be leading the Pleiku portion of my two-day tour. I figured that some territorial agreement between her and Xuân probably corresponded to the border between Gia Lai and Kon Tum provinces.

I would give my motorcycle most of the day off and join the three of them in an SUV.

First, we would visit the former U.S. and South Vietnamese Army Camp Enari site on the outskirts of Pleiku. From there, we'd make the more than thirty-mile trip to the site of Plei Djereng, a former Special Forces camp about twenty miles from the Cambodian border and the Ho Chi Minh Trail.

Both sites were part of the broader American and South Vietnamese effort to bolster the country's western flank against the thousands of PAVN troops situated just across the borders of Cambodia and Laos. Enari, in particular, was one of the set pieces of the large-scale American commitment to the war launched in the mid-1960s.

I climbed into the SUV, and we proceeded west to Camp Enari.

Built in 1966, Camp Enari was a U.S. Army base and garrison for the Fourth Infantry Division. Enari was more of a U.S. Army *city* back then; it was an immense post with a width of over half a mile. Facilities ran 24-7; there were nearly 1,500 buildings with an aggregate area of two million square feet, a 2,800-foot runway, a power grid, a water treatment facility, and the usual tanks, helicopters, and artillery. The camp had all mod cons, including an 8,800-square-foot Post Exchange supermarket with six checkout counters that retailed cameras, clothing, food, refrigerators, records, radios, tape recorders, and electric fans to American soldiers.

Enari was turned over to the South Vietnamese Army in 1970, and with its more modest defense budgets, the base began to fade. Like many "Vietnamized" U.S. Army base-cities, the polish dulled, supply runs slowed, the lights dimmed, and the Post Exchange shelves emptied.

In 1975, the PAVN overran Pleiku, and Enari changed hands again. About half of the former base was eventually subdivided into small farming plots and transferred to local people—a down payment on a promise the Communist Party had made to Vietnam decades earlier.

The other half survived as a People's Army of Việt Nam base. Much of the American construction is now gone.

We drove around the front perimeter of the former Camp Enari. On one side were one-room houses and gardens. Facing them on the other side of the road were the original walls and sentried gate entrance to Camp Enari, cleansed and washed in the French's mustard-yellow paint typical of all PAVN bases.

The driver instinctively accelerated past the welcome gate and guard shack, and its profile blurred. PAVN gate guards don't appreciate civilian automobiles randomly stopping or slowing near military base entrances. Same as anywhere else.

Trang tapped me on the shoulder and told me we would see a helicopter landing strip that had survived the decades since 1975. Our vehicle parked at a small path that wound its way through a hamlet. As I reached for my knapsack at my feet, the sky suddenly opened up, and we drowned in the sound of bellicose rain pounding the thin layer of fiberglass above us.

I suggested we wait in the car for this cloudburst to move on. Trang agreed. Our middle-aged driver was a sweet man, but fidgety. After three minutes of heavy rain, he turned and said it was time to head for Plei Djereng. In his mind, the clock was ticking.

"Not your decision, buddy," I told him. He exhaled and placed his hands on the steering wheel. We waited another four minutes, and the rain ceased.

* * *

The helicopter landing strip is now part of a coffee processing compound. We walked down a muddy path draining rainwater and saw a big concrete slab behind a small workshop. It looked like it could hold ten to fifteen Huey helicopters, and a fragile barbed wire fence framed it.

Ambling and tracing the perimeter, we came to a gate, and I asked Trang if we could step inside and walk the strip.

"Sometimes the gate is open, and you can. Sometimes not," she advised. "Unfortunately, we're not lucky today."

The gate was made of flimsy, waterlogged wood attached to rusty hinges, without any lock or bolt; one of the doors hung at a lazy angle. I realized she meant that we could walk in if the weak gate doors were left open, perhaps due to a strong breeze.

I pushed the sad gate open, and we entered. Strolling on the soggy concrete, Trang mentioned that she and others had months ago asked the Ministry of Sports and Culture to designate a historical relic and preserve this landing strip.

She didn't think they would. I didn't see a strong case either. As a tour guide, it made sense for her to advocate for the preservation of Pleiku's few historic sites. Yet Vietnam's bias seems to be toward purpose-built revolutionary monuments in locations of its choosing, rather than preservation of the American-era antiquities scattered across the country, often on private or military property.

It wasn't a remarkable site, but one that a few Camp Enari veterans had probably returned to visit over the years.

After making small talk for a few minutes, we wandered back to the car. Nearby was an anomaly—a six-foot-long, six-inch-tall concrete foundation in the middle of the road. Built by the Americans, it was once the pedestal for a base traffic sign. Trang said the sign had survived until recently.

One day, it vanished. A Pleiku newspaper later broke an investigative report revealing that an intoxicated motorist had hit the foundation, was ejected from his motorbike, and landed in the hospital. The People's Committee then removed most of the structure.

Trang's theory was that the Committee would return soon for the remainder of the concrete base, leaving her with one less stop on her Camp Enari tour.

* * *

On our way out, our driver barreled past the PAVN base entrance, finally slowing down at a country junction half a mile away, where he exhaled.

We turned and began the trip to Plei Djereng, a former Special Forces camp about an hour from Pleiku. Established to monitor Communist troop movements along the Cambodian border, Plei Djereng would have been one of the war's lonelier outposts.

Photos from the 1960s and '70s show a camp on a gentle rise on the outskirts of a Montagnard village of wooden shacks, with a modest river delta, dense hills, and Cambodia in the background. The infrastructure was paltry, and the camp was little more than a few reinforced bunkers, thousands of sandbags, and rings of trenches.

Plei Djereng served as a launch pad for units of the Special Operations Group (SOG), a highly secret Special Forces unit that the United States government officially denied existed. SOG teams regularly crossed the border into neutral Cambodia and Laos—attacking cargo moving along the Ho Chi Minh Trail, rescuing American prisoners of war, and reconnoitering targets for Air Force and Navy bombers.

They were experts at guerrilla warfare, often finding themselves heavily outnumbered in firefights on the Trail: evading, shooting, and sprinting until they could link up with a rescue helicopter. When extraction came, it was usually under fire.

SOG casualty rates, including injuries, were nearly one hundred percent.

On the drive to Plei Djereng, I asked Trang about the site and its history, learning that this was her first visit. She framed it as newly discovered. But people I knew had been there. That's how it goes sometimes.

The travel was pleasant as charcoal clouds heavy with moisture crept under the scorching morning sun. Hamlets and scattered construction stretched along the roadside. Fifty years ago, this would have been a single-lane dirt road, hemmed in on both sides by jungle and the occasional puff of smoke from a tiny Jarai village somewhere in the interior, nestled under a triple canopy forest.

These days, this land is developed and more sculpted—unfolding in a way that echoes how American suburbs can bleed into one another. Still, in a very Vietnamese way: it's a web of construction materials and dealers interspersed with wooden stilt houses, agribusinesses, cafés, and karaoke parlors. The borders between villages have blurred.

Landscapes are rarely static in this country, particularly in unprestigious settlements along obscure rural roads. New homes are built, roofs are replaced, rooms are expanded, and old shops are razed. Mounds of freshly piled dirt, stacks of bricks and rebar, oversized tire tracks in the mud, and vertical dirt walls bearing the signature of an excavation shovel in the maroon soil all suggest that heavy equipment gets a workout in this part of Gia Lai province.

I sometimes wonder what it's all leading to—and whether construction might simply be a hobby for rural Vietnamese.

We drove past a family of goats scaling a cleared hillside scattered with young saplings; someone had recently passed through with a skid steer loader, clearing the patch of all vegetation for some purpose.

Perhaps it's not about the ends; it's about the means. Perhaps, for the Vietnamese, the enterprise of construction is intentionally never finished because the process is just too joyful.

**

We turned off the road and gradually ascended through Ia Khai, a small village next to the remnants of Plei Djereng.

Plei Djereng presented as an overgrown mound of land with young trees and angular juts that belie the mound's natural curve, suggesting this was no ordinary landscape feature.

I exited the car and surveyed the hill: Plei Djereng was constructed in tiers and resembled a brown wedding cake. Each level was reinforced by rectangular, vertical concrete slabs whose snug foundational fittings had been jarred by the violence of combat, extending out of the ground like protruding teeth.

Unlike most abandoned war sites in Vietnam, this one made perfect sense. I decided I wanted to explore it alone. As I ascended the landmass, I could hear Trang rustling through the brush behind me.

"Be careful of UXO," she warned.

She was right. Many of these bases were abandoned urgently during attacks, or left behind during the American withdrawal or South Vietnam's quick capitulation in 1975—without much attention to cleanup.

The Special Forces handed Plei Djereng over to the ARVN 80th Border Rangers in 1970. The United States repatriated the bulk of its combat troops by 1973. American air support eventually dissipated, and the tiny ARVN outpost became exponentially more vulnerable. In September 1973, the PAVN 26th Regiment overran the camp, killing or capturing two-thirds of the ARVN 80th.

Plei Djereng seemed frozen in time from September 1973; it's still a moonscape today.

Lurking just below the surface of the land I was walking on was almost certainly unexploded ordnance—UXO—along with other remnants I wasn't ready to meditate on. I moved through a fifty-year-old debris field to reach the summit.

Plei Djereng was a perfect Cubist mess, with concrete and jagged perforated steel plating (PSP) and mangled rebar jutting from the ground. Scattered throughout the area were the ruins of lacerated bunkers, their crumbling concrete walls and boulders of debris spilling out from past explosions.

The soil was littered with remnants from the war: shreds of half-submerged green canvas mesh sandbags, rifle cartridges, bomb craters, black rubber combat boot soles, olive drab rain poncho slivers, medicine bottles, and Meals Ready-to-Eat sachets. Fifty years of scavengers passing through typically leave little at these places.

Yet Plei Djereng was a different sort of apparition; untouched, the destruction and debris endured, and it resembled a movie set. It was strangely composed, as though arranged in anticipation of visitors who might never come. The bunkers and rusted remains fit neatly into my imagination, quietly confirming images I'd held for years. Part of me found comfort in this tidy alignment, but another part hesitated, unsure why it felt troubling when reality matched imagination a bit too closely.

The summit remained clear of vegetation, despite having had five decades to grow new trees. Surely, Agent Orange was lurking in this dirt.

I dropped into the remains of a morgue-like, concrete-reinforced bunker and rubbed my palm against the wall. It was smooth and cold—American-made to survive an apocalyptic event. A bouquet of broken concrete slabs accumulated on the floor, the aftermath of an explosion. Peering out, a deep green shag rug of young forest stretched to the horizon, meeting a river and foothills in the distance.

I realized that my feet were planted exactly where American and South Vietnamese youth, aged beyond their years, once stood—keeping watch over the same panorama, brooding over what those foothills might be concealing.

***

Descending a ridge, I passed through a herd of grazing brown cows. I returned to the car and surveyed Plei Djereng one last time, then panned a slow 360 across the horizon. Originally in the shape of a circle, the remnants of Plei Djereng are today ringed by a narrow road, with three or four widely spaced houses facing the mound.

Each house had a small altar supported by a free-standing vertical pole on the curb—about where the mailboxes might be in an American suburban street. Rice crackers filled small bowls at the altars, accompanied by Korean Choco Pies snug in colorful sachets and thimble-sized rice wine glasses.

Trang caught me examining one of the altars.

"The local people are terrified of ghosts from this hill. Ghosts come out at 12:00 in the afternoon and 12:00 at night in Vietnam."

I looked at my watch. It was 12:15.

"The altars are for people to pray for the dead. Regular prayers and offerings keep these ghosts from wandering too much and bothering people."

Given how often in its history Vietnam has been a battlefield, it made sense that the country might have a wandering spirit problem. I noticed the diligence with which the neighborhood altars were tended. All the snacks in these bowls looked less than a day old.

These altars weren't just decorative. People leave offerings at the places where others have suddenly, traumatically, or confusedly died. Ghosts are real, and people worry about them. To join the spiritual community of their ancestors, one should be buried near them in the home village.[3] A person who dies away from home, especially in violent circumstances, becomes a wandering spirit, unmoored from their purpose.

Wandering spirits can harm the living. This is why one finds small outdoor altars at these places of death—offering food and attention, hoping to keep the spirits from troubling the sentient.

Derelict army bases, old battlefields, cemeteries, and forests are crowded with wandering spirits, which might explain why so many Vietnam War sites in the south remain abandoned, even as the rest of the countryside is etched with skid-steer loader tire tracks.

I opened the car door and noticed a Jarai woman with long hair, wearing pink sweatpants and a green plaid lumberjack shirt, prone and fast asleep beside her bicycle under a tree. People here seem to appreciate a midday siesta, and when the urge strikes, some curl up wherever they find themselves—even in a graveyard.

Xuân appeared, commandeering the front seat. It dawned on me that he hadn't been on the hill with us. So, I bit. "Xuân, where were you?"

"Taking care of something," he replied.

Kon Tum

An hour later, the car pulled up in front of the Thành Công Hotel. Pleiku, Trang's territory, was done, and she would return to her office. Like a mother handing off instructions to a babysitter, she reminded Xuân to make sure I ate lunch. She grabbed her purse from the car seat and strode to her motorbike parked on the sidewalk.

Mid-stride, she turned and locked eyes with me. "Take a shower before bed tonight," she said. I nodded.

I retrieved my motorcycle from behind the hotel. The attendant from the night before was standing in the corner of the thinly populated parking lot, gesturing to two couples on motorbikes, demonstrating in precise terms where he wanted them to park.

That afternoon, I would follow Xuân's SUV north to Kon Tum. He said that before departing we'd dine at Cơm Gà Mỹ Tâm (Mỹ Tâm's Chicken Rice), a heritage restaurant in Pleiku's central business district. No objection from me; when a Vietnamese fixer has lunch ideas, they're usually credible. Follow the fixer, and things generally work out. Without a word, the driver took us there.

Cơm Gà Mỹ Tâm has been operating since 1963. Nondescript, apart from its coat of sparkling blue paint, the restaurant sits in a one-story mid-century modern building. Inside were wartime photos of the restaurant's façade, with Willys Jeeps, men in green uniforms, Honda 67s, and Mobylette motorbikes rolling by.

And there it was, in a vintage photo from 1966: the flag of the defeated former South Vietnam hanging over the entrance to Cơm Gà Mỹ Tâm. Though commonly displayed in diaspora neighborhoods in the United States, one rarely, if ever, sees this yellow flag with its three horizontal red stripes here. Overseas, it's a symbol of pride and memory. In-country, it's a provocation: flying it is still one of the more grotesquely reactionary things one can do in Vietnam. I've been here long enough to be jolted when I see this taboo.

I sat down with my companions. Plates of fried chicken legs, tiny bowls of *mắm chấm*, and rice arrived. After a morning of tasting the thick, humid air along the Cambodian border, the tang and heat of the sauce and the juice of the chicken hit the spot, as promised. I needed the salt, sweet, sour, and spice blend that Vietnamese cuisine is known for, and Cơm Gà Mỹ Tâm delivered—no delay, no deviation.

"Why did Trang order me to take a shower tonight? I'm a fully grown man," I remarked as I crumpled my *mắm chấm*-stained paper napkin in my palm.

"To help the ghosts move on and away from you," Xuân replied as he caressed his gums with a toothpick. "It's the same with this restaurant. By stopping here, any ghosts that came with us might decide to stay for lunch and not follow you home."

I'd be exfoliating wandering spirits in the shower tonight, I resolved.

* * *

I rode behind Xuân's car out of Pleiku, along a plateau where the Ho Chi Minh Highway split, skirting the Cambodian border. Twenty minutes in, we pulled over. The site where Lt. Col. John Paul Vann died in a helicopter crash in 1972.

Over his decade of service in Vietnam, Vann became one of the Army's earliest, sharpest, and most controversial leaders. He intuitively understood the war's dynamics and, as early as 1963, after witnessing the ARVN defeat at the Battle of Ấp Bắc in the Mekong Delta, concluded that the American and South Vietnamese strategy wouldn't succeed. But he wasn't a politician, and he had little interest in the nuanced U.S.-South Vietnam diplomatic equilibrium the strategy was designed to maintain. He spoke up often, and was just as often ignored.

Lieutenant Colonel Vann left Vietnam in 1963 after one year of in-country Army service but returned two years later for good. He took a position as an advisor with Civil Operations and Revolutionary Development Support, the U.S. government civilian body that oversaw the controversial Phoenix Program counterinsurgency campaign in the countryside around Saigon.

In 1972, Vann was flying from Saigon to Kon Tum with a celebratory cake shortly after the Easter Offensive siege ended. His helicopter crashed near Highway 14, beside a village cemetery about ten miles north of Pleiku.

Incidentally, I have a friend who visited the site a few years ago and found what he recognized as debris from an American helicopter. He works in the aviation industry, so he would know. I'd seen the same chap identify a bent sliver of Huey fuselage plating while hiking together on Núi Ap Bia, the site of the battle Americans called Hamburger Hill. Two Hueys went down in the 1969 battle, and he'd found a fragment from one of them.

The crash site was in a meadow beside a Jarai village—a cluster of wooden shacks where barefoot children wandered among goats and curious chickens. The cemetery remained intact, and each grave was enclosed by chain-link fencing, with cinderblock walls and a thatched roof.

Unexpectedly, cots and beds sat with the tombstones. Xuân explained that Jarai people sometimes sleep next to the graves of their loved ones. It's part of an extended goodbye, rooted in the belief that the spirit stays close until the worldly connection quietly dissolves.

I saw some movement out of the corner of my eye and turned. A young Jarai man in a camouflage shirt and pants, wearing *dép tô ong* yellow rubber honeycomb sandals, was creeping out from behind a tree twenty yards away, holding a wooden club. He stopped and directed his gaze at us, watching as we examined the graveyard. Between the chain-link fences and this local vigilante, the atmosphere had taken a turn.

We edged past the cemetery and stopped at the site where Vann's chopper went down. We were standing in a blank field, uncultivated, with windy footpaths leading back to the village, framed by old shade trees. A lone Hyundai long-distance bus prowled by on Highway 14, honking its spine-chilling horn at nobody in particular, and then the meadow fell silent again. This quiet, unremarkable clearing was where the American who may have best understood the war—and how to preserve South Vietnam—had fallen.

* * *

An old rumor exists that a group of disaffected ARVN officers sabotaged Vann's helicopter before his final flight. As detailed in the Neil Sheehan book *A Bright Shining Lie: John Paul Vann and America in Vietnam*, Vann was an impatient and direct man. He was hard on his ARVN partners and was known to have made enemies.

Despite his military expertise, ten years spent in Vietnam, and a track record of correctly diagnosing operational problems and suggesting good remedies, his blunt personal style may have limited his influence. The politics of the U.S.–South Vietnam relationship during the war were infinitely labyrinthine; however, many of Vann's communication problems sound like a textbook case of neglecting to honor the concept of "face." Vann scolded ARVN commanders in front of their subordinates after failures in the field, denying them their dignity and the appearance of personal power.

For Westerners visiting Asia, "face" is one of the most difficult—and relentlessly over-explained—cultural concepts to navigate. In its extreme form, it might be described as a custom of having to excuse mistakes, maliciousness, incompetence, and offense on the part of an antagonist, all to help that antagonist avoid losing public respect. Some long-termers go further, seeing this advice as a kind of conspiracy of soft conditioning: a norm that can license terrible behavior while keeping foreigners compliant. One assumes John Paul Vann probably had trouble making the adjustment.

After fifteen minutes of roaming the field, we returned to the car and my motorcycle. I gave a gentle wave to the Jarai fellow with the club. He committed to one in return, but his 1,000-yard stare held.

As we entered the outskirts of Kon Tum, I followed the SUV as it threaded through a maze of shophouses and stopped at a clearing. Xuân had a surprise for me: the site of a top-secret Air America base in Kon Tum. Air America was a CIA-operated airline that ran covert operations during the war, particularly on the Lao side of the border. There were surely CIA sites of different sorts in South Vietnam, but this one—an airstrip—didn't make sense.

We were standing amid a dense neighborhood; that alone didn't disprove the claim, as it had been over fifty years. But the topography didn't support Xuân's assertion. Secret CIA airstrips ought to be level, and this residential area was lumpy, with mounds, hills, and dells.

"Are you sure about this one?" I asked Xuân.

"One hundred percent," he replied, his pupils shifting across the plain houses around us.

A middle-aged gentleman in slacks and an undershirt was loitering nearby, holding a few rolled-up 50,000 Vietnamese đồng notes in his hand. I walked over and asked if he'd ever heard of a top-secret wartime CIA airstrip that used to be here.

"No. I'm afraid not. I don't know a thing about that," he said, shaking his head. Perhaps he was aiming for plausible deniability.

I thanked Xuân for showing me the site and mounted my motorcycle for the last two-mile stretch into Kon Tum, riding solo. We'd see each other again in the morning.

* * *

Poetic Kon Tum. Pleiku's antipode. Unlike its neighbor to the south, Kon Tum is not a cold, engineered Vietnamese city with squares, order, wide boulevards, quiet, statues, temperance, and ideology. It's as though the authorities looked at the two towns at war's end and decided to focus on building Pleiku into the Vietnamese city of note in this part of the Central Highlands. *Kon Tum's backward. Leave it*, they might have said.

Kon Tum is not a postwar creation. One can sense the past here; the small rural city appears to have developed more organically and messily over time than Pleiku. Kon Tum has *tạp hóa* general stores everywhere, and they swarm with personality. *Quán nhậu*, Vietnam's loud, family-run proletariat sidewalk taverns, are three to a block.

Kon Tum's boulevards are wide and uneven, and the shade trees are decades old. The town has hypnotic orange sunsets, and at dusk, the roads carry exuberant shirtless and helmet-less Bahnar boys in shorts and flip-flops, drag racing on souped-up 125-cc motorbikes (Bahnar people comprise the largest ethnic group in Kon Tum). Idyllic Kon Tum refuses to grow up into a modern city.

Kon Tum was historically an epicenter for missionary activity. French Catholic priests arrived in the Central Highlands as early as the mid-nineteenth century. After several decades of growing the flock among Montagnards around Kon Tum, the Paris Foreign Missions Seminary was built in 1935. After reunification in 1975, most French clergy were ordered out of Kon Tum, as the new government asserted control and appropriated most church properties.

Today, the Catholic Church has regained some of its former vitality. The seminary remains active, training future priests in a single-building campus surrounded by grand, manicured gardens. Nearby is the Church of Kon Tum, more affectionately called "The

Wooden Church." Completed in 1918, this quietly beautiful sanctuary blends Roman architecture with the traditional form of a Bahnar communal house, built from rich brown ironwood and rosewood. I've attended Bahnar-language mass here. Services are held several times a week, and the church regularly fills to capacity, with latecomers gathering in the parking lot to follow the mass on television monitors.

Kon Tum anchored Bến Hét, Tân Cảnh, and Đăk Tô, the group of American and ARVN bases protecting Highway 14 from PAVN infiltrations from Cambodia and Laos. North Vietnam believed that controlling the highlands could separate Saigon from the key cities of Huế, Đà Nẵng, and Quảng Trị. Hanoi rightly saw that threatening the Central Highlands would also divert U.S. and ARVN forces from their real mission—defending coastal cities—a strategy the PAVN used repeatedly. There was near-constant combat in this part of the country.

During the Easter Offensive in April 1972, Hanoi sent fifty thousand troops over the Lao border, overrunning Đăk Tô. They moved down Highway 14 toward Kon Tum in May, as most of the town's ethnic Vietnamese—about twenty thousand people—managed to evacuate.

Not having vehicles or the means to pay off a helicopter pilot, the region's Montagnards stayed behind. ARVN Huey crews resupplying Kon Tum often returned to Pleiku empty—or loaded with looted goods. According to interviews with American advisors in Kon Tum, the price for a seat on an outgoing helicopter was 10,000 piastres ($100), paid directly to the pilot. For a Montagnard villager, this was an impossible sum.

The villages to the north became free fire zones, and refugees surged into the town. By late May, the North Vietnamese Army surrounded the city, outnumbering the South Vietnamese defenders and ten American advisors three to one. Thousands were trapped in Kon Tum.

Resupply helicopters landed in a municipal park adjacent to a traffic rotary. Nearby stood the Military Assistance Command Vietnam (MACV) compound—once the municipal nerve center of U.S. military operations, now largely vacated. Crowds of desperate people gathered daily, hoping for a ride out on a departing Huey.

Footage from the siege shows these chaotic scenes—lines of people stretched across the park beneath the statue of the 18th-century emperor Quang Trung, mounted on horseback, saber raised. The crowd grows restless with the rising rotor thumping of every approaching ARVN helicopter on a resupply mission. The statue, the park, and the building that once housed the MACV compound still stand today—familiar outlines in a changed city.

For the next month, the PAVN attacked amid crushing B-52 strikes, artillery, and hand-to-hand combat, but the city's defenses held. After one last failed push to take Kon Tum, the PAVN withdrew in early June. The South Vietnamese defenders counterattacked and declared the siege lifted. American advisors credited the Montagnard fighters—whom they had recruited, trained, fed, and paid over the previous decade—with holding the city. As he flew north to mark the victory, John Paul Vann's helicopter crashed twenty miles south on Highway 14.

* * *

I cruised Kon Tum's main drag at a lazy pace, weaving past Bahnar pedestrians—some in olive drab, others in windbreakers and yellow rubber *dép tổ ong* honeycomb sandals—while marveling at the city's foothills. Eventually, I came across lodging that matched my mood: the Hotel Kon Klor, situated on the city's outskirts, across the street from a wooden Bahnar communal stilt house and adjacent to the Đăk Bla River.

With its spacious lawn and clean wooden cabins, the Kon Klor was an upgrade from the crude cinderblock *nhà nghỉ* guesthouses I had been patronizing. I'd logged more than 250 miles over the previous two days, and my derriere felt like it had been injected with hot lead, so I indulged myself. I dropped my bags and took a walk.

* * *

Spa Massage Bình Dân was an enterprise on the ground floor of a shophouse three blocks down. I noticed the sign, stopped, decided, and entered.

A woman in her twenties, wearing jeans and a T-shirt, led me upstairs to a room crowded with rows of massage tables. Several shirtless Vietnamese men in dungarees lay face-down on the tables, arms draped over the sides, necks craned toward their phones. Some held cigarettes and screens in the same hand, watching soccer matches and puffing occasionally as their backs were methodically pummeled. They were tuned to different games, the soundtrack and commentary clashing in overlapping bursts.

The air was tinged with cigarette smoke. As I lay flat, the woman who had led me upstairs began punching and elbowing my back, causing me to tighten up and wince with each blow. Lacking a mystic, lemongrass, or incense vibe, this place came as promised—a proletariat massage parlor.

Below the clamor of the various soccer telecasts were the sounds of knuckles cracking, skin slapping, backs popping, massage tables straining, and the grunts of men contorting on the tables. The fellow at the table next to mine had his phone volume on maximum. He dropped his cigarette and bellowed "Vàààààààààààààào!" (goal), stretching out the vowel as all exuberant Vietnamese sportscasters do. He asked his masseuse to pause, shifted, and reached down for the smoldering cigarette.

Screening a different match and oblivious to the first guest's delight, another man in the room's far corner interrupted with "Đây! Đây! Đây! Đây! Đây!" (Here! Here! Here! Here! Here!), willing his team to run his scheme.

The seven masseuses on duty chatted with each other as they worked our backs. Suddenly, they were talking about me.

"Do you know where he's from?" one masseuse asked the woman pounding my shoulders with her fists.

"No, I don't. But I think he's Chinese."

"No, I don't think he's Chinese. He looks Western. Chinese look more like us."

"Well, I don't know then."

I cut in, muttering, "I'm not Chinese," between gritted teeth, unsure how my masseuse arrived at her initial theory.

A bit later, the hour was over. The massage was 90,000 đồng (about $4). "Gia bình dân"—proletariat price—she told me.

* * *

I visited a *tạp hóa* a few blocks away and sat on a plastic red stool at the storefront, savoring the late afternoon air with a cold bottle of Dr. Thành's Oolong Tea, a brand I love. A creased and callused old fellow in aviator sunglasses, a pith helmet, and an olive-drab shirt occupied the stool next to mine. Three empty cans of Bia Saigon rested on the pavement. He had a half-full, worn box of White Horse cigarettes and a lighter on another stool in front of him. He was well into his seventies, a veteran enjoying his retirement.

I said hello and told him I was exploring Central Highlands sites from the war. He latched onto the term *chiến tranh* (war), and nothing else seemed to register. That said, a mere "hello" can be enough to conjure up the revolutionary lecture that followed, especially if one's interlocutor has been drinking.

He perked up. "The French, the Chinese, the Japanese, the Americans. None of them could do it. They all wanted our country." He paused for effect.

"Yes, sir," I said.

He was gaining steam. "They couldn't do it. They couldn't defeat Vietnam. The Americans were here for years. The French were here for years. They couldn't defeat us. They fought here, right here, many times. They couldn't defeat Vietnam."

"Yes, sir."

"They couldn't do it. And then the Soviets came...the Chinese, the Japanese...none of them. Then the Kampucheans tried, and now it's the Chinese again. France...the Americans, they came to Saigon and...the Russians went north and then the Chinese...."

Four minutes passed, and he was still rolling. I'd had that same discourse with countless other Vietnamese senior citizens. It's a script. This is Vietnam's modern origin story.

* * *

I thanked the man, crossed the street, and headed to my favorite restaurant in Kon Tum, Cơm Hiệp Thành. This is a sturdy workhorse of a *quán nhậu*, essentially a warehouse with an open frontage. Inside, it's a high-ceilinged structure with harsh fluorescent lighting and fans bolted to the walls.

Vietnamese have a thing about fans in cafés, bars, and restaurants. I'll sit at a *quán nhậu* somewhere, and the weather will be temperate. Without fail, a waiter will arrive and position a five-foot-tall black industrial fan inches from my seat. Next, he'll plug it in, turn it to "high," and blast me with a gale, kicking up dust. Then I'll ask him to take away the unnecessary contraption.

The mint-green dining room was decorated with an art collection, including the ubiquitous sand painting of a herd of wild red, white, purple, and brown horses galloping toward the viewer through a stream with mountains and Chinese characters in the background. This is probably Vietnam's most popular mass-produced painting; it hangs over the country's sofas, in cafés, in dens, behind desks in offices, and in government buildings. I like it so much that I bought one about fifteen years ago. Another poster hung on an opposite wall, a photograph of two white kittens on a red blanket against heart-shaped pillows, with the simple phrase "With All My Love" embroidered on one of them.

For all of its romantic energy, however, the Hiệp Thành is a rowdy country restaurant where rural dads and uncles murder cases of beer together over dinner with their kin. Appropriating a quiet table for one near the open frontage, I passed a table of eight—an extended family out for a meal, with what looked like three dozen empty Bia Saigon cans, chicken bones, and dirty napkins littering the floor around them. Unopened cans of room temperature Bia Saigon awaited them on deck atop the table, next to the stock ice bucket and tongs.

As I dined on plates of ribs and *rau muống xào tỏi*, the familiar sautéed morning glory with garlic, I tuned out the uproar from the drinking festival at the other table.

As usual, the *rau muống* stalks weren't cut short enough, and the serving was a tangled mess of roughage, like a badly coiled 100-foot garden hose, braided and in knots. As I pulled a string of the morning glory from the plate with my chopsticks, it lifted about forty percent of the entire portion with it. This always seems to happen, and unless one is packing scissors, the only recourse is to take the softball-sized bite in one go. Scrumptious but undeniably tough, this mouthful of cud needed seven or eight minutes of chewing.

*   *   *

Working the *rau muống*, I thought back to Plei Djereng, the John Paul Vann crash site, and even the man who walked me through a discussion on modern Vietnamese history just an hour earlier at the *tạp hóa* down the road. I had grown up surrounded by the tumult of the United States searching for a new equilibrium after the war. It was loud, and a decade or so later, it was quiet again. However, there is less tumult on this side of the world, but the war is seemingly the country's background frequency. This history is stamped into the DNA of this land and woven into the people's long-term and short-term memory. The history was actually in the very bones of the man at the *tạp hóa*.

I surveyed Kon Tum's main street: a sparse parade of Bahnar folks passed by on their motorbikes, flashes lit up by flickering streetlamps.

Hill 601

A flock of black drongos convened on the balcony outside my open window the following morning, bickering with each other. Knowing that black drongos are one of Vietnam's more territorial and aggressive bird species, celebrated for their courage in dive-bombing much larger birds of prey that wander into their territory, I reasoned nothing would be gained by trying to break up the squabble. Didn't seem like a great moment for another American intervention.

So I stayed in bed—it was 6:00 a.m. This was much more pleasant than my wakeup the previous day at Pleiku's Thành Công Hotel. I congratulated myself on choosing the Kon Klor.

The air smelled faintly of dust and charcoal, and the sun hadn't yet burned off the night's cool. Eventually, I wandered across the lane to the hotel's canteen and ordered the usual two eggs and *bánh mì* breakfast. As I sipped my coffee, I considered the day ahead.

Xuân and the driver would arrive at 7:30. I would follow them north on the Ho Chi Minh Highway to the site of Bến Hét Special Forces Camp, stopping at Hill 601 and Đắk Tô Base Camp, retracing in reverse the sequence of attacks the PAVN launched from Laos during the 1972 Easter Offensive on its push southward to capture Kon Tum. After Bến Hét, I'd be on my own again, and I planned to make some stops in Quảng Nam province before threading back down to the coast to link up with a friend in Quảng Trị.

They pulled up an hour later, with Richard Marx's "Right Here Waiting" playing on the car stereo at such volume that I recognized it immediately, even with all the windows up. I loaded my motorcycle and tailed their SUV out of Kon Tum onto the plateau surrounding the town.

Ten miles later, we found ourselves pulled over at a warehouse, gazing across the Ho Chi Minh Highway at the base of Hill 601. As we took in the ridge, I noticed a man astride his idling thirty-year-old

Honda Dream II on the road's shoulder, watching us, unreadable. Judging by the appearance of the Dream's delicate front fender, white plastic apron, and rusty black basket, he'd likely been off-roading earlier in the day. The bike was coated in mud, buffalo manure, and tar—caked onto the rims and forks in a half-inch glutinous shell. His clothes hadn't escaped whatever shellacking the bike had endured. His bright purple factory-worker shirt, black slacks, and knackered midnight black *dép tổ ong* sandals were spattered with the same mix.

Balanced between his belly and the handlebars was an aged, royal blue twenty-gallon plastic barrel—the kind used in the countryside to haul spent cooking oil or stews of expired rice, days-old broth, and spoiled vegetables for pigs. In the south, the slop is called *cơm heo*. Our eyes met, and he gave me a warm smile.

* * *

I approached and introduced myself. He carried the fragrance of farm. Hiển (a name that can mean "to reveal" or "to make known") was in his seventies and had moved to this part of Kon Tum province just after the war ended. He said he passes by Hill 601 nearly every day.

"In '76, I found three bodies up there," he told me, nodding toward the hill. "ARVN. Nothing left but bones and cloth. I couldn't leave them like that."

He said he dug three ditches that afternoon and buried them. Then he built an altar nearby so people could comfort the wandering spirits.

He dismounted, motioning to the original altar behind us, a humble structure made of black tiles with an orange pitched roof. The altar looked like a miniature one-room Vietnamese country house, with the front wall missing and an extended, open-air black tile front balcony unfurling from the facade. Under the roof were ten or eleven dusty ceramic shot glasses, a small vase housing six yellow marigolds, bundles of unlit joss sticks in cellophane, and a small, sand-filled bowl from which the stems of dozens of burnt joss sticks poked upward.

About twenty of these sticks were topped with speared upturned cigarette butts. Visitors had stopped, poured a glass of rice wine, and placed lit cigarettes on the joss stick stems, allowing them to burn down to their filters untouched. Cigarettes and wine for the dead.

A small vertical black banner hung behind the bowl, and in the gold lightweight flowing cursive font that Vietnam associates with poetry, or anything profound for that matter, was written *Đồng Sanh Lạc Quốc*. It had the feel of something personal—something Hiển might've added himself.

* * *

Đồng Sanh Lạc Quốc can mean "we were born in the same country," but it can also be interpreted as "co-born and country lost" or "the lost kingdom." As such, the altar straddles a gray area between history and ideology, and this inscription—a quiet detour from rigid public dogma—has somehow survived. It's a rare expression of private feeling made public, an understated subversion of the exultant and sanguine official memory. The patriotic story doesn't always allow much room for nuance or humanity.

War cemeteries in this country are usually understated and speak for themselves. That only those from the winning side, those who *fought the Americans*, are buried in these places is the unspoken piece. Their stories, the shades of their experiences, are swathed with them underground. South Vietnam doesn't figure into the equation, nor do its dead, as Hiển's story suggests.

After the 1972 battle at Hill 601, soldiers from the North Vietnamese side were likely buried with military honors, while the South Vietnamese dead were left where they fell. The privately constructed and unofficially tolerated *Đồng Sanh Lạc Quốc* memorial is one of few that hints at the iceberg of complexity, experience, and sentiment below the above-water tip that is the country's revolutionary narrative. In other words, there are many narratives.

Hill 601, named for its height in meters, was a former ARVN outpost and one of the few hills along the plateau of the present-day Ho Chi Minh Highway positioned to stop or slow a southbound Communist army. During the April 1972 Easter Offensive, PAVN units advancing south from Đăk Tô to Kon Tum attacked the ARVN soldiers stationed there. After hours of fighting, the defenders were overwhelmed and on the verge of collapse.

A desperate South Vietnam President Nguyễn Văn Thiệu ordered two Republic of Việt Nam Air Force jets to strike Hill 601 while close combat still raged on the summit. The ARVN troops weren't warned that their own air force was about to bomb them. The two jets made several passes and dropped their payloads, killing dozens—including their fellow southerners. The craters are still there.

South Vietnam lost 130 men that day; about 700 northerners were killed in action. After the battle, locals explored the wreckage and found corpses and skulls, some half-buried, at the site. Hence the local nickname: Skull Hill. One can only imagine what might be found under the topsoil here today.

* * *

Hill 601 differed from other war sites and memorials I'd visited on this ride. Unlike the purpose-built statues of valiant revolutionaries in every town square, as well as the small, unemotional plaques that speckle the landscape commemorating battles or bases, and the martyr's cemeteries, Hill 601 is darkness. The story that this still-disfigured land tells overrides any propaganda that might be superimposed here. It's atmospherically heavy and leaves one spaced out. Situated right alongside a two-lane highway, cars, motorbikes, and trucks glide past this haunted place all day.

The hill is modest: one can reach the summit in four minutes by way of a 15-foot-wide concrete staircase leading to a memorial. The staircase is weathered and stained with black mold, which appears to drip downwards from outbreaks on the treads and streak the vertical risers. From a distance, the mold resembles dark shadows cast upon the stairs.

Heavy, droopy trees grow on the sides of the hill and cluster at the top, the oldest having sprouted from a burial site created by a bombing run fifty years ago. The hill's shoulders are lumpy with bomb cavities and ditches dug years ago by locals foraging for unexploded ordnance.

At the top of the staircase stood an official memorial under a sign that translates to "Historical Relic of the Revolution Hill 601." The title belies the reality: this is a monument at a mass grave where hundreds of soldiers were unearthed decades ago. Unnerving and undeniably Soviet-inspired, the memorial is made of mediocre ceramic tiles, with brown pieces ascending skyward in the shape of an open book, balanced on its flaps and spine. Some of the tiles are missing; many are cracked. Within it is a black triangular frame.

Vietnamese monuments are generally direct in their composition, and their currency is emotions of heroism, defiance, pride, or shared sacrifice. These currents are often orthodox and collectively embraced, baked into the narrative of struggle. This one, though, gave me nothing to hold onto. I didn't know what it was. It was morgue-cold, impossible to ignore. Whether this effect was intentional is unclear, as official Vietnam can be very deliberate about design. The result could have been coincidental or even expedient—perhaps the builder had access to brown tiles at the time of construction.

I could see my face reflected in the tiles. The funereal result was an unintentional nod to the Vietnam Veterans Memorial in Washington, D.C., with its black granite wall so polished that visitors can see their reflections in the carved names of America's more than 58,000 war dead. There was a small charge of anxiety in standing beside this stele on a lonely hilltop—reminiscent of the unease I felt at my first open-casket wake.

At the monument's foot loomed a large iron joss stick bowl. I lit three sticks. The memorial was enclosed with a low fence and concrete frame, providing enough space for a large plaza around the shrine. Once painted white, the wall was now rusted through. Cream-yellow structures guarded both ends of the entrance gate; at the top of the two short pillars were concrete boxes, each with a single round hole in the middle, under a pitched roof. Incongruously, they resembled birdhouses. Streetlights framed the plaza—lighting one would find on a highway, likely chosen out of convenience rather than design. The structures suggested they no longer worked, as the vertical support poles were rust-covered.

Behind the plaza rose another line of low mountains. A red dirt road passed over the top of the hill, and around it were bomb craters, scrub, and cleared patches that looked like nests for some large creature. Two bundled-up farmers on an overloaded and unquestionably fatigued Honda Chaly hummed by, riding the ridge.

The Honda Chaly is a late-70s/early-80s, 49-cubic-centimeter, 3.2-horsepower mini-motorbike. Long since phased out by Honda, thousands of these twenty-eight-inch-tall machines found their way to Vietnam after the war. Chalys are associated with middle-aged and senior Vietnamese women on wet market runs in the lead-up to evening meal prep. Occasionally, one meets an ironic expatriate who commits to the cuddly Chaly as their daily rider—only to reverse course after fully internalizing the aches-and-pains commitment of commuting on a tiny satirical motorbike.

What rolled through the past wasn't always heavy.

* * *

Coffee trees grew out of the depressions left by bomb blasts. I wandered around—down into craters, back up again—then cut through the brush downwards instead of taking the staircase.

Across Highway 14 stood a newly built temple, its sixty-foot-tall white cement Buddha set just beyond the treeline, the curve of his shoulders and nape rising, from another realm, above the canopy. The sky had turned flat and colorless. He faced away from Hill 601—an orientation that felt deliberate, as if even a figure built to embody stillness could not bear to hold what lay behind him.

Đăk Tô

After descending and returning to my motorcycle, I noticed Hiển had already mounted his Honda Dream, re-balanced the plastic barrel, retracted the kickstand, and pressed the ignition button. I approached him, thanked him for sharing his story, and said farewell.

"You feel it up there, don't you?" he said, looking past me toward the ridge. "There was a man who came every day. Two weeks ago, he stopped. No one knows why."

He gave a quick nod, glanced down, and then pivoted to the road, muttering *dạ, dạ...chào anh*. Then he rolled onto the shoulder and rumbled south on Highway 14, his purple worker's shirt gradually shrinking into the haze at about seven miles an hour.

* * *

Xuân and his driver were leaning on the SUV, smoking cigarettes and sharing a bottle of Dr. Thành's oolong tea. The boys had opted not to make the hike with me.

"What did you see up there?" Xuân asked.

I shared a few observations about the memorial, the bomb craters, and the atmospherics.

"Very interesting," he said. "I've been taking tourists to Hill 601 for a few years, but I've never actually been to the top."

I had a hard time hearing him, but nodded. The car's front doors were open, and the stereo was cranking the 1996 power ballad "Forever and One" by the German power metal band Helloween. Perhaps Xuân's intent was a subtle riff on *Đồng Sanh Lạc Quốc*, but more likely, it was just a coincidence.

First, the Chaly. Now, Helloween. When visiting war sites in Vietnam, I've found that the gloom I encounter is always—always—cut with levity. Something simultaneously ludicrous and endearing.

"Ready to go?" Xuân asked, watching me lower my helmet over my forehead.

*　*　*

The Ho Chi Minh Highway took us north through the country's western high plains. We were approaching the point where the borders of Vietnam, Laos, and Cambodia converge. Our next stop was Đăk Tô Base Camp, also known as "Phoenix Airfield," about 20 miles from the border.

Đăk Tô was an extensive U.S. and South Vietnam Army installation that was ground zero for heavy fighting in both 1967 and 1972. In the first instance, around seven thousand PAVN troops quietly occupied the hills around Phoenix Airfield in the autumn of 1967. One of Hanoi's goals in forcing a battle at Đăk Tô was to divert U.S. forces from population centers along the coast as a precursor to the Tet Offensive that would launch in January.

Once the Americans detected the PAVN positions, they began sweeping the hills. By November, a month-long clash began. The North Vietnamese rocketed Phoenix Airfield, destroying transport aircraft and even detonating the base's ammunition dump. The fight at Đăk Tô culminated in an arduous campaign over several days to seize Hill 875 from the PAVN. Ultimately, incessant air strikes, artillery, and infantry assaults drove the North Vietnamese off the hill and back into Laos.

Hanoi partially succeeded, however. When the Tet Offensive began, about half of all U.S. combat forces in Vietnam had been relocated to the Central Highlands.

The PAVN attacked again in the April 1972 Easter Offensive, sending fifty thousand troops across the Lao border. The North won quick victories against the ARVN at Bến Hét and the garrison at Tân

Cảnh, then overran Đăk Tô Base Camp in preparation for the assault on Kon Tum.

I was riding north on the same road the PAVN had taken south—Highway 14. Hill 601 blocked their advance. After a brutal multi-day fight that ended with ARVN airstrikes falling on their own men, the PAVN took the hill on April 12. Then, inexplicably, they paused their advance for three weeks, giving Kon Tum time to prepare and bolster its defenses. I'd just stood on Hill 601 earlier that day—it looked quiet now, but it had held the line long enough to shift the outcome.

Trailing the SUV, I entered Tân Cảnh. It was a prosaic highlands town with a mixture of ethnic Vietnamese migrants and Montagnards. The road ran around a town square, where two Soviet tanks were mounted on pedestals as a memorial to the 1972 fall of Tân Cảnh and the takeover of Đăk Tô.

One was a T-54 battle tank, freshly painted in olive drab. Next to it towered an exotic-looking ZSU-57-2 Sparka—the Soviet *Zenitnaya Samokhodnaya Ustanovka*, or "anti-aircraft self-propelled mount." With its unfamiliar lines, whitewall tires, and oversized turret, the ZSU looked like something one might see in a military parade in central Pyongyang.

Multigenerational families drifted around the military hardware, some strolling with prams. Children in pirated Disney T-shirts and shorts ran about. A man lay prone on his motorbike saddle, deftly balanced on his back and fast asleep.

As Tân Cảnh unfolded around me, my attention shifted to passing signage. One over a restaurant reading *Lòng Heo Bình Dân* stood out for its redundancy. *Lòng heo* is a dish of boiled pork offal, including liver, stomach, intestines, kidney, and tongue, usually taken with a powerful shrimp paste and bowl of *tiết canh*, or raw duck's blood pudding. Advertising one's *lòng heo* restaurant as *bình dân* is unnecessary: *lòng heo* is about as proletariat as a recipe can get.

A truck hauling pigs passed us, and we rolled by a roadside *quán nhậu* tavern named *Dê Pê Đê*, or "The Gay Goat," a name probably chosen for its alliterative power. This would have been a speck of a town in 1972. It's grown a little, but the square still fades quickly back into valley. The landscape below was a mix of overgrowth, cassava fields, and coffee plantations.

* * *

Some miles up the highway from Tân Cảnh, our convoy came to a vast clearing hemmed in by hilltops on the side of the road, marked by an aging and paint-chipped red sign that read *Khu Di Tích Sân Bay Phượng Hoàng: CẤM XÂM PHẠM*, or "Relic Zone Phoenix Airfield: VIOLATIONS PROHIBITED."

For a country that typically has signage delineating unnecessarily long and superfluous lists of rules for behavior in all sorts of public places, this message was crisp. Swimming pools at hotels, for example, often post all-caps strict screeds that most would consider common sense: "No cats or dogs in the pool," "Unnecessary noise prohibited at all times," "No littering in the pool," "Do not drink the pool water," "Use the restroom instead of the pool," and "No blowing one's nose in the pool."

We rolled to a stop next to a pile of jetsam, broken furniture, and an intact mirror with the phrase *CUSTOMER IS KING* etched on it.

Before me stretched out Đăk Tô Phoenix Airfield, with its 1,300-meter asphalt runway still intact, blanketing the valley floor. The runway was so well-built and preserved that a space shuttle could probably land there today. Overlooking the airstrip were the hills, valleys, and ridges I'd read about from 1967—sites of grueling ground combat where the triple canopies had been sheared by air and artillery strikes, leaving behind shards and stumps. The sky was overcast, but certain crests and parts of valleys blossomed with yellow-green color as the sun peeked through holes in the clouds.

These hills are largely devoid of tree cover even today; aggressive deforestation in the Central Highlands has been a problem for decades, but it's also probable that the surroundings of Đăk Tô Base Camp were regularly swathed in Agent Orange during the war.

I motored down from the road onto the base confines, promptly gunning my motorcycle's engine to 70 miles an hour to cruise the empty airstrip. This was some solid asphalt; the runway was cracked in places, with patches of determined weeds splitting those cracks further, but overall, the pavement held and remained cohesive. Occasionally, I'd pass circular or square patches of off-colored concrete—the former likely bomb craters filled in with cement by U.S. engineers after 1967, and the latter probably once the foundations of control towers, underground bunkers, and other facilities that had disappeared.

I passed a pair of geriatric Honda Waves, one covered in a blue tarp and the other under a blanket of banana tree fronds, sheltered from the now-brutal midday sun that had broken through the clouds. The Vietnamese lovingly take care of their motorbikes. Behind the machines were two scraggy farmers squatting in a meadow in oil-stained baseball hats and long-sleeved shirts. Their eyes trailed me as I rolled by—steady, unsmiling. I gave a quick wave. They lifted their hands in reply, noncommittal, and went on watching, unmoved.

I approached them, dismounted, and removed my helmet. One of the men wore a camouflage army shirt with a patch that read *FRIENSHIP* over the breast pocket. I introduced myself and asked if I might find any relics from Đăk Tô Base Camp here.

"Nothing," one of them replied. "Not at all; nothing but cassava here now," he said, motioning to an expansive cultivated field behind him, with harvested tubers spread out on a corner of the runway, drying.

Xuân appeared and greeted us. Studying the edges of the runway and cassava field, he asked the farmers if they'd seen any war litter recently. The man in the *FRIENSHIP* shirt rolled his eyes, waved his hand dismissively, and said no, implying *Why don't you move along, buddy...*

I followed Xuân off the airstrip and into the cassava field, where he was analyzing the soil, looking for anything worth retrieving. Bits of war rubbish he'd clean up and place on a shelf at his house or office. They would later be shown to friends, enthusiasts, or prospective clients.

"Have you found anything here before?" I asked him.

"Yes," he said. "There's always war garbage at Đăk Tô."

He gestured toward the farmers. "Those two farmers see it every day, and they don't like visitors taking things they could sell to a salvage guy."

We waded through the soil, stepping over shards of sandbags from the war, along with pieces of the white plastic military-issue spoons that came with every MRE packet. Thousands of them must have been torn open here—three meals a day for every soldier at Đăk Tô.

Xuân pried a small plastic bottle loose from the base of a cassava plant.

"This was U.S. Army mosquito spray," he said, brushing off the caked-on soil and handing it to me. I examined it and could make out part of the lettering—tight-set, all-caps, slightly anxious-looking. The government-issue typography of 1960s command posts and war rooms: PELLENT. The old boy was right.

The sunlight had broken through the clouds and lit the ridge ahead. He pointed out a ridge ahead of us.

"That's Charlie Hill," he said.

Another Charlie Hill, I thought.

U.S. personnel kept it simple with nicknames for terrain features that shaped daily life in Vietnam; there must be a thousand "Charlie Hills" and a million "Rocket Ridges" in the former South Vietnam.

"ARVNs and the Americans had to climb this hill and patrol it constantly. If they didn't, the North Vietnamese would creep up and shell the runway," he continued. "It's the perfect spot for an attack like that." He kept inspecting the ground.

I turned into a wild, wooded area that bordered the cassava field. Dried foliage crackled under my feet as I watched the ground for war garbage—or for any more hints in the soil or terrain that this place had once been a base. The woods darkened as I moved deeper, and the ground gave way in spots, sinking slightly underfoot. Given where I was and what had taken place here, those soft spots felt ominous. The air felt faintly charged under the tree cover, like something had just happened—or was about to, a current still racing through the tree trunks.

Then I heard Xuân yelp—about a hundred feet behind me. I backtracked and found him out beyond the cassava field, hunched over in a meadow. He had found two live rounds. Big rounds. Not something I'd want to trip over. Dusting them off, he picked up both and examined them.

"I think these are American," he said.

"Okay," I said, watching him carefully, keeping some distance.

He put them in a canvas bag he brought with him.

"You might want to be careful with those," I added—already deciding I'd be giving his SUV a wide berth on the ride out of Đăk Tô.

"Don't worry," he said. "I'll leave them on the runway and call the authorities later. I can't leave them in the ground."

It felt reckless, but it wasn't unusual. Farmers still stumble across UXO in these parts and usually just pick it up and move it somewhere visible—on a stump, in the road, near the edge of a field—so the People's Committee can deal with it. Xuân wasn't doing anything out of the ordinary.

He paused. "Đi ăn phở, nhé?" (Let's go eat phở, ok?)

A bowl of Vietnamese beef noodle soup sounded good. "Mình đi," I responded.

As we exited the cassava field, Xuân spotted one more item in the soil—the rusted fins of a mortar shell, almost fully corroded.

"This is Russian," he said. "I'll take this one with me." He deposited the UXO on the runway, and I started my motorcycle.

Xuân wasn't the only one collecting. I'd done the same—a shell casing here, an MRE spoon there, a half-buried burlap sandbag. I've talked about it before, in the network, with people who get it. But not so much here. On the page, I've stayed quiet. Xuân moved like someone who knew what to look for. I played the part of the impressed outsider. But we were walking the same field, pocketing the same ghosts—objects that, in some cases, were probably the last thing someone ever touched. It still felt like a game—something boyish and unresolved, dressed up in history.

And if I'm honest, sometimes it still gave me goosebumps. That part never really left.

* * *

"See you at the car," I said.

I rode across the airstrip and back up to Highway 14, where the SUV was parked. Our driver had reclined his seat and was fast asleep. I surveyed Đăk Tô one more time from the road. A gust of wind shot down the runway, lifting Xuân's mop of black hair, and the fast-moving clouds above parted, catching the sun and casting it hard across him as he walked across the hot pavement. Fifty or so years ago, he would've been squarely in the gunsights of North Vietnamese soldiers hidden on Charlie Hill.

He scaled the rise and joined me.

"There are a bunch of phở restaurants on the road ahead," he said. "Don't worry."

"This is Vietnam," I said, smiling. "Finding a phở restaurant is never a worry."

Xuân opened the driver's side door and shook his guy awake. He started the SUV, triggering the car stereo midway through "I Want It That Way" by the Backstreet Boys.

The base had gone quiet. The Backstreet Boys filled in.

* * *

"Follow us," he said, shutting the door as they pulled away. Half a mile ahead, we passed a sign that read *Tắm Heo Quẹo Phải*, or "Pig Showers Turn Right." Beyond the sign was a hut and four large water tanks. Two livestock trucks were parked there, and the drivers stood on ladders, hosing down their cargo. The pigs must have been delighted.

We pulled over at an austere shack with a sign reading *PHỞ HÀ NỘI* in red Cooper Black font, stamped into a white panel. Three Hyundai trucks were parked out front.

The shanty was little more than a corrugated roof on stilts: a burner warming a vat of broth, red plastic tables and chairs, hammocks, and multiple women in floral pajamas running bowls of soup to seated groups of truckers. We sat down, and our bowls arrived before I could remove my helmet.

* * *

"Do you know what this is?" asked Xuân, pointing to a jar of chili paste—the kind that sits on every table in every *phở* shop in Vietnam.

"Yeah, I do," I said, as we passed around the limes, herbs, chili sauce, and fish sauce that *phở* eaters mix into their bowls in highly personalized ratios.

The restaurant doubled as a café, and a group of men in Wellington boots and green jumpsuits sat near us, playing cards and drinking iced coffee.

Xuân and the driver finished their bowls in minutes. The driver produced a box of White Horse cigarettes, and they both lit up. Xuân ordered three iced coffees. A woman called across the room, and her daughter emerged from a hammock, wearing an AC/DC "Highway to Hell" shirt. She grumbled as she tucked her phone into her back pocket and fetched the order.

In between gulps of *phở*, I asked Xuân if any of his family members served in the war.

"Yes, my father was ARVN," he said. "He was based at Biên Hòa."

Biên Hòa was the largest installation in South Vietnam, a joint U.S. and South Vietnamese air base on the outskirts of Saigon. Today, it's a People's Army Air Force base, and the U.S. government is funding a $32 million cleanup effort—half a million square meters of Agent Orange contamination.

"He was there for Tet 1968," he said.

"Is your father still around?" I asked.

"He died several years ago," Xuân replied. "Life was hard after the war. He drank a lot."

The iced coffee arrived just as I gripped the *phở* bowl with both hands and tilted the last puddle of broth into my throat.

"This is the best coffee in Kon Tum," Xuân said, stirring his cup with a tiny aluminum spoon. "It's not the cà phê bệt you guys drink in Saigon. They use a filter here. It's real coffee."

He tipped his polka-dotted glass back, and a river of coffee found its way over a hand-chiseled ice cube, missed his mouth, and leaked out the side of the cup, staining his shirt. He didn't blink.

Iced coffee with hand-chiseled cubes is most smoothly taken with a straw, but Vietnamese cafés rarely serve it with one, so these spills and stains are more common than they should be.

Cà phê bệt is the slang term for street coffee, or "coffee on the flat ground," which construction workers and students drink while sitting on low plastic stools or flattened cardboard boxes, on the sidewalk. Both are highly price-sensitive demographics, and an industry of hustlers exists in big cities to give them an affordable café *experience*—with one caveat: the coffee itself is often fraudulent.

There have been a handful of high-profile police busts over the years of fly-by-night coffee companies that produce cheaply and irresponsibly, seeking to capture markets for *cà phê bệt*. Instead of coffee beans, they roast and grind corn kernels and blend them with chemical emulsifiers, artificial colors, and other toxic additives that make the concoction taste like coffee. I can't imagine what margins would drive a company to this business model, but it seemed like a lot of work to deceive the country's construction workers.

Xuân added, "Never pay less than 25,000 đồng ($1.00) for a coffee," as he licked his thumb and scrubbed at the fresh stain on his shirt.

The price point for a cup of *cà phê bệt* is more like 6,000 đồng (25 cents), which is a siren to construction workers and students. Though they likely know that *cà phê bệt* is poisonous, price overrides health concerns.

We wrapped up and paid the bill.

"How far is Bến Hét?" I asked, checking ahead to our last stop together.

"Forty-five minutes," Xuân replied. "We will be very close to the Lao border there."

The three of us ambled out of the shack, toothpicks in mouths, and motored off—Kon Tum behind us, Bến Hét ahead.

Bến Hét

The site of Bến Hét Special Forces Camp was situated about 15 miles west of Đăk Tô. Jacked up on extra-strong Vietnamese coffee, I followed Xuân's SUV across a chalky plain under a big, open sky. Between the heat and the caffeine navigating my bloodstream, I was fidgety and perspiring, with the chorus of "I Want it That Way" on loop in my head. *The song holds up rather well*, I thought to myself—something I might not have admitted during the tune's peak rotation in 1999–2000. The mind does wander on long motorcycle rides, I find.

One of my more extraordinary insights came on a 2002 trip from Hanoi to Điện Biên Phủ. There were some long stretches of horrible mountain roads on that expedition, little more than mosaics of jagged, uneven boulders. I found myself wrangling the slabs spaced out, conceiving of a painting I wanted to produce: a portrayal of professional wrestler Hulk Hogan in ring costume, despondently sitting in a prison cell. The suggestion was that he may have been arrested during a wrestling match, but the backstory wouldn't be evident because it was a painting, a single frame lacking context.

* * *

Fortunately, Vietnam's heat tends to flush a caffeine overdose through the system quickly, and I gradually regained my equilibrium. As we closed in on Bến Hét, I began seeing old-growth logs stacked on both sides of the road. One encounters shadiness in remote Vietnam; in this case, the logs were likely smuggled in from across the Cambodian border, mere miles away.

As we approached, I remembered reading that Army Rangers referred to Bến Hét as the "most dangerous place in Vietnam" due to its proximity to the Ho Chi Minh Trail.

At the tripoint with Cambodia and Laos, the Trail sprouted an artery that turned east and crossed into Vietnam. The area around Bến Hét, unlike most of the mountainous Central Highlands, offered flatter, more navigable terrain near the border—ideal for infiltration. Because of that, and its proximity to Đăk Tô, Kon Tum, and Highway 14, the PAVN wanted to use this gateway to attack and seize the region. A small hilltop outpost of twelve Special Forces and four hundred Montagnards, Bến Hét sat about seven miles from the infiltration point and stood directly in the PAVN's path.

The camp's mission was to disrupt any incursions. Bến Hét's position offered visibility across the valley floor, extending to the border. The camp had artillery, tanks, and radios, and could call in air strikes on any North Vietnamese Army units that wandered across the border. Infiltrations through this gateway area were frequent, and like a lot of highland base camps, Bến Hét received incoming artillery and mortar rounds nearly every day.

In March 1969, one of the war's few tank battles occurred here. The Rangers began hearing the sounds of engines late one night, with the darkness thickening around them. A few miles away, Montagnard patrols hid as they observed ten Soviet PT-76 amphibious tanks lined up, engines revving.

Bến Hét prepared for an assault. Soon, the PAVN tanks and the base's tanks and artillery exchanged fire. The attackers pushed within 1,000 yards of Bến Hét as they attempted to close the distance and overrun the base. Rangers called in a Douglas AC-47 "Spooky" gunship, also nicknamed "Puff the Magic Dragon" during the war—it saturated the ground with 7.62-millimeter rounds, destroying anything that moved below. Within seconds. At dawn, soldiers surveyed the damage, finding the carcasses of several tanks, as well as North Vietnamese dead who had managed to advance to Bến Hét's barbed wire perimeter.

* * *

Our convoy rolled up to the site. Xuân, clearly having read the same materials I had, greeted me with, "Welcome to the most dangerous place in Vietnam."

We began walking, and Xuân pointed out that Bến Hét was composed of three hilltops. We ascended the middle of the three, where the Special Forces had installed their command bunker and communications equipment. Bến Hét today is abandoned, but amid the orange soil and tangled weeds, shrubs, and vines, the site was still comprehensible.

Reaching the summit via the camp's original one-lane dirt road, I surveyed the famous west sightline that stretched one or two miles toward the high peaks of eastern Laos. Ho Chi Minh Trail country. The crest was knobby, a patchwork of trench networks, foxholes, and the remains of the command bunker, all blanketed in overgrowth.

I hiked and encountered more bomb craters and trenches, shards of green sandbags half-submerged in soil, and in one trench, full sandbags untouched. As I looked over large slabs of mossy concrete, the plateau breeze carried the scent of cow manure. Below me, flatland unfurled with farms, cultivated fields, and a grid of forested land, where neat squares of trees had been felled.

"In front of us is the pasture that the North Vietnamese tanks tried to cross. That's about where they were hit," said Xuân, pointing towards Laos.

It was easy to picture a Ranger standing here that night in 1969, observing flares gently descending, listening to the ominous hum of Soviet tank engines in the distance, moving closer. The scene had a guilty pull, beautiful and unsettling—the kind I still recognized from somewhere I'd never quite outgrown.

* * *

Xuân and I headed back down. Bến Hét's 1,500-foot runway was on lower ground, beneath the hill. It's still there, and nothing grows on the former airstrip. I started my motorcycle and made several passes, imagining the sight of a C-130 transport plane landing there. Original embankments on both sides remained, though in places the berms were twisted—damage from direct mortar hits.

I closed my eyes and found myself thinking of my cousin, who died from Agent Orange-caused leukemia—our family knows nothing about his three years of combat in Vietnam. Perhaps he passed through Bến Hét at some point. Not knowing left that possibility open. Maybe that was the point—the uncertainty established the connection I wanted. We all have our narratives.

I felt a temperature rise, and my eyelids went bright red; I opened my eyes. The sun was moving from behind a cloud, suddenly scorching the abandoned camp. I rode back to where Xuân and the driver were waiting for me.

They were smoking cigarettes, and Xuân had a pair of *tạp hóa*-purchased sunglasses in his hand. As the driver looked on, arms folded across his chest, Xuân was gesturing as though he was trying to sell the glasses to his driver.

I stopped and dismounted as Xuân approached. "I got a phone call this morning. From the local authorities."

I wasn't sure I liked where this was going, but I was comforted that if it were anything but a rent-seeking play, I'd probably be in state custody by now.

"They know everything. They know where you were yesterday, and they knew our schedule today. I don't know how."

I remembered Trang. Perhaps she *was* a minder. But it was equally possible the provincial Department of Public Security had called Xuân, wanting to know who I was.

"So, what's the problem?" I asked.

"Bến Hét is a restricted frontier area. We should have gotten a permit for you."

Ah, the *restricted frontier area* bit. I'd been through this before and began to lose confidence that this story was on the level. Frontier permits are usually required to travel to places like Bến Hét that are so close to the border. But, as my Bản Giốc experience showed, the need for a frontier permit is frequently cited to justify an on-the-spot extortionate transaction once one is already in these lonely border areas.

I sighed. "So, what happens now?"

"Well, I really should take them out for cold beer when I get back home. I'm a tour guide and need to stay on their good side. Everything will be fine if I can buy them a few rounds."

"How much does a case of beer cost around here?" I wondered.

"About 300,000 đồng," he said, with a crooked smile. Maybe $15.

"Sorry, buddy. I have 100,000. Good enough for eight Bia Saigons." Despite the story, I suspected it would probably be one man drinking those eight Bia Saigons this afternoon, and that man was standing before me with his palm out.

"Well, I guess this is goodbye," I said, handing him his tip. "Thanks for everything."

"Thank *you*," replied Xuân. I shook the driver's hand and told him to have a good night. They climbed into their SUV and accelerated, kicking up a small patch of dirt into the Bến Hét airstrip as they made their getaway back to Kon Tum.

* * *

I put my wallet back into my knapsack and took in the 360-degree valley view one more time.

I had a few hours of daylight left, and I planned to traverse more of the border area, frontier permit or not. Ahead was more of the Ho

Chi Minh Highway; I would be crossing into Quảng Nam province to a village called Khâm Đức, with a couple of detours along the way.

It was nice to be alone again, and after Bến Hét, the Ho Chi Minh Highway put on a show. In some sections, Western Vietnam is among the most deserted places I've ridden, but it's not lonely. The landscape went full spectacle—and pulled it off. It's sterling motorcycling.

The long plateau that hosts Pleiku and Kon Tum gave way to young, narrow peaks, and the road followed their shape like it had been drawn by someone who finds switchbacks tedious. There were few sharp turns, but if Highway 14 wasn't ascending, it was descending—constantly shifting between uphill and downhill, never staying level. The tarmac narrowed just as my periphery blossomed into steep cliffs, and below me, unsullied waterways wound their way around hills and through valleys.

Occasionally, I'd pass a Montagnard man with a machete tucked into a drawstring, a homemade rifle slung over his shoulder, and a sack of foraged goods or tools, trudging back to an encampment after checking his high-altitude swidden plot. Sometimes, these fellows would catch my attention and suddenly vanish on the roadside after turning onto a trail I couldn't detect, shrouded in tall Napier grass.

They disappear around corners before I can take a second look—pedestrians on twisted roads like this one, where all my attention is on staying upright and not colliding with anything. At any time, a long-haul bus, a chicken, or a family could appear in the middle of my lane, just beyond a tight fold in the motorway.

That appearance came fifteen minutes later. As I slowly rounded a bend, a stock-still, four-axle Hyundai Trago cargo truck suddenly materialized 20 feet before me. A small pile of tree branches sat between us, a warning to approaching traffic that a stalled vehicle was occupying the lane, ten feet ahead.

The truck cab was open and leaning forward at a 45-degree angle, balanced on the front bumper. A man was bent over the engine underneath, with a tool kit arrayed on the asphalt. To be a truck driver in Vietnam, especially in this part of the country, one also needs to be a mechanic. I quietly rode around the tableau and resumed my journey.

I took in the deforested hilltops in the distance—long, six-foot-high clusters of elephant grass, and the horizon-stretching electricity transmission lines trailing into the faraway valleys and peaks below me. During descents, I had to be mindful of cargo trucks rapidly approaching from behind, taking advantage of the free downhill momentum, and be wary of the same trucks slouching along at four miles per hour on the ascents. The Ho Chi Minh Highway has improved logistics in this part of the country, but Hyundai and Kia freight haulers still inch along on the hills like pack animals.

* * *

I coasted down the mountains into a quaint valley and a town called Đắk Pék. I was there to see another Special Forces camp, this one built in 1962, one more of a long string of modest installations the Americans built along the frontier to surveil the Ho Chi Minh Trail. Đắk Pék was a highland village with a small cluster of Vietnamese shophouses, a school, and a police station.

I followed the map coordinates on my phone toward Đắk Pék camp's original location, which led to a hill on the village's edge. My map told me to walk up the mountain. Instead of dismounting, I rode the perimeter to see if there might be a trail I could ride. I stopped at a yellow-and-white grammar school with a soccer field. The gate was languidly half-open, and since it was summer, the courtyard was deserted. I entered and parked the bike out of sight in a far corner of the compound.

Really, I shouldn't have been in there. I ascended a steep slope on the other side of the hill and reached the top. A dog heard me stumbling through the bushes and brush at the top of the hill and began barking. And didn't stop, wasn't going to stop. So, I headed back.

Rural Vietnam has dogs; some households have one, and others have five or more. These dogs live tough lives, kept hungry and moody through discipline and a primitive lifestyle. They're primarily for security, as social trust here is surprisingly low, even in villages where everyone knows your motorbike.

Vietnamese are constantly wary of theft. I've heard of people working at home when a stranger climbs through the window—only to be confronted with a cricket bat and politely told to leave. Most homes are gated, with safes, roll-down shutters, and walls topped with barbed wire or broken glass. Doors without locks aren't sold, and one usually receives a set of around forty keys when signing an apartment or house lease. In rural areas, encountering ill-tempered village dogs is inevitable.

The hound was in the schoolyard, baring his teeth, growling and drooling. A middle-aged Vietnamese man, elegantly modest in a pair of loose-fitting white men's briefs and nothing else, was standing beside the dog, smoking a cigarette, palm on hip, watching my clumsy descent. An open door behind him revealed his simple quarters. I saw a cot, a mosquito net, and stacks of colorful plastic wash basins.

The man and his dog made up the school's entire enforcement detail. They were the law. The near-nude security guard had me dead to rights. He calmed his companion, held my eyes briefly, and pouted. I slid down the hill as he and his dog inspected me.

I greeted the fellow, and he took another drag from his cigarette. "What are you doing?" he asked in Vietnamese. The fervent yelping restarted.

"Oh, nothing really," I replied. "Just going around."

It was a shady answer. Fortunately, Vietnamese civilians tend not to press for too much information in situations like this. They're pragmatic. We both knew I was cornered, so maybe he was comfortable allowing things to remain vague. It's a situation where "face" can work in one's favor. As long as I was leaving. And I was.

It was a good question: why was a foreigner crawling around in the woods behind a school in Đắk Pék? What was his business here?

"Why do you speak Vietnamese?" he asked.

"Because I studied Vietnamese," I replied.

By this point, I was off the hill and had the bike started. "Hẹn gặp lại, anh" (See you again, brother!), I said.

As I retreated, only then did I notice the police headquarters building next door to the school—close shave. Motoring away from the school gate, I saw the sign: *HISTORICAL RELIC ĐẮK PÉK BASE*, pointing farther up the country lane.

* * *

One block more, and I'd arrived. A second small marker sign, planted on a patch of grass between government buildings and homes, denoted this was the site of Đắk Pék Special Forces Camp.

There was a base here, after all. Nothing remained but the sign, with nothing to explain what it once was. But it was marked. A strange stillness hung in the air. A pasture sat next to one of the government buildings where three broken down, rusted, and retired 1990s Toyota Previa minivans lived. These were the historical relics.

Khâm Đức

I rode the Ho Chi Minh Highway out of Đắk Pék. The road was largely empty, apart from the occasional Hyundai Universe bus overtaking me. Long-haul buses have evolved: twenty years ago, they were more commonly 13-seat Ford Transits, large vans that fit comfortably within a single lane on a two-lane Vietnamese country road. While a few Transits still operate, the Hyundai Universe 40-seat tour bus, imported second-hand from South Korea, is now the alpha hunter of the Vietnamese savanna.

These buses, nine feet wide and forty feet long, occupy nearly both lanes on narrow mountain roads, forcing most other motorists to give them abundant space. This is the vehicle that occasionally appears on my Facebook feed, upside down and in a roadside ditch. Due to drivers often fueled by methamphetamines, alcohol, or hard-wired impatience, it's always the right call to abandon the pavement with all due speed for whatever the road shoulder might have in store when one sees, or hears, a Hyundai Universe on a two-lane highway.

An hour in, I passed a billboard sign that put a lump in my throat: a bright photograph of six radiant Jarai women in matching traditional black skirts and tops with red and white stripes, all wearing orange and red headbands, waving. Below them was the statement *Tỉnh Kon Tum Hẹn Gặp Lại*—SEE YOU AGAIN.

This wasn't the first time that departing Kon Tum province hit me with that familiar melancholy; it's one of Vietnam's best. I was crossing into Quảng Nam on my way to the village of Khâm Đức, once another lonely Central Highlands outpost for American and South Vietnamese soldiers. Fortunately, the descent through Quảng Nam would be gradual, and I had time before I again found myself in crowded coastal Vietnam.

Fifteen minutes later, I came to a stop at Phước Mỹ (blessed beauty), a village at the base of a hill called Ngok Tavak, whose story is intertwined with Khâm Đức's. I'd been to Edenesque villages in Vietnam before, but Phước Mỹ, in western Quảng Nam province, was intoxicating. I turned and rode through the village gate, passing through a tiny farming community of maybe two hundred, tucked in a bowl-shaped valley ringed by Central Highlands foothills. With the 1,000-foot Ngok Tavak lording over me, I motored past cows and dogs loitering in rice paddies.

Phước Mỹ smelled of frangipani, cow manure, and cut straw—heady, but clean. The only sound I could hear was distant Vietnamese electronic dance music; someone in the village probably had a 20-watt amplifier connected to their mobile phone. Shadows were falling on the foothills around the village, lending the trees dark, rich tones that offset the daylight olive drabs. Despite dusk barely hinting at 5:00 p.m., a full moon glowed halfway up the afternoon aquamarine sky.

* * *

This idyllic village figured into the first chapter of the three-day dramatic siege and evacuation of Khâm Đức Special Forces Camp in May 1968. The North Vietnamese Army was retreating to Laos after the Tet Offensive, and units in Quảng Nam were ordered to attack Khâm Đức on their way out of Vietnam. First, however, they overran the roughly one hundred Australian, American, and Montagnard troops that operated a listening post at Ngok Tavak.

The survivors escaped on foot, carrying seventy wounded, with the PAVN in pursuit. After two days of evasion in the jungle, helicopters finally extracted them and flew them three or four miles east to Khâm Đức, just as the PAVN began shelling the camp's 1,500 defenders there.

Legions of North Vietnamese human-wave assaults pummeled Khâm Đức from all sides. American air strikes hit back hard. Napalm and artillery slowed the attackers, but only momentarily. Evacuation became inevitable. As C-130 cargo aircraft and Chinook helicopters began moving troops, the PAVN opened fire. They shot down several Chinooks over the camp's runway. They also downed a C-130 loaded with evacuees—killing everyone on board.

The United States ordered two hundred more airstrikes that day, holding the PAVN at bay just long enough to get the last evacuation aircraft out. B-52s then carpet-bombed the area around Khâm Đức for three days. About fifteen hundred North Vietnamese soldiers died in the battle, along with several hundred American, South Vietnamese, Australian, and civilian casualties.

* * *

Daylight continued to fade. I rode out of Phước Mỹ and pointed toward Khâm Đức. After a few miles, the one-lane road opened into a second lane, with a divider bearing Rose Myrtle and Speargrass flowers. Khâm Đức delivers a VIP entrance.

Street lights appeared every twenty feet, each with a small round sign midway up the pole, flashing colored LED lights that formed the outline of a Communist Party of Vietnam flag draped in lotus flowers; other displays formed textbooks. Beneath the lights were vertical propaganda banners. I stopped for a closer look at one, reading *Nhiệt Liệt Chào Mừng Đại Hội Đại Biểu Các Dân Tộc Tiểu Số Nguyên Phước Sơn Lần Thứ Ba* or "Warmly welcoming the Third Congress of Ethnic Minorities in Nguyên Phước Sơn District." These soft-lit LED signs were, in their way, gorgeous, glowing against the dusky jungle backdrop.

Officially, the signs beamed red, yellow, and white—revolutionary hues. But in the haze, I must have registered turquoise and foam green, too—tones I've always associated with midcentury interiors in Vietnam, and with space-age ads for automobiles or toothpaste in my own country. The color of the business shirts men wore in southern California. Shades of optimism and the future, but corralled. The blue matched my Uncle Stan's 1971 Volvo—something I hadn't thought about in years, but apparently hadn't forgotten. These are the kinds of things that surface after long days on the road, when solo riding starts to dislodge memories in strange, narcotic ways. I didn't know what I was feeling, exactly—just that it felt familiar. And I wanted to stay inside it.

By the time I arrived in Khâm Đức, the streetlights had taken over, and I moved through town in the kind of aimless glide that comes just before sleep, looking for a *nhà nghỉ*.

* * *

I pulled into the first *nhà nghỉ* I saw—Guest House 21 & Yoga House. It sat behind a high concrete gate and a bleached wall, faintly glowing in the streetlamp haze of a residential block. I arrived tired and dirty, dismounted, and strolled around the dim, tiled compound, hoping to find staff. I looked through a cracked-open door and interrupted a woman receiving a massage on a table.

Word must have traveled that a stranger was drifting the premises, because soon the head of the retreat appeared. She was a thirtysomething yogi originally from Đà Nẵng who had moved here several years ago. The courtyard lights caught the edges of her close-cropped hair and the white fabric of her clothes. Her name was Kim (golden).

"What brings you here?" she asked.

"Well, I'm just riding around a bit, and I thought I'd look at Khâm Đức Special Forces Camp in the morning."

"Good. How long have you practiced yoga? Please join us tomorrow morning."

Two moths were circling the courtyard bulb in an uneven in-flight tango. The scent of frangipani hung in the still air.

Instinct told me not to commit to that. "I probably won't."

"You should. Join us tomorrow, please."

"What time does yoga start?" I asked, stalling.

"5:00 a.m. Right out here," she said, pointing to a concrete platform in the driveway under a vinyl awning.

"We'll see. I do want to get up early and see the old Khâm Đức base, and I have a long day of riding planned. How long will you be doing yoga for?"

"Two hours. Every day. So, we'll see you?"

"I don't know," I replied.

She showed me to my room. The concrete hallway was lit by a single bulb, and the cinderblock door frame echoed faintly as I stepped through. It was a cinderblock shell in a concrete building that felt like one of the sandbagged structures that might have once anchored Khâm Đức Special Forces Camp. Apart from the dense constellations of cobwebs in each of the room's corners, it was clean enough, with mid-century modern, asymmetrical, geometric-patterned curtains in white and brown, shielding my window from the outer corridor. A second window was similarly draped.

The fabric reminded me of curtains or shirt collars from another era—the kind of geometry meant to project happiness, whether or not it was felt. I parted the curtains and saw a window with a wall of cinder blocks on the other side. There was no light behind it. Just the hard impression of something pressed close. At least it *had* the second window; one is a luxury for a *nhà nghỉ*. I dropped my bags and took a walk.

* * *

The full moon had held up in the sky, casting a lavender glow over the village. Under that lighting, Khâm Đức felt weightless—slipping slightly out of time. The sky was bright, but the town's lanes were shrouded under trees, and occasionally, a child on a bicycle or a couple out walking would glide past, out of the shadows, caught by the warm yellowish glare from a bulb in an adjacent house.

With each step, a melody grew clearer—strains of Elvis Phương's fuzzy "Sống Cho Qua Hôm Nay" ("Live for Today") floated through the village ether from a shophouse stacked with salvaged Japanese hi-fi gear for sale: tape decks, receivers, speakers as big as suitcases.

It was the earliest, and rawest, four-track demo version—the best version—of a song I love. "Sống Cho Qua Hôm Nay" was one of my first favorites after I fell under the spell of *Trước '75* Saigon rock and roll a decade ago. Elvis Phương came of age with the youth movement during the war. He wasn't establishment, but he was everywhere in South Vietnam. Like many musicians from that scene, he fled the country after 1975—when the Republic of Vietnam fell, and its memory began to live on mostly in exile.

Overseas, Elvis Phương evolved into a kind of Vietnamese Neil Diamond. His was a decades-long, genre-fluid career, always adapting to match the pop moment—from postwar *nhạc vàng* (yellow music), sorrow songs about a country he'd lost and couldn't return to, through the synth ballads of the 1980s. By the mid-1990s, when the constraints on *Trước '75*-rooted and diaspora-inflected expression began to loosen, he began regularly returning to Vietnam to perform for audiences in his homeland.

"Sống Cho Qua Hôm Nay" was Elvis at probably twenty or twenty-two. His Byrds, We Five, Rubber Soul era. My guess is that the demo came out of the mid-to-late 1960s: it perfectly fuses Saigon's youth, glamour, and optimism with the period's psychic undertow—jangly guitars straining to drown out the war.

I followed the sound and found a man in his sixties behind a low counter, sitting quietly, cigarette in hand, watching the street. I asked him if it was Elvis Phương, and he nodded, lit up for a moment, then said nothing more, content to let the song be our *làm quen*. He seemed unfazed that I recognized it, though he might have been. It wasn't background music; we both loved Elvis Phương. Despite the decades that had passed, playing "Sống Cho Qua Hôm Nay" in public like that felt faintly transgressive. I sensed that my new friend realized this.

We stood in it together for a while as the song wound down, the frangipani, the smoke, the evening air, the lavender sky. The song held everything in place for a moment, as if that other Vietnam—the one from grainy film reels and stereo hiss—had slipped back through.

* * *

I found a street-side *bánh xèo* restaurant. The scent hit first—fried batter, herbs, smoke from an open cooking fire, and fish sauce cooling in the air. *Bánh xèo* is a fried rice flour pancake, rolled with shrimp, pork, and herbs inside sheets of rice paper.

I sat on a fire-engine-red plastic chair and matching table inside, beneath fluorescent bulbs that washed the aquamarine walls and evoked the interior of a public aquarium tank—bright on the other side of the glass, glowing, fluorescent.

The husband-and-wife team began delivering dishes immediately, the usual in restaurants with one-dish menus. I indulged right away. Seconds in, I'd nearly drained the bowl of *mắm chấm*. They brought a second, larger one, unprompted. I felt seen.

A sweat-drenched man in workout gear entered and collapsed in a chair near me, resting a pair of boxing gloves on the tabletop. Teenagers, four to a motorbike, rolled by. The boxer sat, rapidly consumed six *trứng vịt lộn*—fertilized duck eggs, steamed with the embryo still inside—and left.

The husband began sweeping the floor and paused to extinguish the cooking fires. It was eight o'clock.

The air still held some of that beautiful meal—fried batter, fish sauce, smoke. I walked back to Kim's *nhà nghỉ* and yoga retreat. After a shower, I climbed into bed and dimmed the naked light bulb hanging from the ceiling. The room was warm and still. So many country towns in Vietnam share a soundscape, and Khâm Đức was no exception.

Sleep came evenly. Through the concrete walls, sounds arrived in layers—two distant karaoke duels in full swing, both singing Vietnamese rumba, the style older people here still adore. A power saw joined the mix, buzzing and biting at the edge of things. Somewhere closer, a group of men shouted "Một hai ba dô!" amid stray voices, plastic chairs scraping tile, and the dull grind of a hard plastic beer crate being dragged across a cement floor. Motorbikes purred past the front gate, one every few minutes, like exhalations. The sound of rural Vietnam tucking itself in for the night.

* * *

I woke at 5:30 to the thunderous sound of New Age music playing in the courtyard outside my room. Recalling the previous day's pointed invitation to practice yoga, I quietly slipped out to see what was happening. Five women were in the Bhujangasana (cobra) pose beside my parked motorcycle, lined up on a bare concrete stage. I was heartened to see that Kim had clients—I hadn't been sure this little compound deep in western Quảng Nam province necessarily had the makings of a yoga destination. My fear the previous evening was that she might not have any students, hence the pressure I felt to show up for this class.

But here we were, at dawn, and Kim had four others with her. I reloaded my bags on the bike as quietly as I could, returned to my room for an instant coffee, suited up, and went to check out.

Despite the ongoing class, Kim appeared at the front desk while I paid my bill.

"What happened? You didn't join us for yoga today."

"Well, I decided to sleep in, I'm afraid." It was 6:15.

"You'll have to come back, then. Are you leaving now? Let me get you a bánh mì before you go. You need breakfast."

"Really, it's okay," I said, smiling and hoping to charm my way into an early release. She followed me out to the courtyard. "I can get a bánh mì on the road," I added, raising my voice just enough to rise above the soundscape. I started the bike.

"No. Give me five minutes."

She was insistent. So I waited. Moments later, she brought me a pair of *bánh mì* in a white paper bag. I put them inside my jacket, thanked her, and said farewell.

* * *

Today, Khâm Đức is a small town of six thousand people. The site of the Special Forces camp was easy enough to find; the Google Earth overview of Khâm Đức depicts an ample ovular space within the town's confines, vacant apart from the faint outline of a runway. I rode for about eight minutes, and then the former base came into view—the one the PAVN had besieged for a few days in May 1968.

Not quite 7:00 a.m., the sun was up. Overnight clouds had congregated around the hilltops that ringed the expanse, and once the sun climbed higher and hotter, it would begin to burn them off. Until then, the hanging moisture held aromatic smoke, carrying tiny droplets of cooking oil and fish sauce from residential cooking fires.

The mist had drifted through the curtilage of the old base and gathered over the 6,500-foot runway. The runway's contours were clear, and the structure was still surrounded by concrete-and-earth berms, originally built to shield it from PAVN or guerrilla attacks. The ring of hills facing me was the same one from which North Vietnamese mortar teams had shelled the base. Large parts of their summits had been sheared cleanly by logging.

The base was silent and all mine, apart from distant fragments of Vietnamese I could hear from nearby houses. Spouses were arguing; parents were calling their children—all part of the ritual of getting a family prepared and out the door in the morning.

I heard the clang of a bell and some rustling of brush. A herd of cows had wandered onto the Khâm Đức runway and was grazing along the berms, sifting through discarded potato chip bags and bricks for tufts of grass. The runway tarmac was remarkably intact, considering more than fifty years of near-zero maintenance since the battle. Bomb craters cluttered the once-pristine airstrip, and the three days of North Vietnamese artillery and American B-52 strikes were still etched into the ground.

I rode my motorcycle onto the runway, weaving through the barrens. I passed open suitcases with clothes spilled out like they'd been tossed from a second story during a divorce. Plastic shopping bags, caught in branches and brush, were settling in for a multigenerational decomposition. Clusters, big and small, of garbage appeared everywhere: plastic water bottles, condom wrappers, concrete slabs, half-burned sofas, watermelon rinds, empty beer cans, decomposing Bia Saigon boxes, random motorbike tires, torched mounds of plastic, tennis shoes, and household furniture that had collapsed into particleboard panels and upholstery shards.

Surveying the litter, I deduced that some people came to this runway to drink and fornicate. This was a massive plot for the town to ignore, in a country captivated by property investment. Perhaps it was because this site, like so many others I'd visited, was cursed—with wandering spirits or other cosmic imprints burned into the soil during those intense few days in 1968.

The former base was no doubt cursed; upwards of two thousand people had died in this confined place, after all. It was so cursed that the town chose a parcel well removed from the site to erect a small monument to the battle. About half a mile from the remains of Khâm Đức Special Forces Camp is the official memorial plaque honoring the expulsion of the Americans in 1968. I found it as I rode out of town.

The plaque is new, and a locked gate surrounds it. About six feet tall and made of black and brown tiles, the stele juts up from its base. Its shape was oddly figurative—like the silhouette of a man with wide shoulders and a high, squared crown rising above his head, long coat flaring slightly as if in motion.

Carved into the black tile is *Di Tích Chiến Thắng Khâm Đức*, or "Khâm Đức Victory Monument." That's it. Saplings with young shoots had been planted around the square, gated plaza, supported by thick sticks tied into pyramids to help them root and grow. The driveway was freshly poured white gravel. The memorial and its space didn't encourage lingering or contemplation, so it felt right to move on.

The stele—a strange figure in tile—striding forward like a 1930s mobster with the pluck to wear a top hat instead of a fedora.

Nonetheless, the past still lived here—just not where the stele said. It clung to the drainage ditches behind the runway, to the hiss of old tape decks, to a song sung fifty years ago by a man who'd since fled the country. It hovered in the lavender sky, in the dreamy blur that settles in near the end of a long ride—when colors bloom strange and time begins to ripple. It was in the silence of the man behind the counter. The monuments spoke loudly, but the war left quieter marks: smudged outlines, atmospheric residue, stray impressions left in the haze. I wasn't sure what I'd come to find. But the more I looked, the more I saw it wasn't buried. It was dispersed.

Hải Vân Pass

Highway 14 turned right some miles north of Khâm Đức and became Highway 14E, which runs east to the Quảng Nam coast. I made the turn and realized that within a couple of hours, I'd be descending out of the highlands and back into the lowlands. Riding out of Vietnam's highlands is always a temporary bummer; the hill country is more scenic, slower, relaxed, and warmer. The drop in elevation tends to trigger a reflexive dread—a return to the denser, more quarrelsome, authoritarian, loud, and hot-blooded lowlands. But the mood rarely lasts: sooner or later, some lowlander with flair always stumbles into view with some gesture that wins me back.

Save for Hạ Long City in Quảng Ninh province, that is. Hạ Long City is the gateway to Hạ Long Bay, once one of Vietnam's most majestic landscapes. It still is, but it now overflows with domestic and international tourists. It's an overcrowded pirate town lacking any savory attributes: rubbish, hustlers running boat tours of the bay, low-grade package tours, hundreds upon hundreds of buses, lousy service, bad vibes, *cao bồi thôn,* diesel fumes, fistfights, clogged toilets, scams, oil slicks, and petty theft.

The goal was to reach Quảng Trị city, once the capital of Quảng Trị province, by day's end. I would meet an old friend, Vũ, who had built a livelihood escorting American combat veterans to the places they served decades ago. This wasn't just another leg of the trip. Quảng Trị had taken a beating during the war, and I wanted to see what lingered—how the land held its scars, and how the people had moved on, or hadn't. I would bypass tourist hotspots—Hội An, Đà Nẵng, Huế—in favor of quieter roads and rural margins.

***

Wanting to linger in the Central Highlands a bit longer, I remembered the two *bánh mì* Kim had given me at 6:30 that morning. I began looking for a café where I could eat them with a fresh coconut and an iced coffee. I entered a village and found a promising outdoor *bình dân* café.

"Do you have coffee?" I asked the woman at the café.

"We don't have coffee here," the woman replied. "Check that café a bit down the road. They sometimes have coffee."

So I did, but that, too, was a bust. I stopped at another café, now outside of the village.

"No, we don't have coffee. We don't have coconuts, either," the owner said.

Vietnam produces excellent coffee in large quantities, but they don't drink as much of it as one might think, particularly in the countryside. Coffee is mainly for export or city-dwellers with curated tastes. Vietnam's robust filter coffee certainly has a following among males in cities. Women aren't big coffee drinkers, opting for juices or complex Frappuccino-type dessert drinks.

That said, there's near-total consensus around the café in Vietnam; there might be four or five cafés per block in cities, and they're often full. City folks like to go to cafés together and enjoy the coffee's luxurious scent, poetically watch the hot water dripping slowly through locally designed single-cup tin *phin* filters, drink gentle sips, linger, take selfies, linger more, and make small talk. Urbanites can idle at coffee shops for hours, uploading photographs of their coffee onto social media platforms.

Country people don't have time for that kind of frivolity; there's work to do. Though one can find cafés in the countryside, finding actual coffee can be challenging. When visiting in-laws or other elders in the countryside, it's said, always bring instant coffee, a flask of whiskey, and a book.

"But we do have Sting," she continued. Unlike the famous English bassist, Sting is a jolt of synthetic energy—a mildly toxic drink of caffeine, artificial coloring, and artificial flavoring. It's a construction worker's drink, gulped before a shift to maximize performance. I gave up and ordered a bottle of water.

I unwrapped the two *bánh mì* and dug in. It was exceptional. Fried eggs and roasted pork were drenched in a succulent, tangy country gravy mixed with locally-made French pâté. The gravy blended with the usual sweet pickles, chili peppers, and cilantro to create an arresting sticky emulsion. The pair was still warm. Christ, Kim had taken good care of me.

* * *

The descent to the coast began in earnest at this point, but I made my peace with it. I was riding into Quảng Nam's Quế Sơn Valley. Quảng Nam was one of South Vietnam's most insecure provinces during the war, quietly accommodating thousands of North Vietnamese troops and National Liberation Front (NLF) guerrillas. Most hid in secret camps in the foothills I navigated that day and slipped down to the valley at night to collect food, lead propaganda and recruitment activities, or visit their homes and families. Some would even sleep in their own beds and return to the hills before dawn the next day.

Most of the Quế Sơn Valley was *de facto* Communist-controlled. Two well-known hotspots from the war are Gò Nổi Island and a cluster of villages nicknamed "Dodge City" by American soldiers for their propensity to deliver serendipitous gunfights.

American troops dreaded patrolling the Quế Sơn Valley, but *not* patrolling meant ceding the region to the Communists. Gò Nổi Island and Dodge City were just ten miles from Đà Nẵng's large U.S. and South Vietnamese base complexes. Despite hundreds of search-and-destroy operations, patrols, and airstrikes, their combined forces had little success pacifying this region.

As I rode through Gò Nổi Island, every modest house I passed was freshly painted, shaded by fruit trees, and immaculately kept. The Ho Chi Minh quote, *Không có gì quý hơn độc lập, tự do!* (Nothing is more precious than independence and freedom!) seemed to appear and reappear on village gates and propaganda banners all along the road.

The veneration was owned; it was as though the island knew it was blessed, carried unimpeachable revolutionary credentials, and felt no need to impress anyone.[4]

* * *

I turned left onto coastal Highway 1, aiming north for Quảng Trị. Highway 1 is Vietnam's original Main Street, a two-lane road that runs 1,000 miles from Saigon to Hanoi, never straying too far from the coast.

On the way, I would be riding over the Hải Vân Pass, a natural landmark wedged between Đà Nẵng and Huế. The pass sits at about 1,600 feet and presents a stunning view of the South China Sea and surrounding hills.

The Hải Vân Pass draws tourists, and visitors to Đà Nẵng usually take a half-day van or motorbike trip to the summit. In addition to the panorama, situated at Highway 1's highest point is a cluster of sun-bleached concrete bunkers and pillboxes originally built by the French Army. Later, the Americans took over this position to protect Highway 1 supply convoys from Communist sabotage.

I pulled over. Ten minutes later, I watched a group of three young, shirtless Western men in banana-print trousers slowly approach on Honda Wins straining against the gradient to haul overloaded Western backpacks to the crest. I'd passed them earlier. Three *Tây Ba Lô* on Honda Wins. Straight out of central casting.

The Honda Win is the frail 110-cc motorbike that took over the backpacker trade after Vietnam phased out Minsk imports. Some bike had to take this mission; unfortunately, it was the Win.

Once the bike was tapped for this assignment, the Win market soon became diluted with Chinese, Taiwanese, and Indonesian copies. To this day, Facebook groups catering to backpackers host earnest, detailed, and unwinnable debates over whether a Detech Win or a Sufat Win—with or without a cheap helmet and bungee cords included in the price—is the better buy. In truth, there's little difference—they all cost about $150 used, and they're all, well, junk. That is, versus an "Original Japanese Win," which can run $2,000 if you're the right kind of gullible.

The point is, a Win (copy or not) outs a young man instantly—*Tây Ba Lô* on a budget, passing through for some adventure and cheap beer. When I started out, it was the Minsk. There were two types of Minsk—the 1980s Minsk and the 1990s Minsk, with a dime's worth of difference between them. So there was far less to debate; they were all reliably unreliable. It made sense at the time, and we loved those machines. Until the first multi-day trip, anyway.

The United Kingdom television show *Top Gear* sent its three hosts to Vietnam for a special episode in 2008. *Top Gear* concerns itself with sports cars and other high-performance vehicles, with most content being auto reviews, auto talk, auto test drives, and auto challenges of various kinds. The *Top Gear: Vietnam Special* episode had the three personalities race low-displacement Vietnam heritage motorbikes from Saigon to Hạ Long Bay on Highway 1 over eight days; they were a 1960s Italian Vespa, a 1980s Belorussian Minsk, and a vintage Honda Cub.

Top Gear: Vietnam Special was masterfully done, driving throngs of twentysomethings to Vietnam to do two- to three-week motorbike trips from Saigon to Hanoi. Previously, riding Vietnam's northwest was chiefly an expat pursuit, while tourists moved about on minibuses. The newcomers traced Highway 1, south to north. The *Top Gear* route. Occasionally, one will still meet young shavers bragging in taverns about how they're here to ride Highway 1, "The Ho Chi Minh Trail," from Saigon to Hanoi.

Hopefully, we've established by now that the Ho Chi Minh Trail was a network of roads that ran from then-North Vietnam's ports and supply hubs into Laos and south into Cambodia, with tributaries that crossed the border into the Central Highlands in western Vietnam. Not the coast, with its wall of American and South Vietnamese bases, helicopters, guns, and tanks. The war would probably have turned out differently if North Vietnam chose to run its supply routes south on the highly militarized Highway 1.

What was odd about this phenomenon was that, apart from the Hải Vân Pass and a few other coastal stretches, Highway 1 isn't especially scenic or enjoyable to ride. It's loud, dusty, and crowded—packed with cantankerous truckers, tourist buses, and the constant blare of horns. Courtesy isn't part of the traffic ecosystem, and trauma care is thin on the ground. If a rider goes down, they're largely on their own. Highway 1 is Vietnam at its most treacherous.

But still, *Tây Ba Lô* ride it—emulating Top Gear, chasing a choreographed thrill.

I once came across a video posted by three young American men doing one stretch of their motorbike adventure in the nude, filming each other riding Wins up Highway 1 wearing only sunglasses, socks, and hi-top sneakers. Not an idea that would occur to me, but there you have it.

* * *

That said, the Hải Vân Pass is a stunning 13-mile ride that should be on anyone's list of great motorcycling roads. Some time ago, the provincial government drilled a tunnel through a neighboring mountain, which diverted most of the nasty Highway 1 long-haul truck traffic from the Hải Vân Pass inland.

One can walk around the summit and visit some of the military bunkers that were there to ward off ambushes; today, the only ambush is from a cluster of vendors selling coconuts, screwdrivers, shoe shines, Saigon baseball caps, pork rinds, nail clippers, gum, and cans of Gold Cow energy drink. Vietnamese touts can be persistent, even when the products and services are impractical. For example, I once had a young man in Hanoi stop me to propose a shoe shine as I was climbing into a taxi.

I bought nothing at the summit. But the show was free: Western backpacker-riders patiently and politely engaging street salespeople well-versed in the Western psyche—they know which emotional strings to pull to prolong their pitches and achieve sympathy sales. I started my ignition. I wove through the six or eight tourist buses parked in both lanes of Highway 1, crossing into Thừa Thiên Huế province. Quảng Trị city was only a hundred miles up the road.

* * *

I circumvented Huế, Vietnam's nineteenth-century imperial capital—melancholic, elegant, and long regarded as the guardian of the country's refined traditions. The war left its scars—especially in 1968, when American and South Vietnamese forces retook the city after a month-long Communist occupation during the Tet Offensive. In the aftermath, mass graves were discovered—some shallow, some forgotten, all full of painful stories that took time to surface.

It was hard to pass through without stopping, but I kept moving. I could easily spend a day or a decade in Huế, but I had my friend Vũ waiting for me in Quảng Trị. I did have time for lunch, so I pulled over at Quán Cơm Phương Nhung (Ms. Phương Nhung's Rice Restaurant) on Highway 1. This *quán cơm* was actually a truck stop, the kind of place I have an irrational confidence in. I spotted several Hyundai Tragos parked out front. Stenciled on the bay window at Phương Nhung's was the phrase CHÚC MỪNG NĂM MỚI! (Happy New Year!). Lunar New Year is more about vibes than a date on the calendar; it's never out of season in Vietnam, and it's expected to see *Chúc Mừng Năm Mới* messaging in summer.

As my eyes adjusted to the darkness inside, I made out gangs of four or five shirtless Vietnamese men at tables, eating lunch while their cigarettes burned in ashtrays and beer replenishments arrived.

Truckers in Vietnam often travel in groups, usually with a handful of drivers sharing each truck. The logic is that a delivery truck must drive all day and night, so these men drive in shifts. If anyone's in a hurry in this country, it's long-haul truckers. They'll drink beer to get them through the day as they drive. Some take methamphetamines.

Peculiarly, they were drinking Mexican beer at this place—Corona, a rather exotic brand for a rural Vietnamese truck stop.

Occasionally throughout the year, a video of some impaired trucker plowing through ten or twenty motorbikes waiting at a red light or similar infraction will go viral. They'll arrest the suspect, and he'll do the perp walk and a hungover interview. Usually something to the effect of "I had too much to drink. I'm sorry, everybody."

I took a table near the wall, adjacent to a hand-painted mural of the cartoon characters Tom & Jerry resting on their bellies. Next to them was a still life that included a large watermelon, a lengthwise-sliced kiwi fruit, a bouquet of flowers, and a bottle of Hennessy VSOP cognac.

Vietnam adores Tom & Jerry, which has been on television there for decades. A large TV bolted to the far wall showed a subtitled

Nicolas Cage film. The Vietnamese like Nick Cage, too. He became a mainstay there after his career tacked and he committed to action fare like *Ghost Rider* in 2007.

I chose a simple dish of sautéed beef, vegetables, and rice. It's most commonly and efficiently eaten with chopsticks, but the woman gave me a fork. Stupidly, I forgot to ask the price beforehand. It's easy to go soft in Saigon, where vendors generally treat foreigners fairly.

I took two iced teas, told the owner how nice the lunch was, and asked for the bill. She came back to me with "130,000 đồng." I asked her to repeat herself. She did, and I knew what was happening. That was outrageous.

Here in the middle of rural Thừa Thiên Huế province, at a truck stop on an unremarkable stretch of highway, at a restaurant that feeds a highly price-sensitive demographic in an already extremely price-sensitive country, she wanted about $7 for a plate of rice and two iced teas. In West Africa, where just about everything is imported, that would not be a shocking price for such an elementary lunch. But this was Vietnam, where wages are kept low and just about all foodstuffs are produced locally. There was no way the men at the other tables were paying more than 30,000 đồng for their plates.

"Are you sure that the bill for lunch is 130,000 đồng? Would you mind rechecking it?"

"Not necessary. I'm sure it's 130,000 đồng. That's how much it costs," she replied.

I took in the room beyond her. Some of the truckers had paused eating and perked up, watching me.

* * *

I learned long ago the consequences of pushing it in situations like this. A friend and I rode our Minsk motorcycles from Hanoi to the north-central province of Thái Bình in 2003. Thái Bình province is one of Vietnam's toughest: the weather and soil are terrible, and it's not bountiful. People there are accustomed to scraping for resources.

The Thái Bình coast isn't beautiful, and we landed in a jaded, dreary seaside village with sand the color of oil and air thick with the aroma of drying squid. The town was the usual rows of welding shops, brick kilns, working-class *phở* stalls, motorbike mechanics, sheet metal wholesalers, and construction sites. The village's soundtrack was the omnidirectional jangle of dozens of power tools.

We dined on seafood at a *bình dân* seafood restaurant inland from the beach. It was a concrete shack with a fresh coat of wedding dress-white paint, surrounded by leftover sand and bricks, evidently recently built.

We might have had six cans of local beer and shared a plate of humble *rau muống xào tỏi*, a family-size bowl of rice, and boiled shrimp from the adjacent sea. Just to underscore the flagrancy: *rau muống xào tỏi* is a well-loved water spinach dish that most people eat six times a week. It's hyper-abundant and nearly free on most restaurant menus. We asked for the bill; it read 2.5 million Vietnamese đồng, roughly $100. Cheeky.

"The bill should be more like 500,000 đồng [$20], no?" I petitioned.

"No, no, little brother. It's time to settle the bill so you boys can go home."

"Eh?" I asked.

"Did you see the size of the shrimp I served you?" he asked defensively. This man had probably hustled for hours the previous three days, earning nothing. Now, a pair of rich Americans saunter into his restaurant and park luxury $250 Minsk motorcycles outside, ready to burn cash on authentic North-Central Coast seafood. Game on.

He was wearing a black oversized leather jacket and smoking Vinataba cigarettes. Vinataba is the flagship budget brand of the state-owned Vietnam Tobacco Corporation. Primarily consumed in the north, these are essentially cigarettes of rolled cardboard stuffed with sawdust. Loose-fitting, suburban-cut black leather jackets are a bad sign in this part of the country; they're gangster.

"Face" can be an unsavory concept. We all knew he was being unreasonable, daring us to cross the line and deny him his face. "Come back in the low season if you want a cheaper meal. This is a holiday town, so things are a little more expensive," he countered. Nonsense. It was November.

My friend tried to force a fair amount of cash into his hand. He refused, so we began moving toward the door.

He followed us out of the restaurant. A crowd of forty more hardscrabble boys in leather jackets gathered, raising the stakes tenfold, along with village women pausing their chores. In Vietnamese, there's a phrase—"camera chạy bằng cơm," rice-powered cameras—gossipy villagers with a radar for controversy. An audience. That's what the villagers were now: watching, waiting, not helping, recording.

Because this was Vietnam, there was a four-foot-high pile of bricks outside the restaurant. The man picked up two bricks. Confrontations can escalate quickly in this country; a switch flips, and suddenly, there are no rules.

I've seen wives chase their husbands with butcher's knives. I've seen people draw samurai swords to settle street arguments. I've seen truckers go at each other, one with a chain and the other with a crowbar, after a fender-bender. I've sat locked in a taxi in a parking lot after a friend got sassy with someone at a *bia hơi*, with the car being pelted with empty 450-milliliter Bia Hà Nội bottles crafted with thick glass thrown by a mob of the victim's friends. Vietnamese, especially northern Vietnamese, are fighters.

Modeling the crucifixion of Jesus Christ, my friend knelt, extended his arms horizontally from his shoulders, and closed his eyes. The man lowered the bricks to his ears and drew both bricks back by a foot, giving him the leverage to deliver a crushing blow.

My friend opened his eyes: "If you're going to hit me with these bricks, I invite you. Let's see you do it."

The leather-jacketed North-Central crowd smiled. The man tensed, considering the consequences of murdering a foreigner at his restaurant in front of his neighbors. The switch flipped back; he couldn't do it.

My partner got back to his feet. To the delight of the villagers, we handed him the equivalent of $20, kick-started our Minsks a few times, and gunned them. As we departed, I saw an airborne brick land in the dirt about ten feet behind us.

* * *

"Okay," I said to the proprietor of the truck stop in Thừa Thiên Huế province. "If you say the price is 130,000 đồng, then the price must be 130,000 đồng."

I gave her the money, she quickly pivoted, and I got back on the road. I reasoned that the inflated payment bought my way out of a nasty thirty-minute argument.

Maybe I hadn't overpaid for lunch. Maybe I'd overpaid for the idea that I could disappear into someone else's present—or someone else's past.

DMZ

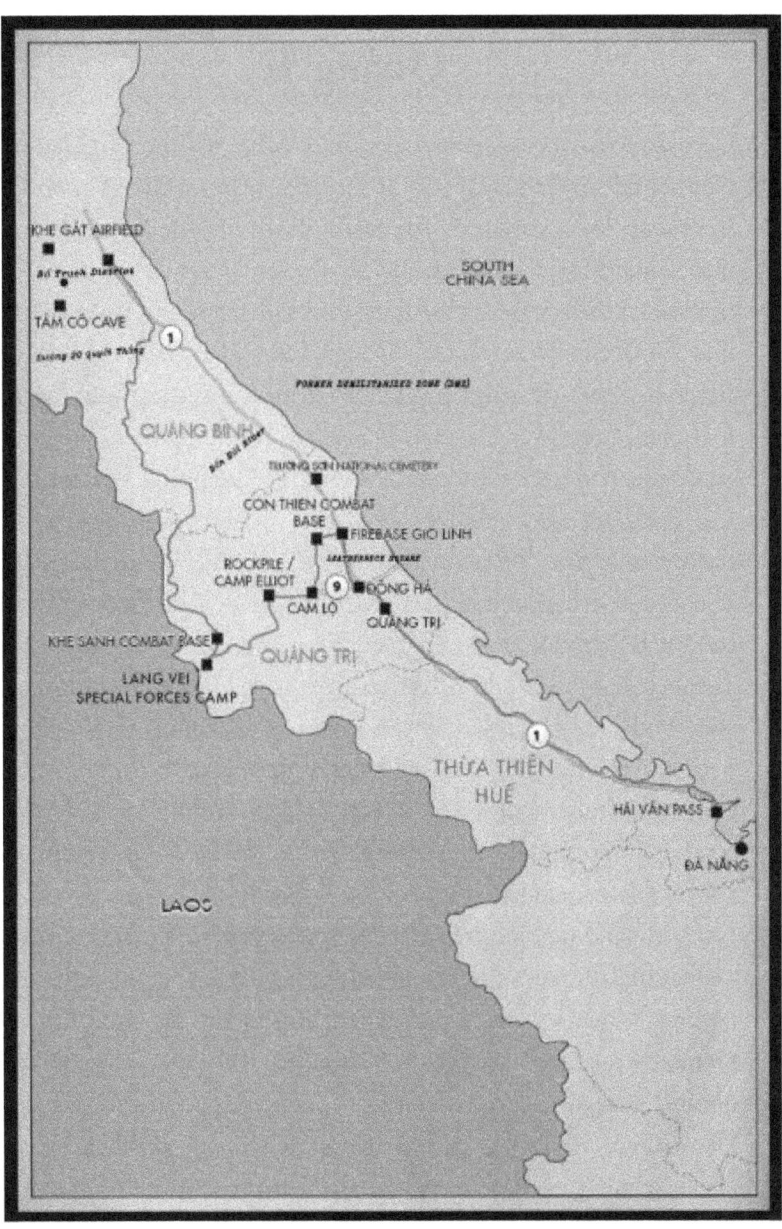

MAP: DMZ

Quảng Trị

Central Vietnam was the war's main stage. In the Highlands, the conflict felt tucked away—in the jungle, or in meadows gone fallow. In Quảng Trị, it surfaced. The Demilitarized Zone froze the conflict into something almost theatrical—seven years of standoff, static firebases, artillery facing artillery, tanks facing tanks, across a known line. Uniforms were visible through binoculars across the Bến Hải River. It wasn't shadows or guerrilla drift. It was spectacle: hardware, foxholes, firepower in plain view from the next hill over. The landscape had been rebuilt to match the tense politics of the age.

The land was smaller here, but the war was bigger. At its narrowest point, Vietnam is barely thirty miles wide. This is that stretch—the bamboo pole between two rice baskets—where the terrain tightened, the walls closed in, and both sides crammed in as much hardware and infrastructure as the space could hold. This wasn't the Highlands, where memory was buried in clay and overgrowth. This was coastal lowlands perforated with pillboxes and charcoal tombs, marooned in wet fields a hundred yards from the road, glimpsed only in passing. *Street Without Joy* country. The towns felt suspended. Light moved slower. At certain times of the year, rain and mist blurred the edges of everything.

Culturally, too, the tempo shifted. Huế is the custodian of the country's identity, less a participant in modernity—and the region seems to take its cue. Central Vietnam still lags a decade or two behind Saigon, even Hanoi. Tradition, conservatism, *bình dân*—these aren't things the region is anxious to shed. They are the baseline. Less Marvel Cinematic Universe. More bicycles. More black velvet. More poetry. More bright silk lanterns—pinks, reds, yellows, blues—against slate eaves or pale yellow plaster. Fewer ambitions, perhaps.

This is also where Vietnam's war tourism industry lives. It's where visitors slot in their DMZ day tour as they try to take in the whole country in two weeks. It makes sense here. There's more *mise en scène*. More signage. More scale. This is where the war posed for the camera. Central Vietnam most resembles the war as we saw it unfold—newsreels, still photographs, and later, the movies.

That wasn't an accident. Central Vietnam had infrastructure. Journalists could get there. There were roads, bases, and comfortable lodging. It was possible to film a war here.

And so this region became the living archive: what the world came to associate with the war.

* * *

Quảng Trị is a small city just south of the former Demilitarized Zone, which once divided North and South Vietnam. During the war, its proximity to the border—where thousands of North Vietnamese troops were stationed just out of view—made it a strategic flash point. The province hosted some of the most renowned American installations of the conflict: Khe Sanh, Cồn Thiên, Camp Carroll, and Đông Hà Combat Base. Until 1976, the city also served as the Quảng Trị province capital.

Quảng Trị city was devastated during the 1972 Easter Offensive. The PAVN overran the province in April, triggering an exodus of Catholics and those with ties to the Saigon government. Northern cadres moved quickly to collectivize agriculture, commandeer housing, and establish a military government.

Two months later, South Vietnam counterattacked. By that point, Hanoi had withdrawn many of its battle-hardened troops, leaving green—and often teenage—recruits to hold the line. They were concentrated in the Quảng Trị Citadel, a walled imperial fortress built in 1814. The ARVN's advance was grinding and costly, fought house by house, block by block. With the help of 5,500

American airstrikes, the South recaptured the citadel in mid-September. Nearly 8,000 South Vietnamese and more than 10,000 North Vietnamese soldiers were killed. Twenty Americans also died.

By the time the shooting stopped, Quảng Trị city had essentially ceased to exist. After the war, the provincial capital was moved to Đông Hà. Today, only four pre-1972 structures remain—bullet-riddled monuments to the campaign's spectacular violence.

* * *

I picked the Duyên Quê (Countryside Charm) *nhà nghỉ* across the street from the Quảng Trị Citadel. It was one of only two guesthouses in central Quảng Trị; most visitors lodged in the more modern and blander city of Đông Hà, seven miles up the road. I preferred Quảng Trị's small-town, leafy vibe over Đông Hà's mod cons. The building was a whitewashed five-story shophouse, maybe twenty feet wide.

I stepped into the foyer, a large tiled room that doubled as reception and garage. A heavy china cabinet strung with Christmas lights was immobilized in the far corner, wedged behind two Honda Waves and a Cub. Ten cases of bottled Aquafina were stacked behind a mahogany front desk. The whir of electric fans muffled the soundtrack of a dubbed Korean soap opera playing on a television in the next room.

A thin man emerged, his messy tuft of gray hair contrasting with his stale white tank top, faded white boxer shorts, and *dép tổ ong* honeycomb sandals—pretty much the uniform of the middle-aged male chief executive officer of a Vietnamese family enterprise. He moved lethargically as he weighed which of his three rooms to assign me, picking up different keys and changing his mind while rubbing his temples with his forefingers.

I detected a faint aroma of rice wine, and his body language suggested he was experiencing a hangover.

He handed me a 330-milliliter bottle of Aquafina and a key, pointing me toward the stairwell before turning and shuffling away without a word. The room itself was more than adequate. I had my own sink, toilet, and shower nozzle, as well as a 10-inch television bolted to the wall at a height of about eight feet, opposite the bed and probably 12 feet away from my pillow.

* * *

It was 2:00 p.m. and probably 110 degrees outside, but I crossed the street and stepped onto a low, arched bridge over the citadel's moat. The water below was still, with lily pads and lotus flowers congesting the moat's outer reaches, drawn to the quiet. The old imperial city's walls have a circumference of about 2,200 yards, roughly 1.25 miles. Some of these brick walls are original and 200 years old, crumbling, breached by vines and heat and time. Large stretches have been rebuilt since 1972.

During Vietnam's pre-colonial era, most of the country's provinces hosted these walled cities that served as imperial embassies for the royal family. French authorities eventually moved in and occupied them, transforming the citadels into colonial administrative centers; later, the U.S. military did, too. Inside the wall is where the mostly teen recruits of the PAVN made their last stand in the 1972 battle. They were surrounded and absorbed sustained fire from ARVN units outside the citadel; those walls are still pockmarked today.

I passed through the main gate. The Vietnamese government has reimagined the Quảng Trị Citadel as a peace park with a vast, tranquil sculpture garden. Sculptors from around the country contributed large pieces, most of which are Socialist Realism-adjacent in style and address themes from the conflict—family, patriotism, and sacrifice. In the middle of the park is a large mound of earth carved into a shrine and altar. As I passed, I watched a group of men in their seventies, PAVN veterans in matching tour company baseball caps, passing joss sticks to each other. Apart from the walls and moat, one original structure remains inside the citadel: part of a crumbling French colonial-era prison.

Beads of sweat multiplied and found each other on my forehead, and I could feel my shirt slowly gain water weight. As I stepped over the prison entrance's low granite threshold, cool to the touch, the air changed—not cooler, just tighter; it had nowhere to go. Tracing an interior wall with my finger, I found myself inside one of the dining table-size cells and stood briefly in a shaft of sunlight. A barred air hole, about the size of a soup can, punctured the opposite wall. Otherwise, the room was sealed. The air was humid, musty, and thick, like it hadn't moved in decades. I stood still and listened. There was nothing.

It felt like I had stepped into a tomb. This was one of the infamous places where Vietnamese revolutionaries once lived miserably, cramped in silence and heat, long before victory. Long before history made them statues or street names. I slowly backtracked and returned to the sunlight outside.

I drifted into a small museum dedicated to the 1972 battle, near the shrine. It was also crowded with older men wearing identical orange baseball caps. As I walked through the photo and document collection, one man tapped me on the shoulder. I turned to face him, and he gave me a quiet thumbs-up. I returned the gesture, and he continued on his way.

Around 3:00 p.m., my phone rang. It was Vũ, suggesting we meet that evening for fried chicken at a sidewalk *bình dân* tavern owned by his high school classmate.

I was still shaking off the prison's silence.

"Sounds like paradise," I replied.

"Okay. I'm outside; meet me at the Citadel South Gate."

Vũ was a local guide who specialized in Vietnam War sites—and unlike many of his peers in the industry, he actually does his research. A lot of guides in Vietnam are young, underpaid, and working off vibes. I'd once been told by a cheerful freelancer that the siege of Khe Sanh was a battle between France and the United States, which, to understate things, isn't good history. But when you're in the business of stuffing rear ends into tour vans at the rock-bottom prices, storytelling loses its importance. If a stalagmite in a cave looks vaguely unicorn-shaped, the line becomes "Local people call this formation 'the unicorn' because it looks like a unicorn."

Vũ wasn't that kind of fellow. He was born in Quảng Trị in 1975 and has lived there his whole life. Most of his clients were aging American veterans returning to the places where they'd served. That number was dwindling. So was the war.

* * *

Vũ glanced at me as we crossed the street. "There are three other pre-'72 sites still standing in Quảng Trị," he said. "Let's go. They're quiet too."

We started with Bồ Đề (Enlightenment) School, a few blocks away in the town center. The school sat on a lane shaded by mature trees, bracketed by two-story houses and small shops. It was once a Buddhist secondary and high school built by monks in 1959. Back then, Vũ told me, nearly a thousand students attended classes here—implying the small, bullet-riddled school before us was once part of a larger complex.

Large sections of the building's outer walls had been destroyed by rockets, and the craters and missing sections were left as-is, presumably as a reminder of the battle. The ground floor and courtyard of the school now serve as a makeshift floral nursery, where a woman in silk pajamas and a *nón lá* conical hat was selling potted plants and flowers. Several customers were browsing that afternoon, wearing motorcycle helmets and holding plastic shopping bags, unbothered by the building's insistent, violent, and melancholy weight.

I climbed the uneven and pockmarked stairs to the second floor; there was a gaping hole in the stairwell's outer wall—a direct hit from a rocket. Another rupture split the roof wide open. At the top of the stairs, an entire section of the outer wall had been lacerated, with rusted rebar rods poking inward from the edges of the blast. I stepped into a classroom.

Along the far wall, an original blackboard still hung in place. Someone had brought chalk in the mid-nineties and written a message—still faintly visible—in the distinctive cursive handwriting style taught in Vietnamese schools. Vũ translated it for me:

Bồ Đề 1967-1972 24th Reunion.
The school is still here.
But where are all the old teachers and old classmates?

As I took in the classroom around me—the dozens of heavy weapons pockmarks, the missing roof sections, and the floor depressions—the statement and question felt like they had come from someone uncertain whether anyone would ever read them.

The message seemed otherworldly. I stared at the message a moment longer. Then my eyes lifted.

Outside, beyond a jagged hole in the wall, a flame tree was in full bloom—dazzling orange against the ruin.

Flame trees bloom in spring. Vietnamese associate these orange flowers with the end of the school year and the beginning of summer vacation. When students say goodbye to teachers, friends, and, gradually, childhood itself.

The timing felt rehearsed. The tree was in full voice.

* * *

We left the school behind and drove to La Vang Church on the outskirts of Quảng Trị city. The road was flat and straight, flanked by rice paddies and telecommunications towers.

The shift from school ruin to spiritual terrain didn't feel like a shift at all.

La Vang is a place where the sacred still feels possible for Vietnamese Catholics. It is believed the Virgin Mary appeared on this site in the early nineteenth century to save the faithful from emperor-directed persecution. In 1820, Catholics built a church here, which was eventually destroyed in another wave of persecutions. It was rebuilt in 1886.

Less than one hundred years later, the Easter Offensive rolled through. La Vang's chapel didn't fall in one clean collapse—it came apart in layers, in single artillery shells. The steeple still stands, tall and tapering, detached from the chapel it once anchored. It rises alone in the center of a flattened plaza, a survivor who never moved on. Beneath it, the original tile floor remains: pale greens, light blues, and cream, geometric Art Deco, chipped but still patterned, like the ghost of a design ethic that belonged to a different Vietnam.

Cannons and rocket launchers razed the chapel's brick walls, or nearly did. They end in torn, saw-tooth edges that look more ruptured than ruined. Rows of pews sit outside under the sky, arranged in the outline of a church that no longer exists. In one corner, a plaque marks the spot where the Virgin Mary is said to have appeared.

And above it, on a grassy rise, overflow seating and concrete sculptures—fairy tale trees with olive-drab mushroom crowns. The contrast stirred something I hadn't thought about in years: discovering the channel from Sherbrooke, Québec on our New Hampshire television. I'd wander there occasionally for cartoons or children's shows—the colors were muted earth tones, the shapes off-kilter, the pacing strangely slow. It was a mesmerizing and alien psychedelia to an eight-year-old boy. It felt like another, perhaps Canadian, planet's idea of Earth's aesthetics.

The concrete sculptures defied dating. They didn't seem to belong to any era I recognized.

On the opposite side of the plaza was another pew area, aligned to face the steeple. Above it stood a spacious replacement church in the distance, probably built in the 1990s or early 2000s. Doing the math, it was possible the congregation had held services outdoors—for twenty years or more, open to sun, rain, and wandering spirits—before the new structure was finished.

It wasn't just resilience. It was ritual, repeated until it became something more mythic.

They kept the footprint of the nineteenth-century church alive in the open air, long after the nave and sanctuary's heart was gone.

* * *

We left La Vang and followed Highway 1 to Long Hưng Church, the last of the four surviving pre-1972 structures. The government hadn't restored it—only stabilized the ruin and left it standing as a memorial. It sat just off the two-lane road, a small chapel in a state of suspended collapse. The paint, once lemon-yellow, had faded to something closer to jaundice. Its front wall faced the traffic quietly, indifferent to the chest-high wild sugarcane growing on the road shoulder. It no longer wanted to be seen.

By all appearances, it had once been a modest mid-century modern church: narrow, efficient, gently geometric. Built in 1955, it was later used as a defensive position by North Vietnamese troops during the battle for Quảng Trị. What remains is a shell: the roof is gone, several walls are missing, and what's left is warped and chipped by hundreds of bullet holes and rocket gouges. Flora spills from the wounds in the walls and bursts through the tile floor, as if the land had grown impatient with the wreckage and begun reclaiming its original geometry, piece by piece.

Unlike La Vang, still alive with its rhythm of pilgrimage, we had Long Hưng to ourselves. I don't think Long Hưng Church gets many visitors. Despite the churn of the highway just beyond the sugarcane, the site felt a little detached from our dimension. Not haunted, exactly—just very, very alone. Even the usual detritus was absent. The sadness here felt physical, like a body that couldn't stop grieving.

A sign outside the chapel read: *Long Hưng Church a relic of the war. This place is the memorial of the bravery of our soldiers and people.*

* * *

The sun was low and the silence still clinging to us when Vũ turned to me. "Uống đi," he said—"Let's get a drink."

We drove back to central Quảng Trị and stopped the car at a sidewalk *quán nhậu* next to my guesthouse. In the shadow of the Citadel and its still moat, the tavern wasn't elaborate: red plastic chairs on the sidewalk, a cooler of Huda and Larue—central Vietnamese brands tied to Huế and Đà Nẵng. On a red plastic table next to the cooler rested a metal snack rack with bags of peanuts clipped to each arm. A middle-aged married couple operated the tavern, and a group of three fellows in their forties, wearing similar uniforms of slacks and polo shirts, gathered at one of the other tables as the afternoon's heat finally released its grip.

Vũ and I each ordered a can of Huda. The three men at the other table had been curiously watching us since we arrived—quiet spectators to the whole sequence. As we sat down, he traded glances with them. Vũ extended his can to mine, and the tap released drops of condensation onto the plastic table.

His first sip was a deep one. "I have to pick up my son from school. I'll be at your hotel in ninety minutes for dinner. Try not to get hijacked by those boys. They'll tell you it's just one drink." He took a second gulp, stood, and departed.

Few pleasures in life rival a sundowner on a plastic chair at a Quảng Trị sidewalk *quán nhậu*, so I gave myself permission to stay for one more.

As Vũ's car pulled away, one of the men called out, "Hello!" I was now alone at my table—visibly alone.

It's rare to encounter a Vietnamese eating or drinking alone; it's simply not a done thing. I enjoy dining alone sometimes, but such solitary lunches and dinners can be hard to engineer, as strangers will sit with me and make small talk out of sympathy.

He motioned for me to join them, his hand mimicking the act of drinking liquid out of a can. I smiled—torn between the lure of a serendipitous sidewalk lager with country Vietnamese and the sense that these guys were reading me a little too well. I had near-certainty on how the afternoon could unfold. It was the wrong night to hand over the controls to these gents.

I thanked the men for the kind offer and quickly emptied my can, lest I succumb to second thoughts. It had been a full afternoon, and the Quảng Trị tour was sometimes heavy—quietly devastating in places. To do the day justice, I decided to avoid the excess these boys promised and instead join Vũ for fried chicken and beer at his favorite *quán nhậu*, a family-run spot in a house on Highway 1. Vũ was closer to kin than they were.

* * *

After we dined, he dropped me off at my *nhà nghỉ*. The Citadel walls were shadows, quiet under a clear, starlit sky. The moon hung low. The calm before the following day's DMZ tour.

Vũ warned me that wandering spirits haunted this section of Quảng Trị. He assured me there would be ghosts in my hotel.

"Bro, your hotel is fifty meters from the citadel. Take care. I'll pick you up in the morning."

I lay in bed that night with the ceiling fan spinning overhead—Martin Sheen's opening scene in *Apocalypse Now*, but without the soft white institutional ceiling panels and hangover. The Duyên Quê, not an officer's quarters in Saigon. Sharing a room with the Citadel's ghosts, perhaps not alone, and too tired to care.

I did have lucid dreams, but then again, a gut-buster fried chicken dinner sometimes does that.

The Tape

I awoke at six the following morning to the sound of a hi-fi on the ground floor; the beat of a Vietnamese cha-cha-cha reverberated across the concrete structure of the Duyên Quê Hotel. Female and male vocalists exchanged flirtations in verse, culminating in a harmonized chorus. It was certainly loud, but the wake-up could have been predicted. *Well, I suppose it's their house*, I thought as I lay in bed. The song ended. Then a pause, lasting about the time needed to replace the cassette in the tape deck.

Then, those familiar arpeggiated piano chords—shy, hesitant. There was nothing disjointed about waking up at six in the morning to "Hello" by Lionel Richie blasting from the ground floor at a hotel in Quảng Trị. On this ten-day trip, it was inevitable.

The war is embedded in Vietnam's cities and countryside. But sometimes, it drifts out of the walls instead—carried by cassette. That morning, it came through a downstairs speaker. No one had changed the tape for my benefit. I was upstairs, out of sight. This was just how things lingered here.

I stayed in bed a little longer, letting the choruses wash over me. The song felt less like a throwback and more like a signal—one I'd heard before, though I hadn't understood it at the time. That understanding came gradually, beginning years ago, on a tour bus bound for Củ Chi. It was the first time I heard "Hello" deployed this way.

My initial brush with Vietnam War tourism came in 1998. I boarded a minibus filled with backpackers, but I knew I was chasing something different. For them, Củ Chi was simply part of the *Lonely Planet Vietnam* itinerary. For me, it was something closer to a pilgrimage. I'd already read *The Tunnels of Cu Chi* by Tom Mangold. I realized then I might be on the wrong bus. I was probably one of the few onboard seeking the illicit thrill of standing on the set of someone else's war—even if I believed a piece of it belonged to me, too. This was the first time I'd actually set foot inside the frame.

The North Vietnamese Army and the Việt Cộng built the 125-mile-long Củ Chi tunnel complex during the war as a network of underground bunkers, supply routes, hospitals, and hiding places—military infrastructure beneath the bombing grid. The tunnel complex served to move men and materiel undetected, and their purpose was to threaten Saigon and influence the villages on its outskirts.

Today, a portion of the original complex is more or less an amusement park. Combat correspondent David Lamb, in 2002's *Vietnam Now: A Reporter Returns*, nicknamed the commercialized former war site "Cộng World."

Tour guides in camouflage shirts lead crowds of visitors through rebuilt and widened tunnels. Tourists crawl through the tunnels and pop up through concealed openings for the Instagram shot. There are food stalls selling cassava and tea (Việt Cộng cuisine), a gift shop with "war souvenirs," and a shooting range where *Tây Ba Lô* can fire vintage M-16s and Kalashnikovs at about $2 per round.

Củ Chi is marketed as both reverent and fun. And in a way, it is—a performance of the war that feels entertaining and strangely clean. But I wanted something that pushed back. Something that required stillness, not spectacle. Something I couldn't walk through and process in an afternoon. I didn't want a reenactment. I wanted to do the work. To stumble into something unlit, alone with the air and the soil.

But it was the only bus I knew about back in 1998, and I went with it. Later, I'd find the right bus.

During the early years after 1995, when Vietnam reopened to tourism, many guides in the south were ARVN veterans. Most had spent time in re-education camps after the fall of Saigon. When they emerged, they tried to rebuild their lives but found themselves quietly locked out of the formal economy. Despite having a medical degree and years of experience as an army surgeon, for example, some took to selling single cigarettes on the street or pedaling *xích lô*—bicycle rickshaws—for tourists.

As the tourism industry grew, a few of these veterans found work as guides—a morsel of validation for skills no longer in demand elsewhere. They spoke English, knew the terrain, were actors in the country's history, and now had broad exposure to the revolutionary narrative. They had a foot in each of the former worlds, North and South. Tourism industry jobs also gave them access to foreign currency, in the form of tips.

In exchange, they had to walk a careful line. Tours led by ARVN veterans muted the southern version of the war, and the emphasis was on the victorious revolution. Most of the rest was left out. In retrospect, it made sense that my guide avoided serious talk on the bus in Củ Chi. The narration was gentle, the soundtrack even gentler. Nothing too sharp that day, as I recall.

Our driver played The Tape on the minibus sound system throughout the eight-hour tour. Our guide stood in the aisle, humming along for much of it. Perfectly unprovocative, The Tape fit right in. I didn't realize it at the time, but it was telling a quieter story—about how Vietnam had moved through its twenty years of postwar isolation.

Expatriates in Vietnam long ago coined the term "The Tape" to describe the cassette compilations of Western love songs that every taxi driver, tour guide, restaurant, and café played in the pre-internet era. The Tape greeted early tourists arriving in the mid-1990s, already mid-track. It stayed in heavy rotation for another fifteen or twenty years. Vietnamese born between 1950 and 1980 know it by heart.

The Tape's origins probably trace back to the 1980s and early '90s, when Vietnam was isolated from the world outside the Eastern

Bloc, a few Scandinavian countries, and some Asian neighbors. In contrast to pre-1975 Saigon—awash in home-grown and imported psychedelic rock, soul, and country—little international pop culture entered the country. After reunification, the Party encouraged Vietnamese to listen to patriotic music and traditional folk songs. The previous era's music was unwelcome in the new political environment and, sadly, many families had already hurried their record collections to the nearest landfill before the tanks rolled into Saigon.

But in the late 1970s, Vietnam began sending more cadres to Eastern Europe and the Soviet Union for education. During their studies, they quietly acquired cassette tapes from Moscow, East Berlin, Prague, Warsaw, and Sofia—bootleg recordings of Western pop. They brought them back home.

This trickle of outside music eventually intersected with broader forces a decade later, during a brief period of *Đổi Mới*-era cultural loosening around 1991, affectionately called the "Saigon Summer." This was Vietnam's *glasnost*: the government relaxed some restrictions on Vietnamese authors and artists, and new cultural and political space emerged. While literature took center stage—with landmark novels like Bảo Ninh's *The Sorrow of War* and Dương Thu Hương's *A Paradise of the Blind*, both reexamining recent history and ideology—music, too, found its way in. Vietnamese of a certain age fondly recall the promise of this period.

That promise took many shapes, some quietly luminous. The window also cracked to the world, and international music flowed in. In 1994, John Denver accepted an invitation to become one of the first Western musicians to perform in Vietnam since 1975. He played seven or eight nights at Saigon's 2,500-seat Hòa Bình Opera House.

Denver wasn't exactly at the peak of his powers in 1994, but that only made his presence more poignant—familiar, non-threatening, and sincere. Saigonese were eager to reengage with the outside world after nearly two decades of isolation, and I've heard that the entire residency sold out. They came for the music, yes, but probably also for what it represented—a reconnection, a small act of welcome. The crowds were surely there for "Take Me Home, Country Roads"—and I like to think they asked Denver to play it three or four times a night, as if willing the outside world to keep singing back. In its way, it may have carried the hush of protest, or at least the warmth of return.

"Hello," by Lionel Richie, was one of the first global hits to drift over the cultural and political wall the Party had lowered.

It became beloved. For those who remember that period, it carried something close to the transcendent—it suited a generation drawn to clean pop production and emotionally direct expressions of love. Its tone may even have traced a through-line back to *nhạc vàng*, the wartime melancholic ballads of South Vietnam whose melodies lingered even after they were driven underground. That "Hello's" vocalist was American was probably no small detail.

"Hello" signaled what might be waiting for Vietnam on the other side of its long season of repression and isolation. It arrived like a postcard from the outside world, suggesting that global life had carried on, and that Vietnam might be invited back in. For a people once closely tethered to France and the United States, I imagine that it felt like a hint that the overdue historical correction was coming. That relationships—once ruptured—could resume.

* * *

A Vietnamese-American friend once challenged me to go deeper on "Hello." He agreed that it wasn't a stretch to hear in it the aspirations and dreams of the Vietnamese people to rejoin the world during the late '80s and '90s. But, he said, the song struck a more literal chord, beginning with its emotional tone.

After the war, millions of southerners fled persecution, making daring escapes by sea or on foot—leaving behind homes, families, and customs. Those who stayed had to restart their lives under a new ruling class that distrusted them, navigating a political and moral order many detested. All had lost family members. To anti-communists, the Vietnam they knew and loved was gone. That sense of trauma lingers in Richie's melancholic voice and the song's arrangement.

In this reading, "Hello" is at its most literal as a metaphor for the rupture of the twenty-year relationship between South Vietnam and the United States. According to my friend, Richie's lyrics trace South Vietnam's unrequited love for the United States—and the betrayal of that love in 1975.

The relationship flowered in the 1950s and '60s, when South Vietnam and America met and grew enamored with one another. There were early red flags on both sides, but the pull was strong, and the bond deepened anyway. It was doomed: history wouldn't allow this epic romance to unfold. The United States cooled in the early 1970s, worn down by conflicts at home that no romance—however intense—could survive. In 1975, it broke off the relationship, and a long period of anguish and self-doubt settled over both former lovers.

In "Hello's" lyrics, the "I" is South Vietnam, and the "you" is America. South Vietnam is alone with its thoughts, sorting through the wreckage of a relationship it had tried to salvage. America, having gone "no contact" after the breakup, is silent—trying to forget the love ever happened. South Vietnam is confused and desperate, making one last, vulnerable appeal to its former lover.

It was an audacious, but elegant, reading. After all, "Hello" wasn't just a ballad. It was a requiem, a confession, a plea. In some way, it was probably protest music. It lingered for a reason.

***

"Hello" anchors The Tape. It's typically track number one. "Careless Whisper" by Wham! often comes next. Followed by "Take Me Home, Country Roads," and some curated ordering of tracks by Air Supply, Lobo, the Carpenters, and Modern Talking. Look for one or two Foreigner ballads, Toni Braxton, the Eagles' "Hotel California," late-career Elton John, the theme from *Titanic*, the Cascades, Barbra Streisand's "I Am a Woman in Love," "Barbie Girl" by Aqua, Boney M, Michael Jackson, solo Peter Cetera, "Right Here Waiting" by Richard Marx, Ace of Base, Michael Learns to Rock, the Spice Girls, "Lemon Tree" by Fool's Garden, Jason Donovan, Leo Sayer, and Andy Williams, for a historically accurate version of The Tape. I made a YouTube playlist of The Tape not long ago, and an experienced expatriate described it as a "lethal dose."

Even ten or fifteen years ago, it wasn't uncommon for service workers to queue up The Tape when a foreigner appeared. Sometimes it played in a car, or a café manager would switch CDs the moment a Westerner sat down. Not that they didn't enjoy it on their own—they certainly did, and still do. But in those moments, the gesture seemed aimed outward. Maybe it was to make the visitor feel at home, with a soundscape presumed to be familiar. Or maybe—more poignantly—it was a bid for recognition, viz., to "start by saying I love you."

But most tourists or expatriates in the 1990s and 2000s, unaware of this multilayered backdrop, rolled their eyes. They labored through the compilation, or asked the waiter to change the music. To them, The Tape wasn't just eclectic, dated, and weird—it was, to many Westerners, bad music. It didn't quite land.

When I heard it on that Củ Chi tour bus in 1998, I didn't yet understand the context, and I remember wondering who thought it was a good idea to pair a lecture on the war's violence with "The One

That You Love" by Air Supply. But I came around. The Tape meant more than I knew.

* * *

Downstairs at the Duyên Quê, "Hello" gave way to "Careless Whisper." I saw the handoff coming a mile away. Since 1998, two things had changed—I'd come to love both songs, and I'd come to understand what they were doing there together.

Leatherneck Square

After "Take Me Home, Country Roads," I rose and pulled on a pair of army pants. I put together a day pack—sunblock, charger, backup shirt. Another rest day for my motorcycle. Business had been good for Vũ the past few years, and he'd recently upgraded to a sport utility vehicle. It was waiting out front, engine running, a Vietnamese ballad playing on the stereo. Several of the sites we'd visit today I'd seen before, but not like this—Vũ cared about getting the story right, and in his way, shared my thrill in chasing it.

I climbed into the passenger seat of Vũ's SUV, and as I did, he turned down the volume on the stereo. The plan was to trace the outline of the DMZ's "Leatherneck Square," named for four big Marine Corps bases marking the square's corners. We would then drive west from Leatherneck Square on Highway 9, in the direction of Laos, stopping at Elliot Combat Base, adjacent to a natural skyscraper formation the Marines nicknamed the "Rockpile." These sites were just a few among the formerly dense network of U.S. and South Vietnamese installations along Highway 9.

After the Việt Minh defeat of France at Điện Biên Phủ in 1954, France withdrew from its former colony, and Vietnam was divided into northern and southern administrative halves along the 17th parallel, roughly the border between Quảng Trị and Quảng Bình provinces. The division was meant to be temporary, with nationwide elections in 1956, under terms set by the 1954 Geneva Conference, to unify the entire country.

Fearing the vote would favor the Communists, South Vietnam, backed by the United States, canceled its elections. Thereafter, the DMZ militarized. South Vietnam—with increasing U.S. backing—began reinforcing the region, expecting the North Vietnamese Army would try to roll across the 17th parallel to unify the country by force.

By the mid-1960s, as U.S. ground troops arrived in large numbers, the area around the DMZ became the most heavily fortified region in South Vietnam—anchored by new combat bases like Khe Sanh, Cồn Thiên, and Gio Linh, all linked by Highway 9. It was here that the United States military pursued some of its most ambitious—and least proven—tactical experiments, including the McNamara Line: a high-tech barrier of sensors, mines, and fences designed to spot infiltrators. It was expensive, fragile, and mostly ineffective.

By late 1968, nearly 100,000 U.S. and South Vietnamese troops were stationed in the DMZ corridor and northern provinces—backed by hundreds of artillery pieces, armored vehicles, and layers of air and naval support. U.S. warships fired from offshore, fighter jets and helicopters flew overhead, and firebases along Highway 9 delivered daily artillery strikes. If the war in Vietnam had a front line, this was it.

Some of it is still visible today, but it's hard to grasp the scale of men, materiel, and attention that was packed into this corridor during the war.

* * *

We entered Đông Hà, the northeastern corner of Leatherneck Square, just north of Quảng Trị city.

"Leatherneck Square alone had 20,000 U.S. Marines. When the Marines first arrived in 1966, Đông Hà was a village. In 1968, the whole Third Marine Division was stationed here. They built a runway, roads, and power station," said Vũ.

We prowled the narrow streets of what is now a small modern Vietnamese city, swerving around women pushing antique bicycles with baskets of dragon fruit tied to their luggage racks. Suddenly, I was launched forward, catching myself with both palms against the glove compartment.

"Moron," Vũ said, shaking his head.

A man on a motorbike, riding in the wrong lane, swerved to a stop just short of our hood, one hand on the handlebars and the other steadying a refrigerator balanced on the saddle. He quickly let go of the fridge to steady the handlebars. Propelled by momentum, the refrigerator toppled onto the pavement with a *thunk*. The man slammed his hand on the car's hood and barked at us.

Vũ steered around him, lowered his window, and returned fire with, "Thôi...ngu thế!" or "Stop it ... dummy!"

The other fellow had zero justification for hurt feelings, so my companion could have said something more potent. See earlier discussion on "face" and the ease with which the rules are warped.

Vũ turned to me, grinning. "Say rồi" (he's drunk). It was 8:30 a.m.

We turned left, joining a long, straight two-lane road. "The original Đông Hà base runway," Vũ said.

After one hundred yards, we turned off onto a narrow lane that gave his car a margin for error of mere inches. Vũ drove in without slowing, and the alley opened into a small plaza surrounded by tightly fitted three-story houses. A massive wartime airport hangar—concrete, curved, and gashed—loomed in the center of the residential plaza.

Vũ killed the engine, and we stepped out. "That scar comes from April 1972, when the NVA took Đông Hà during the Easter Offensive." He showed me a photo from that day on his iPad: a North Vietnamese flag flying from the top of the same hangar. I looked up: a small pink, white, and creamsicle orange victory marker occupied the gash area, and the one-story lemon-yellow Nhà Văn Hóa Khu 5 (Zone 5 Cultural House) building had been built adjacent to the aircraft hangar.

A man came out of his house. He was in his mid-sixties and, by the neat haircut, tucked polo shirt bearing an all-caps *POLO CLUB*

AMERICA across the chest, slacks, belt, and black vinyl loafers, looked to be a recent retiree who hadn't yet found the comfort level to abandon office dress and lighten up. Unlike one of those Jimmy Buffett-inspired longhair retirees one sometimes meets in Florida, say.

He had a small sitting area in front of his home, and the colossal hangar was his immediate view, thirty feet distant.

Dispensing with the *làm quen*, he began at the beginning: "I was young in 1972, but I remember it well. During the war, my family had to frequently move to refugee centers and houses to escape the violence."

I asked if he was from the neighborhood.

"I am not originally from this area," he said. "But my family moved to Đông Hà in 1975, when the war ended. I moved to this house in 1990. This area was still filled with war junk at that time—tanks, burned-out buildings, and lots of garbage."

The three of us stood together, facing the hangar; it was riddled with bullet holes. He drifted back to his balcony, maybe to wait for the next visitor. The man sat and raised his wrist in a casual wave. Though we hadn't indicated we were leaving, perhaps our time was up.

* * *

We drove the fifteen minutes out of Đông Hà to Firebase Gio Linh, which anchored the northeastern corner of Leatherneck Square. As we turned onto Highway 1, Vũ handed me his iPad, preloaded with photos of Gio Linh from 1967 and '68.

Swiping through the pictures, I could feel the heat of the place back then—the rich red soil of this coastal plain, the shirtless, sun-scorched GIs in Ray-Ban sunglasses holding shovels, and the stripped landscape of this base, perhaps the northernmost in the former South Vietnam.

Gio Linh, along with the Marine base at Côn Thiên, formed the top two corners of Leatherneck Square. Both of these camps were only one or two miles south of the DMZ itself; infiltrations, artillery shelling, and small-scale attacks were near-constant at both sites during the war. They were among the most dangerous postings for American Marines.

Gio Linh is right on Highway 1, and Vũ parked the car just beyond a burned-out American M-24 Chaffee light tank that occupied part of the highway breakdown lane.

"Careful," said Vũ, pointing.

On the hood of the tank sat neat stacks of rusty mortar shells and bullets, unexploded ordnance placed there by farmers cultivating this land, which today is a cassava plantation.

Entering the roadside tree line, we climbed over brush that soon opened up into the expanse of the plantation, the former Firebase Gio Linh. Four relatively intact concrete bunkers were still on the site, spaced apart by 75 yards or so, each overgrown with weeds and trees. Wandering through the oppressively sun-soaked field of three-foot-high cassava plants and inspecting the bunkers, I noticed more UXO stacked on each—weathered and rusted, but still not done being dangerous.

They sat in direct sunlight, heat bouncing off the red earth, as if someone had set them out to dry. Fifty years on, it still felt like a place where something could explode.

With UXO underfoot, no shade to speak of, and the heat already pressing in by 10:00 a.m., I persuaded Vũ to cut the visit short.

"Are you sure, bro?" he protested. I was.

As we ambled back to the car, I considered what it must have been like for a Marine in that searing heat, enduring the attacks and artillery strikes, without the option to return to an air-conditioned SUV. Or what it might be like to till this soil in this heat, sidestepping UXO and cultivating one of the world's lowest-margin crops, cassava.

Not a blessed parcel of land, Gio Linh.

* * *

We retreated west on one-lane country roads to Cồn Thiên, a Marine base atop an assemblage of three low-rise hills overlooking the Bến Hải River, which once separated North and South Vietnam. The site was strategically positioned to protect the enormous installation to its south at Đông Hà from the thousands of PAVN troops camped on the other side of the river.

In 1967 and into 1968, Cồn Thiên and the surrounding hills became a daily battlefield. The North Vietnamese sought to push the DMZ southward and lay siege to the installation. Artillery fire was unceasing—about two hundred rounds a day, peaking at twelve hundred in one day in September 1967. That same month, the American press picked up the story: accounts of the siege and the misery of the Marines stationed here began appearing on the nightly news back home.

All told, more than seventy-five hundred North Vietnamese were killed in action that year around Cồn Thiên, and nearly fifteen hundred Marines died defending it.

From experience, Vũ knew where to stop the car, get out, and walk. There are no markers of any kind for Cồn Thiên, one of the war's most reported battles—at least in the American press. Whatever memory this hill held wasn't official. And it wasn't for visitors. We parked on the side of a secluded rural track flanked by meadows and gentle hills hosting young cassava saplings. We climbed over a rickety wooden fence and began an easy ascent along a narrow path. One of Cồn Thiên's three hills is more accessible than the others, and that's the one we chose.

We soon encountered bits of war garbage that had rested here for over fifty years: half-buried sandbags, torn U.S.-issued rain ponchos, shell casings, broken white plastic spoons, medicine bottles, and combat boot heels. Vũ motioned to me and pointed out a shard of white metal sticking out of the topsoil.

"Gold in 1968," he said.

We unearthed it carefully. I recognized the red, white, and blue design instantly—not the modern branding, but the thick-lined tin of an older America. It was a crushed Budweiser can from the 1960s, airlifted into the war zone like so many others. I'd pocketed things before—a sandbag, a ration spoon. Nothing too intimate. Nothing that felt like it belonged to someone in particular. I hadn't written much about it, but I wasn't the only one. People do this, quietly.

The can felt different somehow. A familiar, culturally loaded object sitting in an extraordinary place far away. A gesture toward comfort in what was once one of the worst places on earth.

And still: the thrill. The proximity. That little ripple I feel when touching something that once moved through someone's hand, before everything fell apart. I pictured the Marine tipping it back, tossing it, and reaching for another. In hindsight, this was what I was looking for in Củ Chi in 1998. I slipped the can into my bag. This was a souvenir I'd keep.

Vũ and I finished our ascent. The cassava saplings gave way to a mature rubber tree plantation, and we surveyed the summit of our hill. He pointed out two more hills in the near distance; together, the three formed the entirety of the combat base.

I looked down; amid the rows of rubber trees and dried leaves on the forest floor were the remnants of bomb craters, trenches, and other carved-up land. Compared to Gio Linh's desert-like exposure to the day's extreme sunlight, Cồn Thiên was sheltered, shady, and isolated. It was several miles from Highway 1's constant flow of traffic. It was lonelier, but greener and more naturally overgrown.

I didn't see an altar or anything that acknowledged wandering spirits here. Still, there was a pronounced mysterious atmosphere, as if waiting long enough might reveal something ghostly in the tree line. Tree leaves flitted rapidly without any breeze passing by, and the shrieks of cicadas rose and fell seemingly without any terrestrial prompting, catching me by surprise.

Throughout 1967 and '68, there would not have been a quiet day like this one on this hilltop. This soil probably absorbed more anxiety, blood, panic, and fear over that period than most places in the country. Hundreds of people had perished here.

We proceeded, and shrouded in jungle growth ahead of us was a large, well-preserved concrete bunker with walls that looked 18 inches thick. It was eight or nine feet tall and had a modest footprint. The structure had taken on a dark, moldy patina from decades of humidity and rain.

But the bullet and shrapnel holes that covered both the outside and inside walls made one thing clear: it had taken heavy, sustained fire. I entered and found myself at a shelf and defensive opening in the wall, pointed toward the Bến Hải River, less than two miles in front of me. My view was dense rows of rubber trees and jungle—when Marines were camped here, that view would have been unobstructed, with no trees or vegetation.

Exiting the bunker, I noticed a concrete plaque on the ground in front of the entrance, on which the order *CẤM PHÁ HOẠI* (VANDALISM PROHIBITED) was etched. It must have come from a local authority, though it wasn't clear why this particular ruin was protected. Someone thought it mattered.

I stood for a moment before moving on. The bunker was brutal and compact and strangely intact, a small pocket of preserved violence weathering the jungle's attempt to take it back. I wasn't sure I was supposed to admire it. But part of me did.

I approached it as history. I approached a lot of things that way.

***

We descended the hill slowly, stepping over the occasional cluster of antique but live rifle ammunition on the surface of the trail's red soil. Then we drove south, toward Highway 9, passing several small cemeteries for *liệt sĩ*, or war martyrs. I asked Vũ about these graveyards.

"Local communes built these after the war. As people returned to their land, they needed somewhere to bury the soldiers they kept finding—in rice fields, on footpaths, in the woods. These small cemeteries are everywhere in this region. But you should know that they are for North Vietnamese Army soldiers and southern Communists only; they don't include ARVN dead. We don't officially know what happened to the bodies of South Vietnamese soldiers. It's not something we really talk about."

There wasn't anything to say. He wasn't looking for a response.

Quảng Trị is a bit smaller than Delaware, but it holds seventy military cemeteries, including the National Cemetery on Route 9. About two-thirds of the bodies found on battlefields were identified, usually because a soldier carved their name into their canteen or some other object. After the war, they were temporarily buried, exhumed, and returned to their home villages. Many who could not be identified remained unclaimed in these community cemeteries.

The scale of it all is easy to miss.

***

"These are the guys that won the war?" I asked. "It doesn't make sense."

Vũ and I had stopped at a roadside *cơm bình dân* canteen in Cam Lộ for a lunch of pork-stuffed tofu and *rau muống xào tỏi*. Cam Lộ was the southwest and final corner of Leatherneck Square, south of Cồn Thiên, and once hosted another United States Marine Corps base. Today, all traces of it are long gone; the town is little more than a few *cơm bình dân* restaurants and trucker cafés. Like so many of these sites, it had been overwritten without ceremony. Our table sat on the shoulder of the two-lane highway, with Hyundai Trago trucks kicking up sand just twenty feet away.

We were discussing regional differences in Vietnam, particularly what rural northerners like to have for breakfast. Knowing that Vũ is a central Vietnamese who, like many born and raised south of the 17th parallel, is a bit wary of northerners, I like to bait him with open-ended questions like this one, pretending I find northerners as mystifying as he does. And Vũ plays along, happy to entertain me. It was a game we both understood—regionalism as banter.

"Yes, these are the guys that won the war," he confirmed. Vũ extracted a set of long, white plastic chopsticks from the plastic cylinder on the table and cleaned them with a strip of toilet paper pulled from the roll that reliably sits on every aluminum *cơm bình dân* tabletop in the country. He cited some of the more punishing examples of rural northern cuisine: grilled rat meat, offal stew, sandworm pancakes, and hits from a *thuốc lào* water pipe jammed with extra-strong tobacco.

"These guys aren't morning coffee drinkers, but they do like their rice wine."

According to Vũ, country northerners are often intoxicated by six in the morning, before their workday begins. The rest of the country waits until the afternoon. I wondered how anything would get done in northern Vietnam if this were the case. He had an answer.

"Northerners arrive at construction sites or farms after breakfast, feeling drunk, strong, and cheerful. Once the labor starts, they lose energy. All it takes is another hit from a thuốc lào, and they're back in business—for a little while. They keep this up until lunch, which might be taken at a bia hơi tavern, and the rest of the day is easy."

While it may be hyperbole to say that rice wine and bong hits comprise a "northern breakfast," there is some truth to the theory. I spent a few years in Hanoi and have traveled throughout northern Vietnam. I have personally seen the evidence over 6:00 a.m. bowls of *phở* at country stalls—groups of men noisily burning through bottles of rice wine together, passing around the *thuốc lào* water pipe, and reluctantly sipping their bowls of *phở* beef noodle soup.

This feral breakfast, in Vũ's view, symbolizes the deprivations northerners are willing to endure.

"It gives them enthusiasm, spirit, and courage," he said, resting his case.

Based on this reductive but entirely credible hypothesis, that is how they won the war.

Finishing the tofu and morning glory, we dabbed the corners of our mouths with sheets of toilet tissue, stood up, and climbed back into Vũ's car.

* * *

We drove west on Highway 9 to the former Elliot Combat Base site, at the base of the "Rockpile," a lonely and dramatic 800-foot-tall karst tower overlooking the road. The Rockpile served as a Marine observation post and small artillery base during the war. Its summit plateau measured roughly 40 by 70 feet—not huge, but just enough for a few howitzers, some mortars, and a helicopter landing pad. It was a strange place to put a war—perched, vertical, barely accessible—but it worked.

All reinforcements—Budweiser, C-rations, ammunition, everything—came in by helicopter. The Marines saw the Rockpile and its neighbor Camp Elliot as good duty. The odds of survival were high, especially compared to nearby Cồn Thiên and Khe Sanh. The Rockpile was never really attacked or threatened after the Marines took the monolith in 1966—scaling it would have been absurd, even for the daring North Vietnamese. Yet beneath it ran webs of hidden trails that let Communist forces move through the DMZ with ease. There was no need to take the hill. They already had the ground beneath it.

The former Elliot Combat Base sits in the Rockpile's shadow, on high ground overlooking the valley that winds around the megalith. Today, Camp Elliot is a cassava plantation with a small open-air workshop and an industrial wood chipper. Five shirtless gents were busy operating the machine, crushing eucalyptus and cassava trees—raw material that might eventually get pressed into particle board and sold by IKEA to customers in the U.S. or the E.U. We strolled past the shop and caught the foreman's eye. He smiled like we were regulars. In the United States, two unauthorized visitors to this cassava plantation and wood shop would have been a problem. Not the case here.

We scaled a gentle slope overlooking the shop, dipping in and out of bomb craters that had withstood decades of tilling and planting. The soil looked freshly turned, and it had given up its inventory—poncho shards, sandbags, combat boot heels, and old MRE wrappers—casual litter from another era.

And then I spotted the now-familiar outline of white-and-red mangled aluminum poking through the soil. Another Budweiser can. This one looked deliberately hand-crushed, like whoever tossed it knew they were done for the day. It caught the light in a way that made the wreckage feel almost staged—like something preserved, posed, meant to be found.

I called out to Vū, who was crouched over the soil about forty feet away. He sat down next to me, nodded at the can, and pointed to a small mound nearby that hid the base of an M-16 round.

"You have a keen eye for this stuff," I said.

He looked up. "This is where I'm from."

* * *

Vũ was born in 1975, the year the conflict ended. He came of age in Quảng Trị during the decades-long effort to clean up the vast fields of wreckage the Americans and South Vietnamese abandoned to the soil. Quảng Trị was one of the most bombed places in the history of warfare. Still hidden in the province's folds of land are unexploded rockets, B-52 bombs, mortar shells, bullets, artillery shells, U.S. Navy rounds, cluster bombs, land mines, and grenades.

While Vietnam has made progress in cleaning up unexploded ordnance here since the 1990s and early 2000s, thousands of bombs remain buried in Quảng Trị's jungles and soil. When Vũ was young, UXO was everywhere. He recalled playing catch with friends, using unexploded cluster bomblets.

"We didn't know how dangerous this was. Nobody knew until people started dying. I played hide-and-seek in burnt-out tanks and American cargo trucks."

I nodded like I understood, which I didn't. Not really.

Despite the government's prohibition against the collection of war scrap, people began digging, collecting, and selling in the early 1980s. Vietnam's economy was devastated, and there were few other options in this part of the country. They learned by doing, with zero margin for error.

The government hoped to handle the ordnance cleanup on its own, but lacked the resources for something this big, this buried. Postwar Vietnam didn't receive much assistance from the United States for decades, but now the U.S. and other countries are helping to finance the effort. Even today, Vietnam spends heavily to clear leftover explosives in provinces like Quảng Trị—fifty years after the war. The land still gives hints. Some of them lethal.

Vũ continued, "I've seen this many times. After cutting a shell or a bomb in half, a collector would secure the gunpowder and find a buyer. Most of it went to fishermen so they could catch fish using explosives.

I was in class when I was eight or nine years old, and in the middle of a lesson, I heard an explosion outside. The school emptied. Three guys were sawing an artillery shell right next to my school. When we got outside, their remains were hanging from the branches of the shade tree they were working under. Bones and skin were everywhere, and there was so much blood. There was nothing we could do, so we went back to class. It was horrible."

I didn't ask any follow-up questions. I wasn't sure there were any. I'd felt it before—uneasy admiration, dressed up as curiosity. It still caught me off guard sometimes.

I placed the Budweiser can in my bag, and we quietly returned to his car. We drove east, retracing our steps back toward Quảng Trị.

As we did, I imagined how this now somewhat prosperous-looking countryside might've looked in the late 1970s: a moonscape of craters, destroyed military vehicles, maybe a few birds of prey circling overhead, and debris fields stretching to the horizon. Scavengers picking through what remained.

And there would have been children like Vũ, independently navigating the junkyard. It had always been easier to imagine the hardware than the kids climbing over it.

The car went quiet, and Vũ played a CD of Vietnamese pop music.

* * *

Forty minutes later, we entered Đông Hà, circling a towering statue of Lê Duẩn that rose over the city's main artery. Americans know Ho Chi Minh but never really knew Lê Duẩn. Maybe that was their oversight. South Vietnamese knew who he was. He was the Communist Party General Secretary from 1960 onward, having quietly sidelined Ho through internal maneuvering. He was the figure most responsible for North Vietnam's decision to reunite the country by force.

His imposing granite form was about twenty-five or thirty feet tall, overlooking the boulevard and his hometown. Like just about every V.I.P. Vietnamese revolutionary, Lê Duẩn was handsome. As we passed the statue, I wondered if it was a coincidence that so many Vietnamese Communist leaders throughout history cut such dashing figures: the adoring, if slightly performative, term *Ba Ông Râu*—The Three Beards—is often used to denote Karl Marx, V.I. Lenin, and Ho Chi Minh.

Vũ and I revisited his classmate's bar that night for another round of fish sauce-soaked fried chicken and Bia Saigon. The tavern sat in a small country house, with sun-faded red plastic tables scattered across the front garden. Like the night before, the owner—a woman in her forties—greeted us with a scuffed green plastic crate of 500 milliliter Bia Saigon bottles, a bottle opener, and an ice bucket and tongs.

We savored the evening, eating and drinking for a couple of hours as long-haul trucks passed us on Highway 1, horns blaring. Other customers came and went amid the backdrop of chirping crickets and a karaoke session underway at the house next door.

Several of them knew Vũ from school and, along with the restaurant owner, teased him about being a teenager who was friendless, a lousy student, frail, and positively luckless with girls. Vietnamese can be direct and tormenting with those they are fond of, and he took it gracefully. It was the kind of noise that warms a cold day.

* * *

Vũ dropped me at my *nhà nghỉ* just after dark. Our time together was done. He and I had been meeting like this for years—I drift into town, we walk the war, we catch up at a *quán nhậu*. We both knew we'd do it again.

"Hẹn gặp lại, bro," he said, pulling me into a one-armed hug as we shook hands.

I entered the lobby, peered into the living room, and then turned to the front desk to raid the bottled water. The CEO who'd checked me in was lying in a hammock in his underwear, head turned to the television. He stirred and approached as I leaned in to grab as many bottles as I could carry.

Unbothered, he shook my hand. "I'm drunk," he said. "I've been drinking beer all day. I feel very happy."

I told him I'd been at the *quán nhậu* with Quảng Trị's best fried chicken, with my friend.

"I've had a couple, too," I admitted. Hearing this, he let go of my hand and gave me a long embrace, rested his palms on my shoulders, and wished me a good sleep. I didn't know what this was, exactly. But it felt like something I'd keep.

Western DMZ

I awoke to the sound of an electric cold-cut metal saw caterwauling through stainless steel sheeting at ground level next door to my *nhà nghỉ*. I glanced at my phone: 6:40 a.m. Construction had started. I roused myself and prepared a Trung Nguyên G7 3-in-1 instant coffee from a sachet. Vũ had plans to meet an American veteran and his son today. They had flown from the United States to Đà Nẵng, and this would be the father's first trip back to Vietnam.

I would ride Highway 9 to the western end of the DMZ, solo, toward the Lao border. My first stop was Lang Vei Special Forces Camp, just west of the better-known Khe Sanh Combat Base. From there, I'd continue north into Quảng Bình province.

Quảng Bình was the southernmost province in the former North Vietnam. During the war, the region hosted thousands of Communist soldiers, most of whom passed through en route to Laos via the Ho Chi Minh Trail, ultimately infiltrating South Vietnam for combat. Riding into Quảng Bình meant I would be crossing the former DMZ alone on my motorcycle, an act that would have been the height of stupidity back in 1968 or 1969.

I packed and descended to the front desk. My man emerged from his hammock in underpants and the same tank top; he looked pale and wilted, with bags under his eyes and a slack jaw.

"Chào buổi sáng, anh"—"Good morning, older brother," I said extra cheerfully, stretching out the *ào* in *chào*, the way carefree southerners do sometimes.

"Un ... Anh đi a." — "Right. You going?"

The same man who gave me a long hug before bed last night.

I paid my bill, and he hurriedly retreated to his hammock.

* * *

As I ambled out of Quảng Trị, the sun was low in the sky, rising over Highway 9. A light mist lingered, and the hills were washed in cool greens and blues. Smoke from outdoor kitchens curled above the one-room houses as I motorcycled past Cam Lộ and the Rockpile. From there, settlements vanished for twenty miles of quiet road as Highway 9 curved south, and then west to Khe Sanh, roughly eight miles from the Lao frontier.

I arrived at Lang Vei an hour later. It was once a lonely observation post meant to track activity on the Ho Chi Minh Trail, about three miles over the Lao border farther west. Special Forces personnel trained Montagnard villagers on weapons, defensive tactics, English language, and first aid at Lang Vei. In theory, the goal was to train allies—but in practice, it was to co-opt the Montagnards into defending South Vietnam. Over time, many of these locals and their families settled on base.

In early February 1968, amid the broader Tet Offensive, Lang Vei became a target. The PAVN intended to push eastward along Highway 9, overrunning American and South Vietnamese positions as part of the larger shock and awe campaign.

At the same time, a separate war and revolution had long been underway across the border in Laos—one the U.S. had been entangled in for years, once considered the key front in Indochina. For Hanoi, the Lao frontier was strategic: the Ho Chi Minh Trail ran through this borderland, and the Communist Pathet Lao provided cover for its operations. The Lao revolution, too, would conclude in 1975 with a Pathet Lao victory.

The North Vietnamese took a small Royal Lao Army base near the border, and 350 royalist troops, weary and demoralized, evacuated, trudging into Vietnam at Lang Vei. They were met by twenty-four American Rangers and five hundred Montagnard fighters.

In the early hours of February 7, a group of North Vietnamese PT-76 tanks and troops crossed into Vietnam, following the path of the fleeing Lao troops. The tanks rose from the western treeline, quiet and deliberate, almost spectral in the half-light. The American, Montagnard, and Lao resistance was lightly armed. Desperate, they called in air and artillery strikes, but the tanks kept advancing. Still, the defenders gave ground slowly, and a U.S. Marine task force arrived to help them withdraw to Khe Sanh, less than seven miles inland.

Following the Rangers and Marines were six thousand Montagnards, their families, and the Lao troops. Most weren't allowed to trail the Marines and Green Berets into Khe Sanh Combat Base, as the Americans were suspicious that PAVN spies had infiltrated the group.

After fending for themselves for three days in the forest around Khe Sanh—locked out of the base they had followed the Americans to—the Lao were eventually airlifted back to Laos. The Montagnards dispersed into the countryside. They had fought beside the Americans. Then the wire closed behind them. More than three hundred defenders and ninety North Vietnamese troops were killed in the battle. Though seven North Vietnamese tanks were ultimately destroyed, this was Hanoi's first successful use of armor in the war.

*   *   *

Lang Vei today is a minor tourist site on Highway 9. The draw is a single vintage Soviet PT-76 tank on display atop a concrete foundation on the eastern side of the road. I pulled over and parked my motorcycle. About ten Vietnamese tourists had scaled the foundation and explored the tank, posing for group photos. Two men were asleep at the base of the display. I began photographing the tourists photographing themselves with the tank. Soon enough, some turned their phones on me, capturing me as I photographed them photographing each other. Perhaps the Vietnamese, too, enjoy a meta-joke. Or maybe the sight of me in the scene was simply unprecedented.

I crossed Highway 9 and found the actual site of Lang Vei Special Forces Camp, unmarked, just beyond the road shoulder and the tree line, on a plateau with a view to Laos to the west. Untouched since the 1968 battle. Dozens of bomb craters still pocked the plateau. This would have been the route that both the retreating Lao troops and the North Vietnamese tanks took to approach Lang Vei. I counted six or seven half-destroyed concrete bunkers, a well-preserved trench network, and trails that stretched for a hundred yards in several directions. I wound my way along the trails, pushing young banana trees to my side, and I began noticing dozens of bullets and unspent cartridges lining the trail—still there, half a century later.

Somehow, this was all familiar to me. Growing up, I was surrounded by this *mise-en-scène* in Hollywood films and my imagination while reading war memoirs. Lang Vei was so abandoned and thus well-preserved that it could have been the set for *Missing in Action IV*. In a way, it already had been—nothing had been packed up.

* * *

I was still groggy from the fried chicken party the night before and realized I needed another coffee. I rode east toward Khe Sanh and found a serviceable *bình dân* café on the ground floor of a two-story country home just outside town. The café was empty except for two men in their forties, sitting together and gently murmuring over glasses of *nước chanh* limeade. An instrumental guitar version of "Scarborough Fair" played on the hi-fi.

As I luxuriated in drinking a cup of authentic Central Highlands coffee in the Central Highlands, I realized that the ride north into

Quảng Bình province would be along one of the Ho Chi Minh Highway's most remote stretches. Though by last check my tank was three-quarters full, I wondered if I should fill up now—according to my map, the road ahead had no villages for many miles.

I approached the men at the other table to gather intelligence. The conversation stalled almost immediately, possibly because my Vietnamese was lousy or they were accustomed to a proper Khe Sanh accent. Or, they were too overwhelmed to process Vietnamese spoken in a foreigner's voice.

"Hello, brothers. Are you healthy? I am riding north today," I said, showing them the map on my phone. "Will there be any villages or gas stations on this road?"

They paused, trying to make sense of it—a foreigner speaking Vietnamese in their local coffee shop was not an everyday event. After repeating myself, one of the men gestured to his friend.

"He ... he's the one you want to talk to. He knows everything."

"Sure," I said, and repeated my question to the other man. He seemed very focused on me, trying to follow the gist. I was literally watching him think. There was no answer, so I asked again.

I waited, but the confused pause showed no sign of letting up. Neither of us was feeling very confident about this exchange any longer.

He finally looked down, shook his head slightly, and replied, "Ehhh ... không," his voice trailing. "Not really."

It didn't feel like a strong *no*. I asked, "Should I ride back to Khe Sanh town and fuel up before going north?"

He struggled, fixing his gaze on his tennis shoes. After a long pause, he said, "Ưn," which sort of means "affirmative." Often, a non-committal affirmative.

"Thank you, older brother," I said.

After finishing my coffee, I rode back five minutes to Khe Sanh town. There, I found a petrol station. My tank was nearly full, so I added a dollar's worth of fuel. I got back on the road and eventually passed the café again. A quarter mile beyond it was a large, well-lit gas station, bustling with customers and open for business.

This communication breakdown reminded me of motorcycle travel in northern Vietnam in the early 2000s, before the days of smartphones and digital maps. Vietnamese analogue maps were notoriously inaccurate and misleading, and the country's roads lacked signage. Yet other details were faithfully communicated: without exception, every bridge in rural Vietnam, even those twenty feet long, had signage on both sides announcing the bridge's name, length and height, the year it was built, and its load estimate. To most motorists, this is useless information.

Getting lost on one of these trips would put one at the mercy of northern villagers, who'd mastered the immediate geography of their surroundings but were often a bit foggier on the world outside their hamlet. Pulling over and asking for directions inevitably drew a crowd, jostling for a look at the map. Three or four villagers might argue about the best way to get to the next intersection or village a mile away, and they would ultimately fail to achieve consensus. There might be extreme variances in their advice: some would say north, some would say south. Normally, one would have to roll the dice at this point, get to another village, and start the ritual anew in search of an exit strategy.

* * *

Khe Sanh Combat Base was a mile up the Ho Chi Minh Highway, the same road that would take me across the former DMZ later in the day. Today, it is one of Vietnam's better-preserved war sites: the layout of the former base is understandable, and bunkers and trenches have been rebuilt, letting visitors walk the grounds of the Battle of Khe Sanh, arguably one of the twentieth century's more momentous sieges. There's also a museum and an intact runway. I have visited Khe Sanh many times over the years, as it is accessible and the anchor stop for the country's many minibus backpacker tours to the DMZ out of Huế.

Most Americans of a certain age know the name Khe Sanh. Between January and July 1968, around forty thousand North Vietnamese troops surrounded and besieged this big, remote Marine base on the western end of the DMZ. Khe Sanh Combat Base sat in a valley, vulnerable on all sides to surrounding hills. The North Vietnamese attacked from those heights, and the United States saw a parallel between Khe Sanh and Điện Biên Phủ, the 1954 battle in which French troops were defeated in another valley surrounded by Communist Việt Minh forces attacking from a ring of hilltops. Based on this historical parallel, the United States poured reinforcements into Khe Sanh, determined to hold the base at all costs, incurring thousands of casualties in the seemingly interminable six-month battle.

It is now understood that the siege was more likely designed to concentrate and distract American resources at Khe Sanh, enabling Hanoi to launch the 1968 Tet Offensive and simultaneously attack more than a hundred other military and civilian targets elsewhere in South Vietnam.

In the Khe Sanh Combat Base parking lot, I was greeted by several cheerful men in pith helmets and polo shirts peddling vintage dog tags and wartime Zippo lighters, most of which were of questionable authenticity.

They walked with me as I moved through the grounds, pointing out the old C-130 cargo transport aircraft in its final resting place on the camp runway, an M-48 Patton tank parked nearby, and a U.S. Army Huey helicopter, which had been lovingly restored. They also directed my attention to the hills surrounding the base, pointing out where PAVN units had been positioned, and what roles they played in the siege, with the breezy authority of men who'd explained it a hundred times before.

I thanked them for the quick-hit tour and made my way to the octagonal-shaped base museum. The museum is relatively small, about the size of a two-car garage. Yet, it is triumphant. I followed the battle's timeline through documents and black-and-white photographs displayed in glass cases. The pictures were invariably exultant, with Communist troops storming Khe Sanh, loading artillery shells, hauling supplies, or scrutinizing maps in the field—always smiling, always purposeful.

Alongside the visuals were recovered guns, bombs, radios, uniforms, and other combat articles from the era. As usual, the final chapter focused on Khe Sanh today, with emphasis on the region's revolutionary credentials: like all towns in Vietnam, Khe Sanh contributed to the national effort to achieve poverty reduction and scientific and technological advancement under the banner of socialism.

After concluding my loop on this visit, I lingered at the museum visitor register. The open book was on a podium; I hadn't noticed it on previous trips.

Flipping through the pages, I was captivated by the contrast between foreign and Vietnamese messages. Foreign visitors felt sadness and shame for what America did in Vietnam. One visitor from Canada wrote, "The tragedy of this place knows no bounds." Others quoted popular songs of the era, such as "War. What is it good for? Absolutely nothing," attributed to Edwin Starr, or "Give peace a chance—John Lennon."

Fair enough, all of it, as these are unassailable sentiments from Western tourists seeking some measure of atonement.

Vietnamese language comments, however, were much more confident, often variations of "Việt Nam Muôn Năm!" (Vietnam forever), "Việt Nam Là Vinh Quang!" (Vietnam is glorious), or simply "Tôi Yêu Việt Nam" (I love Vietnam). This contrast was revealing.

Perhaps these were foreign visitors at the last stop on a DMZ tour—a long day of visiting former American and ARVN bases, absorbing narratives of the American War, imperialism, devastation, and the staggering wrongness of it all—and were now ready to speak. They wanted to add to a narrative, any narrative, or at least be heard.

But maybe they missed the point: the museum's Khe Sanh narrative, the revolutionary narrative, is largely celebratory. The war wasn't a mistake. It was the only choice. It was a painful rebirth, but it had to succeed. And it did.

While the sorrowful tourist quotes were sincere, this Western narrative seemed unimaginative, redundant, and even out of place in this context. The museum presents Khe Sanh as a symbol of a people's struggle against overwhelming odds, fierce combat, ingenuity, strategic and organizational brilliance, loss, and ultimately the vanquishment of an enemy. The story is decidedly not one of victimhood, apologies, reconciliation, and peace.

I closed the visitor's book and stepped out. The two narratives clashed quietly, two versions of a story side by side, one side in particular not really seeing the other. It's not often I get to witness that kind of friction in the space between history and memory, all on one page.

Quảng Bình

At Khe Sanh, I rejoined the Ho Chi Minh Highway, the scenic, two-lane road that connects Hanoi and Saigon via western Vietnam. I'd ridden a stretch of it earlier in the trip, through the Central Highlands. Environmentalists have long scorned the highway as bloated, destructive, and largely unnecessary, especially since most of the country's population centers and logistics traffic are concentrated to the east.

However, big infrastructure projects are embedded in Vietnam's DNA; they're irresistible. A project that commemorated and paved sections of the country's most ambitious infrastructure effort—the wartime Ho Chi Minh Trail—while simultaneously pushing out public resources to underserved provinces ahead of the quinquennial Communist Party National Congress in 2001, was self-evident. *Of course* Vietnam was going to build the Ho Chi Minh Highway. Construction began in 2000.

Perhaps the environmentalist critics weren't entirely wrong. From Khe Sanh, the well-paved and eerily underused road grew increasingly quiet. No hamlets were to be seen, and neither buses nor trucks were blaring horns or performing aggressive overtakes.

The mountains unfolded—the Annamite range, stretching along Vietnam's western frontier. This was a wild section of Vietnam. The forests I rode through were as lush as anything I'd ever seen, with heavy-limbed trees and furry branches towering on all sides.

The road wound upward, empty and slow. I climbed through thirty miles of ridge lines and switchbacks, taking nearly two hours.

At some point, I crossed the former DMZ and entered what had once been North Vietnam. The absence of markers or monuments suggested that the old boundary held little interest for Hanoi or the two provincial governments.

If these forests could speak, the conversation would be rich. The land was undoubtedly once host to networks of trails and camps hidden beneath the triple-canopy jungle—covert movements of PAVN troops and gear, American aircraft soaring overhead.

The road began a gradual descent but continued to throw switchbacks and hairpin turns my way. After three hours, I encountered my first pedestrian: a lone man wobbling down the road, carrying a large stick and wearing camouflage army surplus.

Even at a berth of twenty feet, his spicy aroma of pilsner and *thuốc lào* tobacco smoke was unmistakable. I marveled at his ability to find a party on one of Vietnam's most windswept roads.

By that point, I'd entered the familiar terrain of mild road delirium. The same mental haze that once had me plotting a Hulk Hogan-in-jail painting on the road to Điện Biên Phủ—and the encounter triggered a memory of a 2009 ride through western Laos. On that occasion, I passed a pickup truck on the shoulder, ringed by Lao farmers. A man in the cargo bed was handing out Kalashnikovs—one for each of them. I figured I didn't have "need-to-know" clearance, so I kept my eyes focused straight ahead.

Twenty minutes later, I came across a tiny settlement and then another. Approaching a third, I was pulled forward by the siren call of gaudy, deafening Vietnamese electronic dance music. I slowed and crawled past what must have been fifty motorbikes—Honda Dream IIs, Chalys, and Waves—lined up on the Ho Chi Minh Highway beside a crowded outdoor tent.

The marquee was made from scaffolding poles and vinyl tarps, but carefully dressed: red and white fabric draped in pleats, floral arches framing the entrance, and dangling beadwork swaying gently. Beneath the crowded canopy, guests sat at long banquet tables, calling to one another across stacked cases of beer.

It was a rural street-side wedding party. Outside, three flushed, middle-aged men sat on red plastic stools, drinking cans of Bia

Saigon and lazily passing around a bamboo *thuốc lào* pipe, its smoke curling out from the top of the cylinder. When they spotted my face through my helmet—a foreigner's face—they whooped and motioned for me to stop. One man hustled to the middle of the road, waving his arms. A chance informal invitation to a roadside wedding reception.

I smiled, saluted, and gently rode around him. Having been through it before, I knew the chances that I'd find myself vigorously intoxicated within twenty minutes of pulling over were close to 10,000 percent.

* * *

Moreover, I had an appointment to keep that day. My destination was the Phong Nha Farmstay, operated by Ben Mitchell and Lê Thị Bích, an Australian-Vietnamese couple. They had built a boutique hotel in Bích's ancestral village, located in the Bố Trạch District of Quảng Bình Province, adjacent to the wildly beautiful Phong Nha-Kẻ Bàng National Park. Ben is an adventurer and conservationist, locally known for his contributions to exploring and preserving this stretch of the Trường Sơn.

Visiting Bố Trạch offered a rare chance to understand what things were like on the northern side of the DMZ—a region barely footnoted in American history books. Bố Trạch had been a key staging ground for PAVN troops and supplies moving toward the front, either across the DMZ or down the Ho Chi Minh Trail. As the Trường Sơn foothills bottomed out into flatland, the air temperature rose, and I turned off the Ho Chi Minh Highway, riding northeast toward Bố Trạch.

I arrived at the Phong Nha Farmstay an hour later, approaching the front desk still in my helmet, combat boots, gloves, armored knee pads, Kevlar-reinforced jacket, and jungle fatigues, with motorcycle saddlebags in hand. Across the lobby, the hotel manager sat on a sofa with a French family, casually walking them through tour options for the next day.

Seeing her supervisor engaged, the concierge sweetly suggested I take a swim in the Farmstay's beautiful pool while waiting. I reflected on the logistics of the recommendation: I would have to ask around to borrow a men's swimsuit, and if successful, remove all my muddy motorcycle gear, boots, gloves, and jacket in the poolside men's room. I'd then need to find a place to store that gear, take a shower, swim, exit the pool, request a towel, shower again, dry off, dig through my bag for clean clothes, dress, haul everything back to the front desk, formally check in, and finally lug the dripping swimsuit and loose gear to my room.

A pre-check-in swim felt impractical. I smiled through my motorcycle helmet. "Thank you very much for the suggestion. But I think I'd like my room first."

The manager then saw me and handled it gracefully, inviting the other guests to flip through a brochure while she checked me in.

* * *

I dropped my bags in what were easily the classiest quarters of the trip, a warm, tropical-style room with wood flooring, a massive bed with clean sheets, a reading lamp, a lush restroom, and a glass door that opened to a balcony overlooking a landscaped garden. It felt like I'd stepped into someone else's holiday.

I met Ben a few minutes later, and we set out to tour Bố Trạch in his 1968 Willys Jeep—built in Toledo, Ohio, and shipped to Vietnam by the U.S. Army. Ben's Jeep rode rough, and the shock absorbers had largely retired, but it was a joy to travel in a vehicle with so much history.

Most American vehicles from the war era aged out of commission long ago and were scrapped. But a few survive, kept alive by ingenuity and patchwork repairs. In Saigon, I still encounter the occasional late-'60s Ford Thunderbird or early '70s Mustang—somehow functional despite their age, thanks to Bondo and resourceful hands. A neighbor of mine in Saigon even owns one of the five known remaining Harley-Davidsons left behind by American military or civilian personnel: a beautiful 1968 Sportster. I've said plenty about Harleys already, but '60s Sportsters—especially those marooned in Saigon for 50 years—get a pass.

Bố Trạch felt like a rural idyll. We rattled through verdant country lanes walled in by bamboo groves, gardens, and the occasional one- or two-room farmhouse. Avocado, guava, lychee, and grapefruit trees lined the road in casual abundance. Buffalo and oxen wandered freely, and kingfishers rested on electricity wires, surveying conical hat-wearing farmers bent over in their paddy fields.

The Edenic calm masked a much darker past. Quảng Bình was a hub for the revolution and, consequently, violence for vast stretches of the twentieth century. Ben drove me to a patch of fallow land near the Farmstay, where a single pillar stood in a field. It looked out of place—tall, narrow, moss-covered, and alone.

"This pillar was half of the original temple entry gate," Ben said. "It's the only thing that survives from what was once a village here—probably two hundred houses and one thousand people."

He paused, then added, "During the revolution and colonial era, Quảng Bình was essentially one big Việt Minh guerrilla base, Bố Trạch included. The province was insecure, and the French Colonial Army terrorized this village in the late 1940s. During the American War, Bố Trạch was a staging area for northern troops headed to South Vietnam. American air strikes destroyed the houses and shops that were there. B-52s atomized Bố Trạch."

As the war with South Vietnam ramped up, northern soldiers bound for the front often spent time in this PAVN forward base—resting, regrouping, and completing a final round of combat training before deployment across the DMZ. Phong Nha itself was an entrepôt. Supplies were trucked in, stored in caves throughout the region, and quietly ferried south by smaller vehicles, bicycles, or porters along the Ho Chi Minh Trail.

Before the United States committed major forces to South Vietnam in 1965–66, North Vietnamese troops could cross the DMZ on foot with relative ease. But as the U.S. fortified Route 9 in Quảng Trị with a chain of large bases and strong points, the north began redirecting its forces and supplies through Laos and Cambodia instead—upgrading and expanding the Ho Chi Minh Trail.

North Vietnam routed some of its most important arteries through Phong Nha. Ben and I prowled along Đường 20 Quyết Thắng (Highway 20, or "Victory Road"), a feeder route that wound west toward the Lao border. It ducked through triple-canopy forest, slipped beneath stream beds, and passed caves used to conceal trucks during daylight hours. In the hills, it threaded into the broader Trail system that crossed into Laos and beyond.

So much moved through Quảng Bình—troops, trucks, weapons, fuel—that it became one of the most heavily bombed provinces of the war. PAVN anti-aircraft guns shot down hundreds of American aircraft above Quảng Bình. Around 30 percent of the bombs dropped on the province never detonated. Unexploded ordnance remains a serious threat, having killed nearly 3,500 people and injured another 5,000 since the war ended.

* * *

Ben turned the jeep off Victory Road, and soon we pulled up to the Bomb Crater Bar—an unadorned bamboo hut of a tavern on the shore of the Son River. Plastic tables and low chairs rested wherever the last customer had moved them, beneath a stand of swaying bamboo. Faint water rings lingered on the tabletops. Two enormous craters pocked the grounds, remnants of a 1971 B-52 strike on a fuel storage tank. The river moved past in slow, silty coils as we each ordered a glass of *nước chanh*, or fresh lime juice.

Ben had been in the district for more than a decade, and was accustomed to talking about Phong Nha with visitors. He was effectively one of the region's tourism ambassadors—though the role didn't always sit comfortably.

"It's like Serengeti around here in September," he said, motioning to the valley around us, backed by the foothills and peaks of the Trường Sơn and Hoành Sơn ranges near the Lao border. "After the first rice harvest of the year, these paddies are filled with grazing cows and buffalo. Despite the breakneck development here, it's still magical. September is my favorite time of year in Phong Nha."

He turned his attention to the tourism boom that had arrived in one of Vietnam's least urbanized provinces—a sweeping change that started with a discovery.

"Sơn Đoòng Cave. Sơn Đoòng Cave has changed Quảng Bình for good," Ben said. "A cave so big that a Boeing 747 could fly through it."

It all started with a Vietnamese teenager named Hồ Khanh. In 1990, he was out hunting in the jungle when he lost track of his friends. A storm rolled in, and he ducked under a tree to wait it out. When the rain finally eased, he looked up—and saw clouds drifting out of a cleft in the side of a cliff.

Curious, he followed the mist and stumbled upon a gargantuan cave entrance. Eighteen years later, Khanh showed it to a group of visiting British cavers. By then, the government had designated the region Phong Nha-Kẻ Bàng National Park, which was recognized as a UNESCO World Heritage Site in 2003. But the cave was still something of a secret. The British team was stunned, and they returned two years later to take formal measurements. It was over five miles long and about 1.4 billion cubic feet. Sơn Đoòng didn't open to tourism until 2013.

When it sniffs an opportunity, Vietnam's tourism industry moves with maximum velocity.

"Phong Nha is going to be spoiled, sadly. We're trying to convince the government to apply the brakes, but it's been a slog," Ben remarked, referring to the dozens of new low-end hotels and restaurants around Phong Nha town. Shabby hotels had sprouted up everywhere, practically overnight. Families had retrofitted their homes as guesthouses. A land grab was on, and paddy fields had become construction sites.

"Money is rushing in from Hanoi; none of this is planned out in any way, and it's all being done as cheaply as possible. Quantity over quality, unfortunately," he continued.

Ben had a point. But demand for tourism had exploded over the previous decade, as Vietnam entered middle-income status. The country now welcomes more than 15 million foreign tourists and 80 million domestic travelers annually. Chinese, European, and Korean tourists had joined the flow.

Despite official hopes to grow the high-end segment, most of the country's tourists are budget-conscious and travel in large groups—through tour agencies or informally with extended families. Vietnamese developers and entrepreneurs know this demographic well and are comfortable striving for quantity in a landscape of ultra-thin margins: room rates are cheap, booze is cheap, karaoke is cheap, buffets are cheap, and bus tours are cheap.

The result in places like the northern hill station Sa Pa, the ancient city of Hội An, and the Riviera-aspiring Nha Trang is severe overcrowding, haphazard infrastructure, noise pollution, and streets and beaches filled with rubbish. The ambiance that once made these places special has quietly vanished.

Ben had good reason to worry that Phong Nha, one of the most breathtaking parts of the country, was starting to resemble other once-charming places—places whose decline many Vietnamese and long-term expats quietly mourn.

We finished our *nước chanh* and drove back to Ben's Phong Nha Farmstay. Adjacent to his hotel, construction was underway on a second facility—a set of high-end villas with swimming pools and mountain views. He noticed a disagreement between several of the workers he'd hired, so we pulled over. I couldn't make much sense of their dispute, but their confused faces suggested they were struggling to communicate even with each other.

Like many countries, particularly in this part of the world, Vietnam has countless regional variations on its national language. Geography, migration, and conquest have shaped its diversity. Some would argue that the borders, language, and even the idea of Vietnam as we know it today have only existed for about two hundred years. Even within regions, provinces are further divided by hamlet and village. Differences in accent, vocabulary, and grammar create communication barriers, even between neighboring hamlets.

Their foreman helped them straighten things out. Ben turned to me. "If you hired six people from six different hamlets across Quảng Bình to lift a table into the back of a truck, you'd be surprised how long it would take. They'd spend most of the time trying to express, translate, re-translate, and agree on a plan that everyone understands."

At that, Ben and I parted ways for the evening. I returned to my palace of a room and took one of the complimentary ice-cold Bia Saigons that had been waiting in my refrigerator out to the balcony. I sat in front of a panorama that stretched for miles, in stages—a huge tract of paddy, Victory Road, the Son River, and the Trường Sơn mountain range in the distance. Clouds gradually embraced the setting afternoon sun.

Formerly the critical forward base of the war, Bố Trạch District was now a postcard.

Sơn Đoòng, and everything that came with Sơn Đoòng, was outpacing this place's older identity. They still coexisted, for now. And maybe that was what drew me in—the friction. Not history as it was kept, but as it kept showing up. I said I was here for what endured. But part of me kept watching what was slipping away.

* * *

I went to the poolside restaurant for my evening meal. Below me, farmers worked the paddy fields in the valley, while others rested beside their grazing cattle.

I listened to a pitch from my waiter. The Farmstay, I learned, had Quảng Bình's most outstanding chef, a gentleman imported from Hanoi.

Despite noticing some Western favorites on the menu—and realizing I was craving my first pepperoni pizza in a week—I felt some pressure to try their kitchen's *chef-d'œuvre*. It was *bún chả*, a Hanoi specialty. *Bún chả* is an apocalyptically succulent rice noodle and barbecued pork dish served with a sweet broth and herbs. Having lived in Hanoi, I know *bún chả* well, but I was told <u>this</u> *bún chả* was a revelation. It was a tourist recommendation, an opportunity to discover a dish in the pantheon of northern cuisine.

As we've discussed, Vietnamese tend to firewall lunch and dinner dishes from each other. *Bún chả* is not one of those grand dinner dishes normally paired with an alcoholic beverage.

Some Vietnamese I know were amused when they saw photos online of President Barack Obama and celebrity chef Anthony Bourdain eating *bún chả* together during the president's visit to Hanoi in 2016. The media was a PR coup for the trip, designed to impart good vibes and go viral. But someone had advised them to dine at a street *bún chả* restaurant at night and be photographed drinking bottles of Bia Hanoi while eating.

Bún chả is a midday food, slurped with a glass of iced tea. Or it's a nighttime snack. That's the extent of it.

"Why are the Americans drinking beer with *bún chả*?" was a question I heard more than a few times after the photos and film clips began circulating. "Who would *do* that?" was another refrain.

A rough equivalent, I suppose, would be a photo-op of the Prime Minister of Vietnam dining on a double cheeseburger and a mug of piping hot clam juice for breakfast in Washington, DC.

I folded. Based on the recommendation, I committed the peccadillo anyway, ordering a bowl with a can of Bia Saigon. It was unquestionably delectable *bún chả*, but the whole thing felt a little weird.

Đường 20 Quyết Thắng

I met Ben again the following morning. He introduced me to his childhood friend Stu, a recent émigré from Australia. Stu had retired from a career as a firefighter and moved with his family to Phong Nha, joining Ben. The three of us set out that day on a motorcycle trip—not to visit Sơn Đoòng Cave (which requires a ten-day guided underground trek), but to explore many other lesser-known caves and sites from the province's history as a staging ground for the North Vietnamese Army.

After visiting many former American and South Vietnamese base sites, I would see what things were like on the other side of the DMZ. The situation, I assumed, was much more austere. And I was right—the North Vietnamese Army had spent much of its time in Quảng Bình's caves.

We rolled onto Đường 20 Quyết Thắng (Highway 20 Victory Road), winding along its curves beneath the shade of drooping bamboo groves and tropical canopy. This natural roof opened, and we soon found ourselves out of the forest, ringed by distant peaks, karst formations, and cliffs.

Fifteen minutes in, Ben slowed, and we pulled over at a *tạp hóa*, a general store in a dilapidated wooden shack. The sun was climbing; it would be hot soon. Across from the *tạp hóa* were a few tall and narrow bald karst peaks, their lower flanks covered in vegetation that reached the road.

"Giáp's Cave," Ben said, pointing to a spot halfway up the nearest peak.

There, a circle of exposed rock surrounded a dark opening. Local legend holds that North Vietnamese Army Commanding General Võ Nguyên Giáp, who vanquished the French Colonial Army at Điện Biên Phủ, visited PAVN soldiers camped here in the late 1960s.

A boy emerged from the back of the *tạp hóa*, barefoot and wearing the red-and-gold Vietnam national soccer team kit. He looked about twelve years old. Being a salesman, he motioned to the shelves of his parents' shop, which were stacked with bottles of La Vie drinking water, sachets of single-use shampoo hanging in perforated strips from the ceiling, and cases of Bia Hanoi and Bia Saigon stacked side by side on the floor—a neutral offering astride the former DMZ between north and south. Beyond the beer were Sting energy drink, gum, Dr. Thanh's oolong tea, nail clippers, and sunglasses.

After acknowledging the largesse, Ben asked him about the cave.

"I'll show you," the young man said, and we followed him across the street.

We trailed the boy up a dirt path that ran straight up the mountain. It soon narrowed into a verdure tunnel, and we crawled along at a steep, 60-degree angle until we came upon a cement staircase. At the top of the stairs was a small entrance to the cave. Parts of the rock wall around the entry had been sheared off, likely from an American air strike. The air inside was cool and moldy; the light seeping through the entrance soon gave way to darkness.

We turned on our phone flashlights, illuminating a platform at the room's far end. Unexpectedly, it was an eight-inch tall, eight-foot-wide stage carved from rock—something public, ceremonial, tucked inside a space meant for hiding.

Feeling faint gusts of breeze on my cheeks and ears, I imagined General Giáp holding court on this stage, surrounded by troops. On less opulent days, this dais might have been used to deliver news updates, lead discussions on Marxist-Leninism, perform revolutionary theater pieces, and give speeches to young North Vietnamese recruits.

"Here's something," Ben said. "I've met more than a few locals who have fond memories of waiting out bombing runs in these caves while watching newsreel footage of American students burning their draft cards back home."

"To the soundtrack of a diesel generator running the projector," I added.

Camaraderie, fear, disillusionment, and patriotism likely mingled in this room. I imagined the space lit by candles or kerosene lanterns for these events, with groups of recruits cast in heavy shadows. Soldiers and volunteers would have squatted on the floor in dark green army clothing, Kalashnikovs at their sides, sandals cut from truck tires on their feet.

As I approached the stage, I noticed the smoothing and dipping in the cave floor—calluses left by ten or fifteen years of revolutionary audiences squatting together in this spot.

Ben illuminated a wall with his phone, revealing graffiti in white paint: names like *Vĩnh* and *Tuyết*, alongside a *72* and faded patriotic slogans that once stretched across the wall.

"These were very likely written by soldiers and volunteers during the war," Ben said. "We see a lot of graffiti in white paint in caves like this."

There were a few empty cans of Red Bull energy drink on the floor, along with used Styrofoam clamshell takeout containers and disposable chopsticks inside single-use pink plastic bags, handles tied in atonement knots. The atonement knot is a signature Vietnamese move upon finishing a takeout meal—a measure to soften the transgression of abandoning the bags in place as litter. It was clear someone still came here now and then to sit with a Red Bull. It could be teenagers. Then again, it could also have been someone who served in this cave fifty years ago, returning for a picnic lunch to feel the cave's aura once again.

The boy who escorted us to Giáp's Cave stood brightly backlit at the entrance. We made our way back to him slowly, and it occurred to me that, though ascetic, musty, and dark, this cave didn't ooze horror and tragedy in the same way that the battlefields down south sometimes did. There seemed to be a signature of bravado in the ether. Those who passed through here were certainly fearful of the future, but many were also confident—bound, in part, by solidarity and shared deprivation.

In the south, things get left behind. Trash, mostly—often on a dramatic scale. In the north, it felt different. A soda can, a plastic bag knotted shut. Not quite offerings, not quite litter. Signs that, rather than abandoning unwanted articles, someone came back. We followed the boy in Vietnam national team kit back down the trail, bought some drinking water at his parents' shop, and gave him some pocket money as a thank you.

***

We rode along another road flanked by distant karst formations en route to Khe Gát Airfield, a few miles away. In Quảng Bình, there were concealed airstrips used only occasionally by the People's Army of Việt Nam Air Force during the war—there were simply too many American fighter jets overhead to risk scrambling the country's few combat aircraft here.

PAVN engineers built Khe Gát Airfield in 1969. The airfield straddled the Ho Chi Minh Trail, giving it access to supplies and anti-aircraft cover. In early 1972, as part of a mission to strike back at the American carrier-based aircraft that regularly bombed Phong Nha, North Vietnam disassembled two Soviet-built MiG-17s and brought them down the Trail in pieces. The planes were reassembled at Khe Gát, and one flew a daring attack mission on U.S. Navy warships in the Gulf of Tonkin, scoring a direct hit on the destroyer *USS Higbee*.

This was actually a historical round-trip; the *USS Higbee* was one of two vessels involved in the Gulf of Tonkin Incident, eight years earlier. After the strike, the pilot bailed out over the Gulf of Tonkin, with U.S. Navy aircraft in pursuit. He was rescued by a Vietnamese fishing boat and celebrated across Vietnam, Cuba, Eastern Europe, and the Soviet Union.

Not all aircraft stories were that cinematic. There's a Quảng Bình legend about a teenage conscript stationed with a gun at the summit of a coastal hill. American carrier jets flew right overhead, en route to inland targets. Not eager to draw fire—or return it—he supposedly aimed behind the jets, just enough to maintain deniability. Pilots figured it out and started tipping their wings as they passed. A nod from above, a pass from below. An understanding, however brief.

We came over a rise, and the road straightened, flattening out into a horizon of woolly karst formations. It was clear why the airstrip was built here—this stretch of land was perfectly level. The jungle was cleared on either side of the road, and wooden country houses and general stores dotted the panorama. Ben motioned to the road ahead, and I opened the throttle for half a mile.

I sped past wooden houses on my left, with families sitting out front, chatting or fixing motorbikes. Turning around, I noticed a parallel dirt track running alongside, with a rusty blue sign with white lettering that read *Di Tích Lịch Sử*, or "Historical Relic." I turned off the runway to have a look and realized I was riding on cobblestone—likely part of the original Ho Chi Minh Trail.

Adjacent to the trail were two mammoth bomb craters, probably 18 feet deep and 45 feet across. Between 1967 and 1969, when things were at their loudest, the United States likely bombed this part of Quảng Bình daily. Ben descended and stood in the middle of one of the pits. He looked tiny.

* * *

We motored on, looking for some shade, pulling over at a *tạp hóa* with a roadside rack of colorful, cheap plastic brooms meant to catch the eye. With water and snacks in hand, we drifted back to the awning and sat on some aged folding aluminum chairs around a red plastic table.

"That airstrip—the Cuban government sent a construction crew to Vietnam in 2010 to re-pave and expand it into the road you see today. It was to recognize the runway's contribution to the war and the propaganda victory against the Americans. They don't really—" Ben was interrupted mid-sentence.

"Where are you boys going, here?" I heard from behind me. Then I scented manure and turned my head. A middle-aged man was standing there, smiling and holding a pitchfork. He wore camouflage pants and shirt, a green ball cap that read "SÀI GÒN", and yellow *dép tổ ong* honeycomb sandals. His face was weather-beaten.

"We are just riding our motorcycles around. Phong Nha is beautiful," I replied.

"Well, why don't we all go back to my house and drink some beer?" he asked. With his free hand, he mimicked the motion of holding a can of beer and dumping the contents into his mouth. Then he pointed to a small village a few hundred meters away.

If a piss session with a group of foreigners is potentially on the table, middle-aged rural Vietnamese men can be some of the most spontaneous people in the world. They're happy to drop what they're doing and fervently engage. It was still well before noon.

"I'm right over there. Let's go," he said.

"No, but thank you, older brother," Ben said.

The gent smirked. As he walked away, he took one last look at us and shook his head in astonishment as if to say, *suit yourself, fools.*

"The Cubans still like to needle the United States once in a while, don't they?" he smiled as he finished his water.

Having turned down an offer to get loaded with a farmer in rural Quảng Bình, we nevertheless regrouped for the trek to Rượu (rice wine) Cave, the next stop on Ben's tour. Rượu Cave was once just that—a revolutionary rice wine factory installed inside a cave to avoid American air strikes.

Thirty minutes in, Ben and Stu detoured, slowing their motorcycles under a lavish karst peak. They pulled over next to a large round hole, probably two feet in diameter and six feet deep. Its walls were smooth inside, worn to a polish.

"That's a hiding spot," Ben said to me. "Teenage volunteers in the wartime Vietnam Youth Brigade were assigned the task of cleaning up Victory Road after American air strikes. If an American jet was looking for targets on the road and didn't find any, they would fire missiles into the sides of these karst formations to cause rockfalls and landslides to block the road. If the landslides stopped traffic, the Americans would eventually have their target."

He continued. "The Vietnam Youth Brigade's job was to clear the road. If a jet were in the area, North Vietnamese anti-aircraft guns would start shooting. The jets would shoot back. Anti-aircraft guns were positioned everywhere on this road. When the guns went off, the Youth Brigade Volunteers would hide in these holes."

I dropped my kickstand and ambled over to the hole in the wall. I wasn't going to squeeze into it, but it looked reasonably comfortable, akin to a prehistoric Japanese capsule hotel pod. It was probably still used occasionally, as it would be much cooler than the air outside.

I imagined a teenager nestled inside, head resting on palms as they peered out and watched American Navy jets swoop by like meteors, with anti-aircraft guns spitting out shells in their wake. One of the twentieth century's most fateful dramas unfolding in front of them, as they cheered on their comrade aunts and uncles above them on the hill, shooting at the bad guys.

* * *

Twenty minutes later, we pulled over in front of a small, one-room country house, looking for the entrance to Rượu Cave. Ben was disoriented, so he flagged down a man in his late sixties, rolling past on a beat-up Chinese Hontai Dreamer. The man looked well-fed, wearing the obligatory baseball hat, an oversized oxford shirt, and yellow rubber *dép tổ ong* honeycomb sandals.

We asked him where the cave was. He paused, pulled a phone from his pocket, and made a call. He nodded mid-conversation, then hung up with a grunt.

"I can take you there," he said, "but first, I need to drop off my bike at home. I'll ride on the back of your bike. Give me one second," he said to Ben. The man turned his Dreamer toward the one-room house we'd stopped at, rode in, and parked. What a coincidence.

He then jumped onto Ben's bike, and Stu and I followed them on a narrow, half-mile-long footpath that ran through a meadow, past three grazing buffalo, through a large mud puddle, and into the jungle. We stopped, dismounted, and made the short walk up a rise and into a cave, clearing walls of vines as we hiked. No wonder we needed directions.

Rượu Cave is so exquisitely hidden that I could only conclude that it was strategically crucial. Rice wine was likely used as an antiseptic, fire accelerant, barter item, and sterilizing agent during the war. More importantly, it was one of the few pleasures a northern soldier might enjoy before crossing into Laos and moving down the Trail, and leadership had set up a factory to make it available in Quảng Bình. The wine distilled here served the dual purpose of supplying troops in the Phong Nha staging area and PAVN troops in the field in South Vietnam.

Big jugs of rice wine from this factory were carried down the Ho Chi Minh Trail to the base areas at the front. PAVN soldiers didn't take their R&R in exotic places like the Philippines, Australia, or Japan, as the Americans did. Most took their R&R in the field, usually just far enough from the front to be safe, or in rear areas in Cambodia and Laos. Some would spend a few days drinking rice wine in Quảng Bình during their break from combat. A bottle or two of rice wine from this factory essentially *was* a PAVN soldier's R&R. From a morale perspective, the facility was probably infinitely more valuable than any airstrip.

Rượu is quite essential to Vietnamese men. Northerners, in particular, treasure it. Beyond the sharp-tasting white lightning's intoxicating effects and the joyous camaraderie it inspires, rice wine is often infused with herbs and other natural medicines that deliver healthful properties to the drinker.

To supercharge the simple health benefits of *rượu*, distillers will add snakes, geckos, blackbirds, seahorses, worms, scorpions, and lizards to wine and let the cadavers marinate in clear glass jugs. Infused *rượu* is creature-specific and is also marketed in gift bottles, with, say, the flawlessly positioned lethally coiled cobra still inside. I recall a Hanoi tavern in the early 2000s that disposed with the showmanship entirely, selling *rượu* by the glass from a 55-gallon aquarium with a spigot, in which all of these different forest creatures marinated together for an especially invigorating multivitamin-like fortified wine.

According to conventional wisdom, these more exotic wines assist with one men's health problem in particular: virility. However, these medicinal properties can also give *rượu* drinkers convenient cover for a drinking hobby, something their spouses typically shun.

Rather than simply telling his wife he's going for drinks with the lads, a Vietnamese man might frame it as helping to fulfill the family's wish for more children—suggesting that he will stay for a single cup and come home. The issue with the standard recommendation of one cup a day for impotence is that most men struggle to stop at that one cup, often coming home well-oiled instead, only to pass out on the sofa and undermine their best intentions.

We followed our friend through the vines and were greeted by another decades-old staircase, this one carved from karst. We climbed it and hunched through the cave's entrance. Inside, this cave was lighter, with multiple entrances, exits, and openings—exposing the distillery to sunshine and air, which made sense given the precision work that took place here.

There were three large and connected rooms, and the man who brought us there wandered around silently, his fingers clasped behind his back. He had been there before and seemed focused. We asked him about certain features inside, and he quietly pointed out rusting steel racks still bolted into the walls—presumably for hanging distillery equipment—and a set of tables carved from rock, where vats of rice wine in various stages of preparation once sat.

Maybe he was a quiet fellow. Or maybe, in his mind, he was somewhere else—remembering life as a young boy working in this factory, sneaking sips of rice wine on the job. I followed my intuition.

"Did you ever work here?" I asked him.

"Sometimes," he said quietly, peering at the wall. We left it at that.

I followed his gaze. More white-paint graffiti covered the walls inside the cave. Someone had painted a *67* on the wall, and another had inscribed *Thịnh thân một người làm việc bỗng hai đi đến đắp cho đồng bào miền nam ruột thịt*, which roughly translates to, "One person working for two, for our southern brothers, flesh and blood of the same country."

It landed harder than I expected. Right in front of me—an antidote to all the noise: communism, democracy, patriotism, freedom, way of life, revolution. The big words that float above places like this, passed between textbooks, documentaries, speeches, and plaques.

This could have been propaganda, but it didn't feel that way. It looked homemade. A distiller's gesture, maybe—something that lifted the room, or maybe to remind whoever might come later what it had felt like to be there. Not fighting for ideology, but for the people beside you. No slogans, just sentiment. For many, it was that simple: *flesh and blood, the same country.*

I thought back to Hiền, the farmer on the Honda Dream I'd met at Hill 601 in Kon Tum several days earlier. He built the altar at Hill 601 with the small vertical black banner that read *Đồng Sanh Lạc Quốc*—"We Were Born in the Same Country."

They were both private thoughts, left in public. They were layered and complex. Side-by-side, they were unresolved—not because they lacked meaning, but because they suggested too many. Stories within a story, unspoken but claimed. These weren't monuments. They didn't need to be.

I'd come looking for history. I kept telling myself that. But what held were moments like this—mute, unmarked, unofficial. Things we can miss unless we're standing still.

* * *

The four of us silently made brief eye contact and nodded. It was mid-afternoon, and Ben had one more spot he wanted to show me. We retraced our steps and dropped our friend at his house, thanking him for bringing us to a place we'd have surely missed. He shook all of our hands, holding our palms for a moment, and thanked us—likely for the good excuse to revisit Rượu Cave, which was essentially in his backyard. He sauntered away slowly and disappeared through his front door, passing a crowing rooster. The three of us accelerated as I wondered if those days in the cave had been a halcyon time of that man's life—or just the part that held its shape longest.

We parried more hills and karst cliffs to visit Tám Cô (Eight Ladies) Cave on Victory Road. After fifteen minutes, we pulled over at a spot framed by high karst peaks that came up to the roadside. There was just enough space for a small parking lot and a one-room building. Next to the building was an opening in the rock wall. I walked over. It was the entrance to an underground cave.

Stairs covered in a bright red carpet descended from where I stood, lined on both sides with bright yellow daffodils in pots. The entrance's reds and yellows matched the color tones of Vietnam's national flag. The stairs turned left and were consumed by rock walls closing in. I could not see any further. I took off my helmet as Ben approached behind me.

"It's off-limits, mate," he said.

Women played a central role on the Ho Chi Minh Trail. Most northern combat troops were men, but over 70 percent of the 170,000 volunteers who kept 1,300 miles of the Trail open were women. They bravely defused bombs, filled bomb craters, managed way stations, moved supplies, ran hospitals, built infrastructure, and operated anti-aircraft guns. Most were in their late teens or early twenties and came from farm households. Many lived in caves.

One day in November 1972, B-52s bombed a way station at this location and destroyed an anti-aircraft battery. The blast triggered a landslide that blocked the entrance to an adjacent cave. Inside that cave were eight women volunteers between the ages of eighteen and twenty, childhood friends from a village in Thanh Hóa province, sheltering from the bombs. Over several days, Trail volunteers and soldiers tried to reopen the entrance. After nine days, they could no longer hear the eight women inside calling for help. Eventually, they stopped trying. In 1996, the government cleared the entrance to the cave and found the remains of the eight women; they were sitting in a circle together when they perished.

They returned their remains to their village in Thanh Hóa and built this shrine. The red-carpeted stairs and the daffodils suggested that the space was sacred and off-limits—perhaps only for use by the eight spirits as they wandered in and out of the cave from which they had departed this life. No one else.

I turned to Ben, and we both exhaled.

"Yep," he said.

Later, the three of us mounted up and rejoined Highway 20, cruising at a slower pace than before. Things felt a little somber, but visiting war sites often brings these moments, these stories, these realizations.

Crossing the DMZ may have shifted something in the air. The places we visited today didn't challenge the revolutionary narrative so much as complicate it with feeling. They didn't undermine it. They just made it harder to dismiss.

In its stripped-down solemnity, Tám Cô Cave may have been the most mournful place I saw—not despite the victory it marked, but because of what it cost.

Rượu Cave, like so many others in Quảng Bình, felt shaped by the austerity, simplicity, and even innocence of the conscripts who passed through.

While I'd been south of the DMZ, tracing the outlines of U.S. and South Vietnamese base cities—built for permanence, now mostly vanished—north of the old border were caves, bamboo, rubber sandals made from truck tires, and stories of combat breaks that amounted to little more than a bottle of rice wine and a few hours in a hammock, half a mile from the front.

North-South conditions differed. The narratives came later. The rest was lost in the retelling.

I didn't feel proud, or mournful, or especially enlightened. I just thought about rubber sandals and rice wine, and how little it sometimes took—for PAVN soldiers, for ARVN troops, for Montagnard militias—to stay in it, whatever *it* was to them.

I used to think I was chasing something else. Something just out of reach—someone else's memory, maybe. A story I wasn't part of, but couldn't stop circling.

* * *

Thirty minutes later, we arrived back at the Farmstay and called it a day. I showered and made my way down to the restaurant, sitting down to a candlelit dinner for one. The same waiter approached me with an open menu in hand. I raised a finger, smiled, and ordered the pepperoni pizza—a tourist's order.

A house band was setting up in a small corner of the restaurant, a singing duo from the Philippines. Filipino singers and bands are ubiquitous in Vietnam and usually stick to popular covers, which aligns nicely with their Vietnamese audiences who know "The Tape" by heart.

This duet, consisting of a male guitarist and a female vocalist, ran through a standard set list of love songs and higher-energy rockers. Brian Adams, REO Speedwagon, that sort of thing. Something in the room tipped me off. Maybe the tempo, maybe the way the guitarist looked at the floor. I knew it was coming.

The opening lick of "Sweet Child O' Mine," by Guns N' Roses.

I loathe Guns N' Roses. This performance was now in danger of going off the rails. I waited it out, reading a Boston Red Sox blog on my phone. As one of an audience of four, I decided to take control and raised my hand as the singer stretched out the final *mi-i-i-i-iiine*.

"How about some country music?" I asked.

They were happy to oblige, producing "Take Me Home, Country Roads," "Jolene," and "Sweet Home Alabama" in succession.

"How about that?" the guitarist asked, smiling. Classic country purists back home would debate whether Lynyrd Skynyrd or John Denver belong in the same class as Dolly Parton—or even have anything in common with each other, for that matter.

But in Vietnam, such trivial concerns wash away quickly.

Afterword

From Quảng Bình, I rode south back to Đông Hà the following day to put my motorcycle on the southbound Reunification Express train and fly back to Saigon. Before I did, I kept an appointment with the Trường Sơn National Martyrs Cemetery on the old DMZ. To close this trip. It was July, just a few days before War Invalids and Martyrs' Day. The cemetery was immaculate: lawns mowed, tombstones made lustrous, flowers laid, grounds swept.

This national holiday is dedicated to honoring the sacrifices and contributions of martyrs, Vietnamese Heroic Mothers, veterans, those who spent time in prison for revolutionary activities, and the many citizens who were victims of war. It is a time for veterans and families to visit cemeteries and remember the fallen. Trips to these cemeteries happen year-round, but visitor numbers tick upward in July.

Upon arriving, I noticed an antique-white dove perched on a revolutionary statue at the entrance—on the head of a Kalashnikov-clad comrade, arm-in-arm with another, towing a rocket launcher. It felt orchestrated, but it wasn't: the dove took flight, dropped, and darted to a telephone pole in the corner of the parking lot as I pulled in.

Trường Sơn National Martyrs Cemetery spreads across a rise above the Bến Hải River—the former boundary between North and South Vietnam—where more than ten thousand North Vietnamese soldiers are interred. I dismounted and walked the grounds. The land gave hints here, too—not scattered or obscured, but aligned and visible. Navigating the labyrinthine rows of gravestones felt like tracing the country's geography. Since most northerners joined and served with others from their villages and districts, the cemetery maintained unit cohesion by grouping gravestones by province.

Reading the gravestones evoked yet again the youth of Vietnam's war generation. Like the Americans and southerners, they were mainly between the ages of eighteen and twenty-one. Many of the markers are those of unidentified soldiers, with the phrase *Chưa Biết Tên* (name not known yet) accompanying the date they fell. I found the *chưa* (not yet) in this context poignant; someone was still trying to answer this fundamental question for the young man buried below.

I wandered to the plaza's center, passing rows of graves from Cao Bằng, Tuyên Quang, and Quảng Ninh provinces. On the rise to my left, I spotted two crumbling French Colonial–era bunkers, overlooking the river delta in the distance. The national cemetery, it appeared, was built on a former enemy position, and it echoed the founding logic of Arlington National Cemetery.

Arlington National Cemetery was founded during the American Civil War, when Union soldiers began burying the dead beneath the front lawn of Confederate General Robert E. Lee's estate in northern Virginia. That initially modest cemetery now contains the graves of about four hundred thousand who fell in the country's wars.

* * *

I arrived at the main shrine, a gold-and-gray concrete structure resembling a star, shooting skyward above a large altar of joss sticks. Beyond the star and altar stood a low wall of charcoal-colored tablets, inscribed with *Tổ Quốc Đời Ghi Công Các Liệt Sỹ* (The Fatherland Forever Recognizes Your Sacrifice).

That promise is reflected in the government's efforts, as Vietnam's people and institutions continue to honor the sacrifice of their veterans. Every year, the country spends about $1.4 billion (about 1.5% of the national budget) on programs to support veterans, and gestures of gratitude—both symbolic and material—remain visible. Over nine million "revolutionary contributors" or their families receive some form of support. But the scope of that support still varies.

The year before, I'd visited Bình An Cemetery outside Saigon. During the war, Bình An was South Vietnam's national cemetery, but after 1975, it lost its government patron and fell into disrepair. That day, a man in an olive drab uniform let me through the gate, but not before carefully checking my identification and residence permit.

Today, upkeep is quietly financed by the overseas Vietnamese community, but maintaining a 58-hectare, 12,000-plot cemetery requires significant investment.

Bình An is a lonely place. Though fenced, gated, and lightly guarded, it is largely overgrown with weeds and mold. Fallen branches lie across the graves. Tombstones are chipped and broken. Funerary portraits of the fallen young southern soldiers are fading. Yet most graves have identical white censers, and on the day I visited, during the rainy season, they were full of waterlogged joss sticks.

For the hour I spent there, I saw no one—not a visitor, not a groundskeeper, not even a passing motorbike.

Still, someone is doing their best to mind these graves—leaving joss sticks, tending censers, and reminding both us and themselves of the humanity of the fallen southerners. Bình An Cemetery might be one of the most forlorn places in the country, and in many ways, it was like the other consequential yet neglected places I'd visited on this trip.

* * *

A group of men in matching crimson baseball caps lingered in front of the altar; they looked like a veteran tour group awaiting a formal program. Most were in their seventies or eighties, and they clearly knew each other. I joined them, noticing a tour company's logo on the front of each hat.

With a patriotic song playing over the public address system, a uniformed official ascended the podium near the main altar and welcomed the group. He introduced the cemetery layout and discussed the history of some individuals and PAVN units interred there. He closed his remarks by thanking his audience and their families for their sacrifices, and invited them to spend the afternoon exploring the tableau and remembering.

He finished his comments, and the group began milling about. Someone behind me took my wrist, and I turned as he clasped my hand and shook it with both of his. He was probably in his late seventies and was smiling. Soon, several others from the same demographic joined us, many wearing the same style of beard Ho Chi Minh once wore.

"Cháu là người ở đâu?" he asked. I told him I was from the United States and asked where they were from.

"We're from Hà Tĩnh province, Nghi Xuân commune," he said. "We traveled here last night. Do you know *The Tale of Kiều*?"

"Of course," I replied. He was referring to Vietnam's national epic—a long, tragic poem from the early nineteenth century.

"Nguyễn Du was born in Nghi Xuân," he replied. "That's where we come from."

Vietnamese are nothing if not writers and poets. Much of the country's revolutionary history originated in Hà Tĩnh and Nghệ An provinces, north of the former DMZ along the North-Central coast. These fellows had serious credentials.

"Did you all serve together in the war?" I asked.

"Yes," he replied. "325th. Trường Sơn," referring to his unit and the Central Highlands. He circled back: "Nguyễn Công Trứ is also from Nghi Xuân." Another national poet from the same period.

I hadn't realized that, but it didn't matter. We slipped into a warm *làm quen* zone. They'd been planning this trip for months, and had all come by bus to the DMZ and Trường Sơn National Martyrs Cemetery.

They asked me about my family and what had brought me to Vietnam. I gave them my best answer to each question. That I was American wasn't provocative—they'd surely encountered Americans before, long ago.

As for closer to the present day: a 2015 survey—the year before President Obama's visit—found that 94 percent of Vietnamese viewed the United States favorably. The United States polls better in Vietnam than at home.

They learned I had relatives who served against them in the war. No one flinched. "You're welcome here," one man said, and the group dispersed to explore the cemetery.

I slowly wandered back to my motorcycle and watched the Hà Tĩnh veterans ascend a tombstone-covered slope. A *làm quen* session at the national cemetery—with combatants from the People's Army of Việt Nam's 325th Infantry Division, on the eve of Vietnam's equivalent to Memorial Day—was probably how this trip was meant to end.

* * *

I grew up steeped in a loud, messy dialogue about the war—who fought, who resisted, who reconciled, who betrayed whom.

Vietnamese my age grew up with a story of revolution—cleaner, prouder, more linear than the truths both North and South carried in the past and in the present—retold until it settled into national memory, whether or not it aligned with the family one. The Republic of Vietnam's complicated story survived—quietly, at home; openly, abroad—held in diaspora communities, family memory, and the kinds of silences too nuanced for the official version.

From an early age, I learned how electrifying the American narrative could be, at least from the lens I inherited. I chased down all the films and books—the same chase that brought me to Vietnam in 1998, and earlier, in my imagination.

On this trip, I still told myself it was about history. Maybe it was. Or maybe that was just the high-register version of the story I preferred.

Even knowing the American frame obscured more than it revealed, I stepped into it anyway—from the Pittman Apartments all the way up to Trường Sơn National Martyrs Cemetery, and at every point in between.

The thrill never fully left me—of standing inside someone else's war, tracing the edges where these two stories touched. I kept looking for the point where time might circle back and let me in, even knowing one can only get so close. Even knowing that, in some way, I was trespassing.

I walked the perimeters. Let the ritual loosen. Tried to touch what was still there. And sometimes, I put it in my pocket.

Eventually, what stayed weren't explanations, but gestures. Not monuments, not answers—just small moments left behind, on their own terms, to remind us what it was like to be there. Single frames, left unframed. A bomb crater where nothing was interpreted. A landing zone turned cassava field, without inscription. A tour guide who censored himself. The buried violence of a sandbag poking through the soil. A waterlogged censer in a cemetery no one officially tends. A roadside altar. A man who remembered hiding in burned-out tanks. A group of veterans in crimson caps, asking if I knew *The Tale of Kiều*.

These weren't clarifications. They were *làm quen*—small, human crossings between past and present, between strangers who weren't entirely strangers. The narratives all still evolve yet run in parallel lines, to a large extent. The official and unofficial stories rarely meet. But on the ground, people sometimes did. And sometimes, if I moved slowly enough, the land gave hints.

Glossary

bánh mì

World-famous Vietnamese baguette sandwich made with grilled pork, pate, pickled carrots and daikon, cilantro, cucumber, chili, and mayonnaise. It's known for its crispy crust and soft, airy inside. One of the most popular street foods in Vietnam.

Army of the Republic of Việt Nam (ARVN)

United States-allied South Vietnam's national army between 1955 and 1975.

bia hơi

Magnificent locally-made pilsner unique to northern Vietnam that has been around for more than a century and has historically been priced for the proletariat. It is served in a small sidewalk bar or, in some cases, a grand beer garden with plastic stool and table seating for a thousand people. *Bia hơi* also can denote a tavern itself, or the northern equivalent of the southern *quán nhậu*.

bình dân

Term that describes something common, working class, or rural. *Bình dân* is also a business marketing or service category in Vietnam, targeting budget-conscious customers.

cao bồi thôn

Slang term for petty *bình dân* hustlers or those at the very bottom of a formal or informal organized crime hierarchy with the lowest amount of criminal prestige and influence.

cơm bình dân

"Ordinary person rice," a marketing classification for a certain type of communal canteen-style restaurant that delivers cheap, quick, and filling proletariat lunches.

Democratic Republic of Vietnam (DRV)

In our context, the former "North Vietnam." Led by the Communist Party of Vietnam and established in 1945, when Ho

Chi Minh declared its independence from French colonial rule in Hanoi. Despite France's post-WWII attempts to reestablish control over its former colony during the First Indochina War between 1945-54, the DRV maintained control over much of northern Vietnam, ultimately securing its victory with the French defeat at Điện Biên Phủ in 1954, which a year later led to the division of the country into North and South Vietnam. The DRV, or North Vietnam, existed until 1975, when it unified with the Republic of Vietnam (South Vietnam) after the fall of Saigon, leading to the creation of the Socialist Republic of Vietnam.

dép tổ ong

Cheap, ugly, durable yellow rubber shower sandals with a honeycomb pattern on the sandal's upper, that have been a staple of working class and rural menswear in Vietnam for forty years. *Dép tổ ong* are associated with the country's self-reliance during the economically difficult postwar period and thus are fondly remembered.

di tích lịch sử

"Historical relic," *di tích lịch sử* is the Vietnamese term one should use on an online map to discover lesser-known sites preserved as part of the country's cultural and national heritage.

đồng

Vietnamese currency.

Đảng Cộng Sản Việt Nam

Communist Party of Vietnam

Đổi Mới

Translates as "renovation," and refers to the economic and political reforms initiated in Vietnam in 1986, transitioning from a centrally planned to a socialist-oriented market economy, encouraging foreign investment, decentralizing economic decision-making, and building private enterprise while maintaining

Communist Party leadership, leading to thus far four decades of economic growth.

hẹn gặp lại
Informal term for goodbye, or "see you again."

Ho Chi Minh Highway
A 750-mile, two-lane, north-south road that connects Saigon and Hanoi via parts of the original Ho Chi Minh Trail in mountainous western Vietnam.

mía đá
Popular street drink made from the fresh juice of pressed sugarcane stalks served over ice.

nhà nghỉ
Inexpensive, aggressively simple, family-run hotels found all over Vietnam; some of these urban rest houses serve as "love hotels," where extramarital affairs or certain dating rituals might be conducted.

nón lá
Traditional Vietnamese conical hat made from bamboo and palm leaves, commonly worn to protect against the sun and rain.

nước chanh
Everyday drink made from fresh lime juice, water, and sugar, served cold.

People's Army of Việt Nam (PAVN)
North Vietnam's national army, also referred to as the North Vietnamese Army (NVA).

phở
Vietnamese beef noodle soup.

quán nhậu
Southern Vietnamese term for a vigorously proletariat outdoor or semi-outdoor restaurant/tavern. Southern equivalent of the northern *bia hơi*.

rau muống xào tỏi

Staple dish of sauteed morning glory / water spinach that most Vietnamese eat upwards of six times a week. Hyper-abundant and nearly free on most restaurant menus.

Republic of Vietnam (RVN)
South Vietnam, the anti-communist post-colonial southern Vietnamese state, existed between 1955 and 1975.

rượu
Rice wine with intoxicating effects, often infused with herbs or other natural medicines with healthful properties. Distillers sometimes add preserved snakes, geckos, blackbirds, seahorses, worms, scorpions, and lizards to rượu to fortify the wine and improve health outcomes for the consumer, usually a Vietnamese man.

tạp hóa
Vietnam's family-run general stores, groceries, corner stores, bodegas, and convenience stores, usually situated in a shophouse.

thuốc lào
Water pipe/bong made from a section of bamboo; Vietnamese men pass the time by smoking a highly potent (so high a concentration of nicotine that it's used to make pesticides) tobacco through this communal pipe.

Tết
Vietnamese Lunar New Year, the country's biggest holiday, marked by family reunions, honoring ancestors, giving red envelopes, and traditional foods, lasting several days and beginning on the first day of the lunar calendar year.

Việt Cộng
Informal, loaded, and usually derogatory abbreviated term for "Việt Nam Cộng Sản" (Vietnamese Communist), denoting irregular Communist forces of South Vietnam, also known as the National Front for the Liberation of South Vietnam, who fought against the

South Vietnamese government and U.S. military during the Vietnam War.

Việt Minh

Communist-led nationalist movement founded in 1941 that fought for Vietnam's independence from French colonial rule, in many ways the National Liberation Front's ancestor.

xe máy

Motorbike, or what an American would call a "scooter." Usually with a 125-cubic centimeter engine.

About the Author

Arrested for underage motorcycle riding in 1985 at the age of 14 while cruising Manchester, New Hampshire's French-Canadian West Side with a friend—after that friend's older brother handed him the keys at a keg party—Stephen F. Berlinguette has been riding motorcycles since he was 13, when his own older brother first taught him how to work a clutch and shift gears.

The arrest landed him in the back of a police wagon, sharing space with a heavily intoxicated, perspiring, shirtless French-Canadian man in dungarees and hi-top basketball sneakers, followed by a few hours in a holding cell. On the ride home from the station, his parents laid down the law: "No motorcycles."

It didn't stick.

He'd already been placed in the saddle of a Honda CB350 as an infant, and by the time of his arrest, he was surrounded by bikes, memories, and family mythology. His father, a former Matchless owner with deep regrets about the "former," passed down a love of riding through motorcycle camping trips and stories about annual pilgrimages to Laconia Bike Week and the "Blessing of the Bikes" in Colebrook, New Hampshire. His mother rode her own Suzuki.

Eventually, the rule became "motorcycles." He kept going—from a 6,000-mile cross-country USA ride on a 1974 Honda CB750, to wrenching on a temperamental BSA Lightning, to more reliable Hondas, Triumphs, and Yamahas in the years since. He's ridden all over Laos, Rwanda, Liberia, and Vietnam, where he lived for nearly a decade. He wants very badly to move back.

He spent fifteen years working for the U.S. Agency for International Development (USAID) overseas before losing his job in 2025 when the Trump Administration dismantled the agency.

He studied History at the University of New Hampshire, and International Relations at the Johns Hopkins University School of Advanced International Studies.

He has a son, Oscar—the greatest boy in the world.
https://www.etsy.com/shop/RoyalKingDynasty
https://facebook.com/sfberlinguette

[1] The Spratlys and Paracels are contested archipelagos in the South China Sea, known as the "East Sea" in Vietnam. These islands are claimed by Vietnam, China, and, to a lesser extent, the Philippines and Malaysia. The Paracels were seized by China in 1974, expelling South Vietnamese forces who had controlled them since the French occupation. For Vietnam, the Paracels are considered stolen territory. The Spratlys are more complex, with both Vietnam and China making competing claims based on historical evidence, such as old maps and artifacts unearthed from the islands themselves. Around thirty-five years ago, China began militarizing features in the archipelago, followed by Vietnam doing the same, escalating tensions. The rivalry between China and Vietnam is deep-rooted, fueled by centuries of Chinese territorial ambitions. Vietnam's bitter history with China includes a thousand years under Chinese suzerainty and multiple invasions, including a brief but fierce border war in 1979. Natural resources in the East Sea, including oil and gas reserves, only intensify the dispute. For many Vietnamese, nationalism and anti-China sentiment are essentially one and the same.

[2] Ironically, Vietnamese sometimes express their fondness for cash with the phrase *Tôi yêu Bác Hồ*, or "I love Uncle Ho," as founding father and revolutionary Ho Chi Minh's face is engraved on the bill of every denomination of the Vietnamese đồng currency.

[3] Before Buddhism, Hinduism, Taoism, Confucianism, Islam, and Christianity arrived in Vietnam—through trade, conquest, and exploration—people worshiped ancestor spirits. Ancestor worship is identity: tied to home, village, and city. The spirits of the deceased stay on, guiding, protecting, and preserving the family line. Nearly every home has an altar: a wooden shelf, candles, bowls of fruit, rice wine, a joss stick holder. Photographs of the deceased hang above. Offerings are made—food, drink, and paper money burned into currency for the afterlife. The relationship is transactional: protection in exchange for remembrance. During Lunar New Year, meals are first served to the ancestors. Only then does the family eat. Not all spirits are kind. Evil ones roam. Newborns are vulnerable; parents take precautions: no compliments, no tempting fate. Some give their children bland names: Two, Three, never One.

[4] I find that people from Quảng Nam province in central Vietnam tend to be a bit reserved compared to southerners, who seem more outgoing. At one of my offices in Ho Chi Minh City, I had to pass a security desk each time I used the restroom. The security guards would greet me and ask how I was doing whenever I walked by, meaning a greeting on the way to the restroom and another on the way back. Every single time. For someone who visits the washroom frequently,

that amounts to an awful lot of pulse-taking. That certainly wouldn't happen in Quảng Nam. However, the province has a cheerful side: Quảng Nam is now known for the "Hội An Banana Shirt." For whatever reason, these locally-tailored, short-sleeved shirts made from a silk textile featuring bunches of bananas have become extremely popular in Hội An, especially among Korean tourists. I'm unaware of any special connection between Hội An and bananas, but someone made a link a while back and started selling clothing made from banana-themed textiles. It has turned into a bit of a social movement for Northeast Asian tourists. Visiting Hội An now, one notices that every third or fourth tourist encountered will be wearing some form of banana-patterned attire—be it a shirt, hat, skirt, shorts, or baggy trousers. To whoever started this trend, it was a fine idea; bravo.

www.ingramcontent.com/pod-product-compliance
Lightning Source LLC
Chambersburg PA
CBHW020922090426
42736CB00010B/1001